北大版对外汉语教材·公共选修课系列

汉英对照

学习中国书法

Chinese Calligraphy

韩家鳌　〔美〕童若春　〔美〕谢国骥　编著

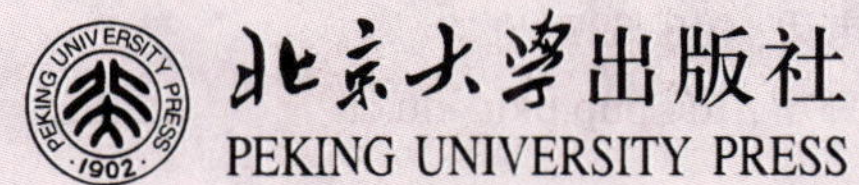

北京大学出版社

PEKING UNIVERSITY PRESS

图书在版编目(CIP)数据

学习中国书法/韩家鳌,〔美〕童若春,〔美〕谢国骥编著. —北京：北京大学出版社，2008.10
(北大版对外汉语教材·公共选修课系列)

ISBN 978-7-301-14312-4

Ⅰ.学…　Ⅱ.①韩…　②童…③谢…　Ⅲ.汉字 - 书法 - 对外汉语教学 - 教材　Ⅳ.J292.1

中国版本图书馆 CIP 数据核字(2008)第 152777 号

书　　　　名：学习中国书法
著作责任者：韩家鳌　〔美〕童若春　〔美〕谢国骥　编著
责 任 编 辑：沈　岚
标 准 书 号：ISBN 978-7-301-14312-4/H·2079
出 版 发 行：北京大学出版社
地　　　　址：北京市海淀区成府路 205 号　　100871
网　　　　址：http://www.pup.cn
电　　　　话：邮购部 62752015　发行部 62750672　编辑部 62752028　出版部 62754962
电 子 邮 箱：zpup@pup.pku.edu.cn
印　刷　者：北京大学印刷厂
经　销　者：新华书店
　　　　　　787 毫米×1092 毫米　16 开本　13.75 印张　320 千字
　　　　　　2008 年 10 月第 1 版　2008 年 10 月第 1 次印刷
定　　　　价：50.00 元(含 1 张 DVD)

About Authors

Han Jia'ao (韩家鳌)is a member of the Chinese Retired Professors Association. His past careers include principal of Tsing Hua University High School, principal of Beijing No.4 High School, Vice President of the Beijing College of Education, and member of the Board of Directors of the Calligraphy Research Group in the Beijing Education Association. 1992–1994 he was a consultant to Hong Kong Baptist College School of Continuous Education in Chinese Language Center. In 1964 he taught calligraphy, aesthetics, traditional art, and other Chinese subjects in the Tsing Hua University, Chinese Department. He was Editor-in-Chief of the three volumes *Basic Knowledge In Calligraphy* (《书法知识基础》) and author of *Dictionary of Pronunciation in Kun Qu* (《昆曲字音》).

Rebecca T. Hsieh (童若春) Chinese-American. She received the Bachelor of Art Degree in English Literature from Evansville College, Evansville Indiana, and Master of Science Degree from Catholic University of America in Washington D.C. U.S.A. She is a member of the Board of Directors of the Chinese Calligraphy Education Group, and a member of the Chinese Language Teachers Association (CLTA.). From 1985 to today, she teaches different levels of Chinese Language courses at Towson University, and Johns Hopkins University Baltimore, Maryland, U.S.A. She initiated a Chinese Calligraphy course at Johns Hopkins and has been teaching this course since then.

Richard Hsieh (谢国骥) Chinese-American. He received Bachelor of Engineering Science degree (1957), Master of Science degree (1959), Master of Public Health degree (1964), and Doctor of Public Health and Preventive Medicine degree (1966) all from the Johns Hopkins University, Baltimore, Maryland, U.S.A. 1966–1994, he served as a Health Scientist Administrator in different professional capacities of the U.S. Public Health Service, Department of Health and Human Services. He retired from the position of Director of International Programs of the National Library of Medicine in 1995.

前　言

　　这是一本汉英对照学习中国书法的教材。

　　在这本教材中,我们讲解了基础的书法知识,教初学者掌握中国书法的基本技能。

　　为了加强教材的系统性,我们把书法知识(共十一章节)安排在教材的前半部分,而把技能训练(十四个练习)安排在教材的后半部分。

　　教师讲授书法知识,不必受教材先后顺序的限制,可根据自己的需要取舍,还可以补充一些内容和图片,以增强课程内容的丰富性和趣味性。

　　书法是一门技能性很强的课程,一定要贯彻精讲多练的原则。学习书法的最终目标,不是检验学生掌握了多少书法知识,而是要求学生把汉字写得得体、美观。

　　在国际社会对汉语发生浓厚兴趣的今天,中国书法也必然会引起国际社会的重视。希望这本教材能够把初学者领进书法的大门,并由此对中国的传统文化有所了解。

　　在编写的体例上,中文的文字说明部分用的是简化字,而范字和例字中有很多繁体字,目的是在教材中保留汉字的原始形态。

　　这本教材既适用于教学,也适用于自学。

作　者

Foreword

This is a Chinese-English bilingual book for learning Chinese calligraphy.

In this book, the basic knowledge of Chinese Calligraphy is covered, along with techniques of brush writing. In order to have a more systematic teaching material, the basic calligraphy knowledge (eleven chapters) is arranged in the front part of the book; and the calligraphy practice (fourteen chapters) is placed in the rear part of the book.

This basic calligraphy book is recommended as a one semester college course; it is also suitable to use as a self learning primer. When used as a textbook in classrooms, instructors should not feel bounded by the sequence of the subjects in the chapters, but rather to select and rearrange as she or he feels suitable. Indeed, instructors should also feel free to supplement contents in this book with any additional materials such as stories and figures to increase the richness and interest of specific topic.

As more people around the world become interested in Chinese language, they realize that writing and speaking are inseparable parts of learning this important language. We hope this primer will help them with both aspects of the language and further, provide a better understanding of traditional Chinese culture.

In this book, simplified Chinese characters are used in the text of the book. However, many traditional characters are used in the demonstration and exercise sections for teaching.

Authors

目　录

Table of Contents

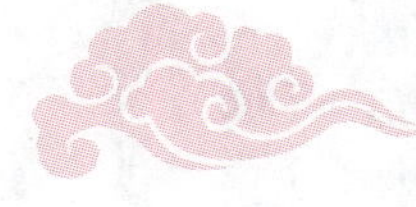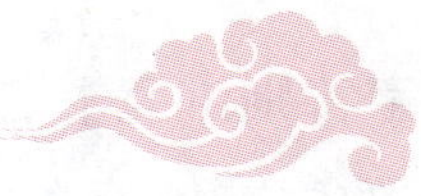

第 一 章

Chapter 1

什么是书法？为什么汉字会成为艺术品？

What is Chinese calligraphy? How can Chinese characters be art?

　　什么是书法？书法是书写文字的规则和技巧。从古代到近代，中国人书写汉字的主要工具是毛笔，所以中国的书法就是中国人民使用毛笔书写汉字的规则和技巧。

　　汉字特别讲究书法艺术。北大教授季羡林在《书法文化与学者眼界》一文中说："在中国的优秀传统文化中，书法实在是占有很重要的地位。"

　　汉字是中国人民（主要是汉族）进行书面交流的主要工具，它的实用性极强，但它为什么又会成为观赏价值很高的艺术品呢？主要原因有两点：

(1) 汉字是方块字

　　汉字最早的形状是象形文字，与欧洲各国文字的原始状态是一样的。古埃及文、巴比伦文、腓尼基文也是象形文字，与汉字形状很相似（图1）。今天西方的拼音文字都是从古埃及文发展来的，古埃及文传到腓尼基，腓尼基人觉得这些象形文字太繁难，于是挑选出少数象形文字作表音字母，互相拼合成词，这就是今天欧洲拼音文字的最初形状。拼音文字成为一种纯粹的符号，完全失去象形的姿态，而中国的造字方法把文字固定在形体上面，所以汉字没有发展成拼音文字，而形成方块字。方块字因其外形的特点，由八种笔画拼合成字，比拼音文字的单一线条丰富得多，例如"福"、"寿"等字都能写出 100 多种字样，"宝"字可以写出一百多种字样，这就为汉字成为艺术品创造了非常好的条件。

古埃及圣书字	日	月	山	水	目
巴比伦文	日	手	鱼	屋	
腓尼基文		手	蛇	屋	目
古汉字	日	月	山	水	目

图1　古象形字

What is Calligraphy? Calligraphy is a method for the inscription of written language. From ancient to modern times, the brush has been the principal tool for Chinese people to write the Chinese language. Thus, Chinese calligraphy is the method by which Chinese people write their language, using a brush.

Why, then, can Chinese Calligraphy be considered an art? Professor Ji Xianlin of the Beijing University said in his essay *The Culture of Calligraphy In the Viewpoint of Scholars*, "Among Chinese cultural heritages, calligraphy occupies a most unique position."

Chinese people have always used Chinese characters as the basic tool in written communication. Since it already possesses this significant practical value, why would it also be a highly appreciated art media? There are two reasons:

(1) Chinese characters have a square construction

The modern monosyllabic Chinese characters are descendants of ancient Chinese pictographs. The ancient Chinese pictographs resemble their counterpart in Euro-Egyptian pictographs, e.g., the ancient languages of Egyptian, Babylonia, and Phoenicia. (Figure 1)

The phonetic spelling alphabets of modern day western languages were derivatives of ancient Egyptian pictographs. When ancient Egyptian pictographs passed on to Babylonia and Phoenicia; the Phoenicians felt the pictograph characters were overly complicated. In response, Phoenicians selected, from among their pictograph characters, a few which would come to form phonogram. They then combined those with other pictographs to become basic semantic units, that is, words. Eventually, this evolutionary process made European languages into phonetic languages, and completely divorced them from their original pictograph language. Chinese, on the other hand, fixed its evolution of written language in pictograph characters. Thus, Chinese characters did not evolve into a phonetic language; rather, they continued to maintain their square construction. Each character in a square is constructed from 8 different types of strokes which affords each character a variety of forms and appearances.

The square character has a much richer variation. For example, the Chinese character "fu" (fortune), and "shou" (longevity) can be written into more than 100 different forms, and the Chinese character "bao" (treasure) can be written into more than 100 forms and appearances. This square block contributed to make Chinese characters a good art media.

（2）软笔书写

　　毛笔是软笔，有弹性，书写起来，有粗有细，有顺有逆，可方可圆，可转可折，所以能写出千姿百态的字来。相比之下，拼音文字用硬笔书写，变化就很少了。但是，在中国，书法艺术发展到今天，用硬笔来写汉字，也能写出非常美观的字来，被称为硬笔书法，这是什么原因呢？这是因为，将软笔的使用方法搬到软笔上来，使硬笔书写发生了质的变化；另外，由于硬笔的书写工具不断地改造创新，使硬笔书法也产生了粗、细、方、圆等软笔书法所具有的效果。所以说，硬笔书法的基础仍在软笔。

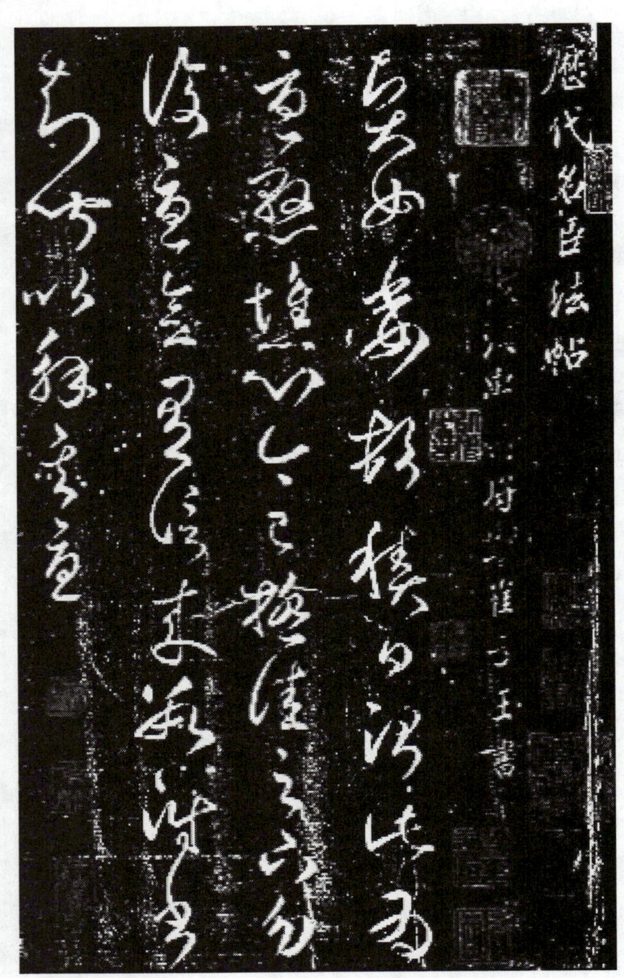

*《贤女帖》

---

(2) Chinese writings use soft brush pens

In their writing, Chinese calligraphers have used soft tip brushes from ancient times to the present. Soft tip brushes possess a characteristic resilience, in that their soft tips will quickly bounce back to their original shape. When in use, the soft tip can accommodate an up-lifting stroke, a down-pressed stroke, or a twirling motion stroke. This character allows the flexibility of writing a thick stroke, a thin stroke, a forward motion line, a backward motion line, a squared shape, a round shape, or a clipped motion shape. This is the wonder of using such brushes in calligraphy writing. In contrast, using a hard tip pen to write a phonetic language can only produce a limited number of variations. However, modern day calligraphy artists in China have experimented with the use of hard tips to write Chinese characters, and succeeded in the creation of some beautiful calligraphy. Actually, the hard tip artists have developed hard tip techniques with the same basic principle as those used with soft tip brushes. That is, using hard tip pens to achieve a variety of stroke requirements such as thick, thin, square, or round strokes.

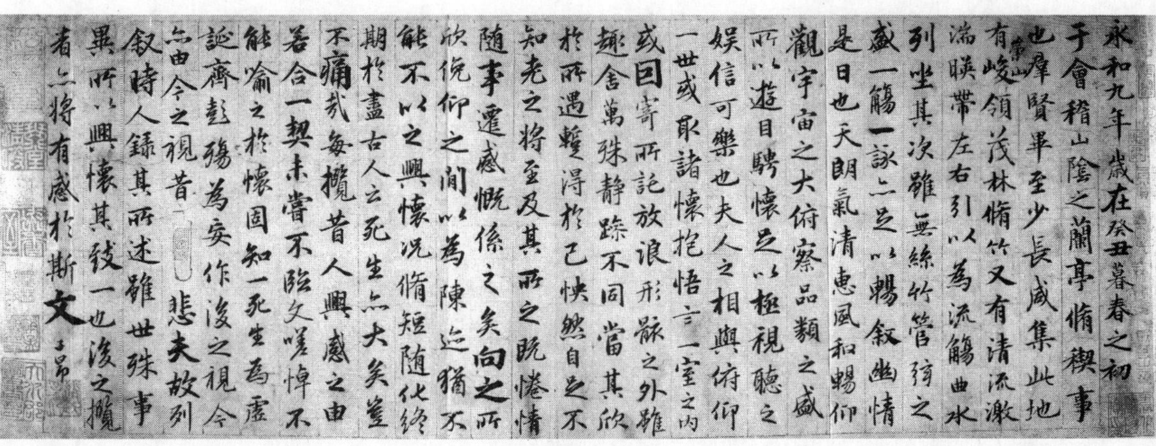

*《兰亭序》

Chapter 2

汉字的字体是怎样演变的？

How did Chinese characters evolve?

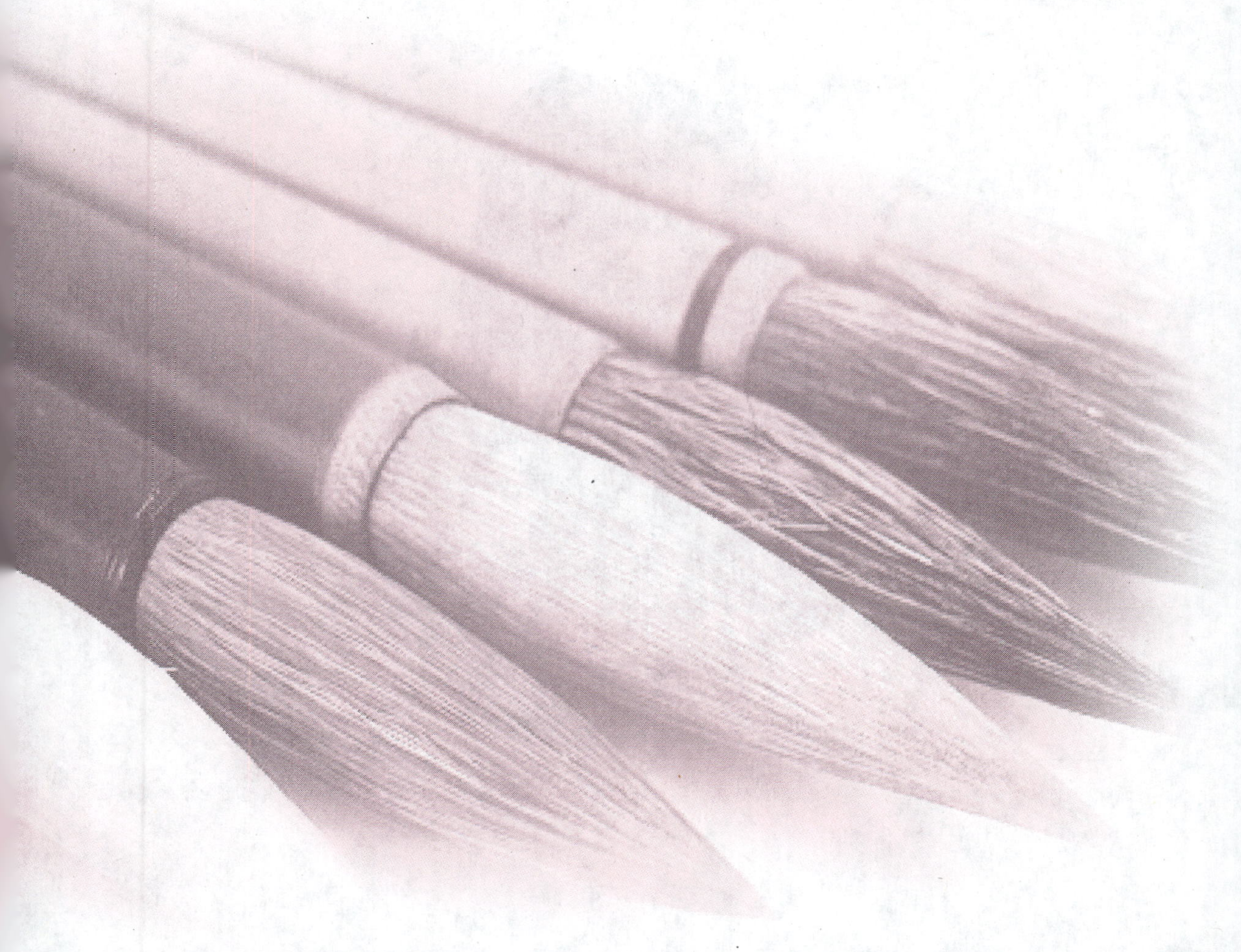

现代汉字的字体基本上只有两种：一种是楷书，[1] 一种是行书。古代汉字的字体除了楷书、行书以外，还有篆书、隶书、草书。

（1）篆书

篆书是汉字最古老的字体，具有明显的象形特点。

在中国殷商时代（约公元前 16—公元前 11 世纪），刻在龟甲和兽骨上的甲骨文（图 2），是中国最早的成系统的文字，上面记载着占卜、祭祀等活动内容。甲骨文多数是用刀刻的，字的线条细瘦。

西周时代（约公元前 11 世纪—公元前 771 年）出现了大量铸刻在青铜器上的金文（图 3），金是铜器的意思。青铜器中以钟和鼎最为常见，钟是古代祭祀、宴享时所用的乐器，鼎是古代的烹饪器，所以金文又名钟鼎文，内容多记载有关祭典、赏赐、征伐、契约的事。金文的字体比甲骨文圆活、自然多了。

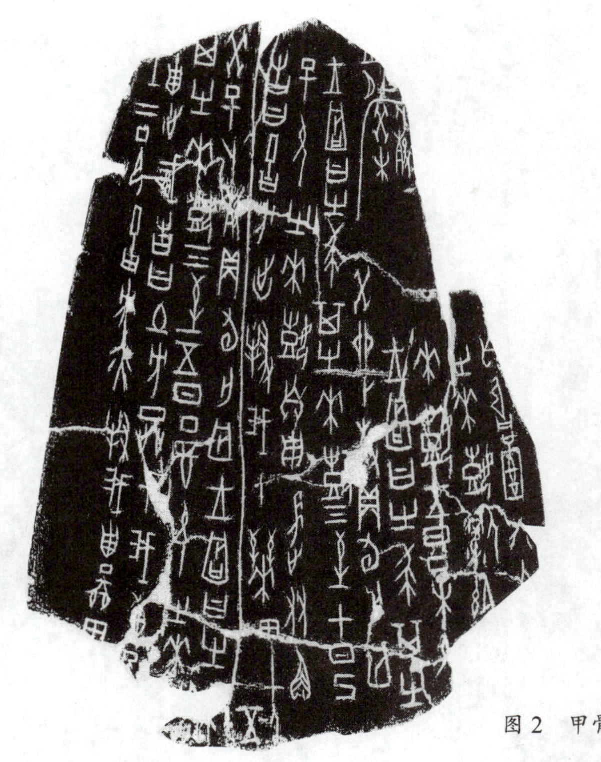

图 2　甲骨文

---

1 广义的楷书就是指正体字。狭义的楷书，是现在通行的字体的一种，其他还有宋体（宋代雕版印书通用的字体）、仿宋体（仿刻北宋刻本的一种字体）等。

Today, two Chinese scripts are in common use: one is the Kaishu[1], and the other is Xingshu, However, there were several earlier forms of Chinese writing in addition to Kaishu and Lishu, namely Zhuanshu, Lishu, and Caoshu.

(1) Zhuanshu (seal script)

Zhuanshu is the oldest script of Chinese Han writing, and carried the most obvious features in pictorial characters.

From 16 BC to 11 BC, China's Yin-Shang era, inscriptions carved on tortoise shells and animal bones were called Jiaguwen. This earliest Zhuanshu script, Jiaguwen (Figure 2), recorded events, divinations, and supplications to their gods. Because bone inscriptions were carved by knives, (strokes) lines in characters appeared thin.

From 11 BC to 771 BC, the Western Zhou dynasty, inscriptions appeared on bronze utensils. (Figure 3) Because they were on metallic material, bronze inscriptions were also called Jinwen. Jin means metal; and bronze utensils, like Zhong and Ding are mostly made of metallic materials. Zhong were bells or musical instruments used in major celebration ceremonies; and Ding were cooking utensils used in the preparation and enjoyment of food and drink. Jingwen were inscriptions on bronze material and the contents of the inscriptions concerned primarily the recordings of national events such as ancestor worship ceremonies, performed by the royal family, military victories by famous generals, and the conclusion of important national agreements by royal officials, etc. These bronze inscriptions appeared much smoother than the earlier carvings on tortoise shells or bones.

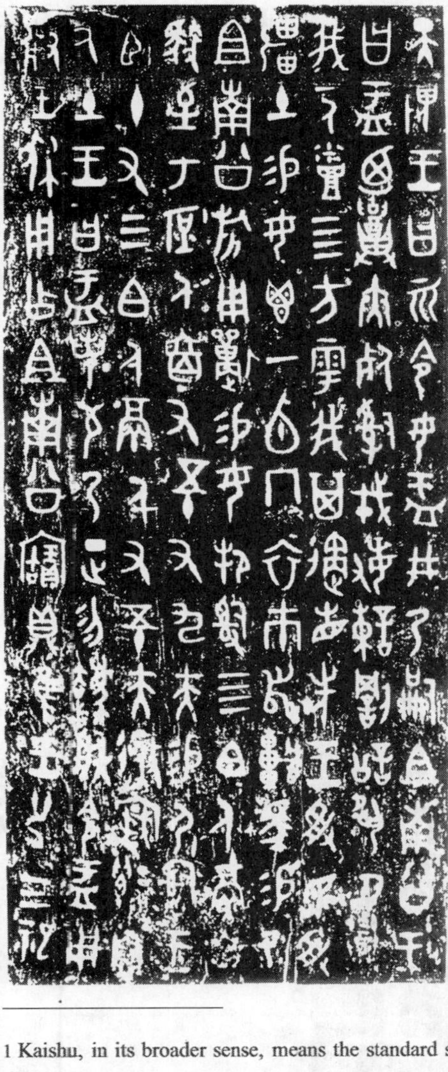

图 3　金文

---

1 Kaishu, in its broader sense, means the standard script. In a narrower sense of the term, Kaishu, is only one kind of several standard writings in general use now. There are also Songti, (the script used in the Song dynasty for carving purposes), Fangsongti, (the carving script used in the copying of carvings of the Northern Song dynasty), etc."

公元前 770 年以后，开始了春秋(公元前 770—公元前 476 年)战国(公元前 475—公元前 221 年)两个历史时期。战国时期出现了中国书法史上很有代表性的石刻文字——石鼓文(图 4)。石鼓文是战国时秦国的文字，记录了秦王游猎的情况，因为刻在十个鼓形的石头上而得名。石鼓文的产生大约在公元前 300 年左右，它的字体比金文更为均匀整齐、严谨端庄。

有一种与石鼓文同属一系的篆书字体叫籀文，为当时的标准字体，周宣王的史官名叫籀的用这种字体写了教儿童识字的教材《史籀篇》，共十五篇，可惜早已亡佚了。

籀文和石鼓文统称大篆。

公元前 221 年秦始皇统一中国后，由丞相李斯等将文字加以改造、简化，确定了新的字体形式。历史上把李斯等整理后的字体称为小篆。小篆是秦始皇统一中国后采用的标准字体，它在汉字发展史上具有重要意义，它是秦代社会通行的字体。立于泰山山顶的《泰山刻石》(图 5)是小篆的代表作，相传为李斯所书。

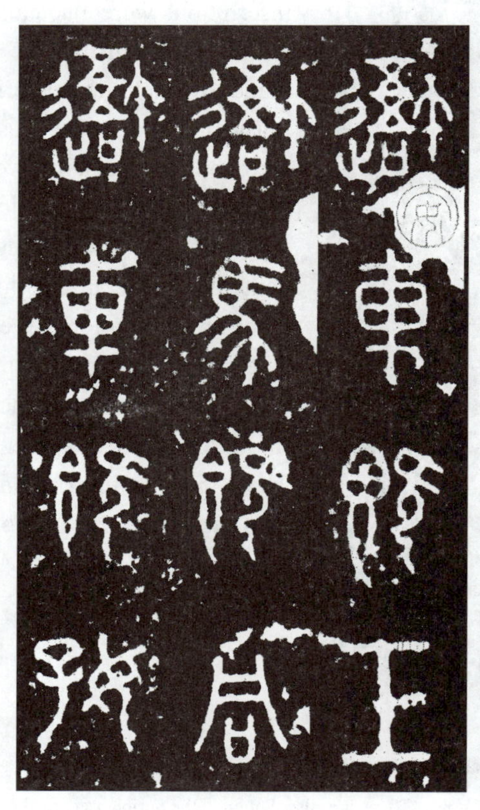

图 4　石鼓文

After 770 BC, China began the Spring and Autumn period, (770—476 BC) and the Warring States (475—221 BC). During the Warring States period, the famous calligraphy style of Shiguwen appeared. (Figure 4) Shiguwen was the language of Qin during the Warring States period. It primarily recorded royal hunting events. They were named Shiguwen because carved inscriptions were found on ten stone drums. The first appearance of Shiguwen was in 300 BC; strokes in Shiguwen writings appeared more uniform in thickness; and the appearance of scripts were more standardized than Jingwen.

One style of writing belong to the same group of writing as the Shiguwen was Zhouwen, Which is the standard style writing. Zhou Xuan King's royal historical staff called "Zhou" used this style writing to compile an elementary reading learning material—*Shi Zhou Pian*. There were fifteen chapters, but unfortunately all have lost in time.

Zhouwen and Shiguwen are called Dazhuan.

In 221 BC, Emperor Qin unified China. His Prime Minister Li Si standardized Chinese writings, thus appeared the more uniform and simplified Xiaozhuan. In history, Chinese writings appeared before the unified Qin was called Dazhuan, and the new writing standardized by Li Si was called Xiaozhuan. Xiaozhuan of the Qin dynasty has a special significance in the evolution of written Chinese because it is a unified national writing script. On the top of Mount Tai, there lies a stone carving which is a representative piece of Xiaozhuan, commonly known as the *Tai Shan Stone Carving*. It is believed that the carved characters were written by Li Si. (Figure 5)

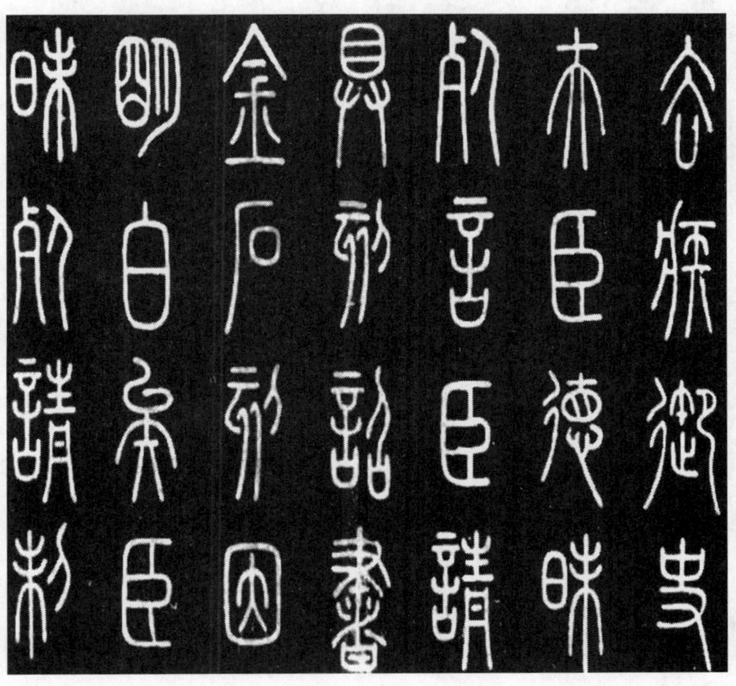

图 5　小篆《泰山刻石》

（2）隶书

隶书也分两种：秦隶（图 6）和汉隶（图 7）。

秦隶又称古隶，是秦代使用的字体之一。秦代的小篆是官方使用的标准字体，用于比较郑重的场合；隶书为下级人员日常使用，用于非正式的场合。因为篆书笔画繁多，书写不易，为减省篆书的繁难笔画，化圆为方，变曲为直，出现了秦隶。秦隶可说是篆书的潦草写法，所以称为隶书。

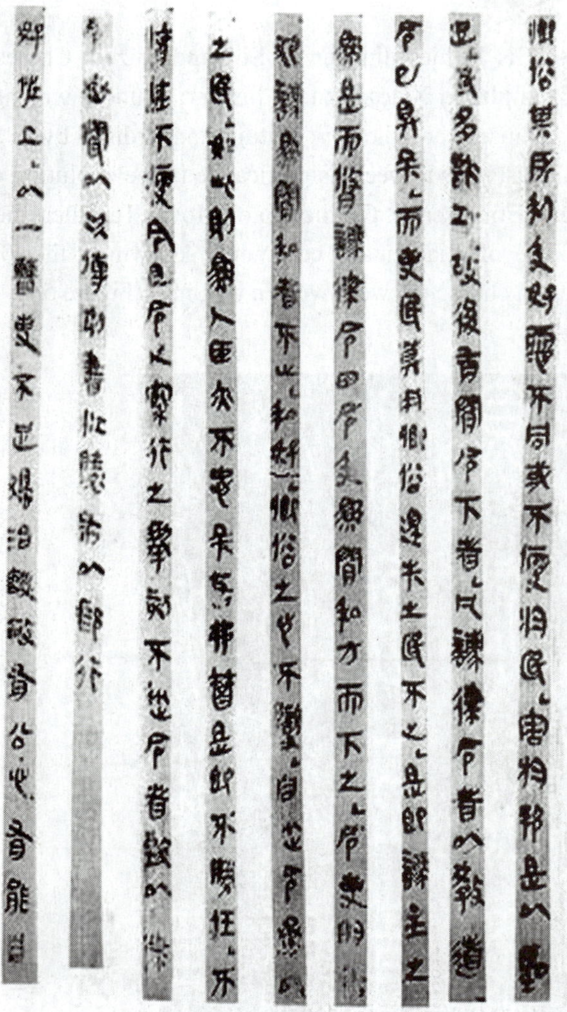

图 6　秦隶《云梦睡虎地秦墓竹简》

(2) Lishu (clerical script)

There are two styles of Lishu: Qin Li (Figure 6) and Han Li (Figure 7).

Qin Li is also named Gu Li. It was one of the writing scripts used in the Qin dynasty. At that time, Xiaozhuan was the standard writing script used by high officials in formal occasions; Lishu was an auxiliary writing script used by lower echelon officials in official occasions of lesser significance.　Because Zhuanshu was characterized by complicated strokes and was difficult to write well; round strokes in Zhuanshu became square strokes, and curvilinear strokes became straight strokes in the Qin Li style scripts. Qin Li is like a cursive writing style of the Zhuanshu.

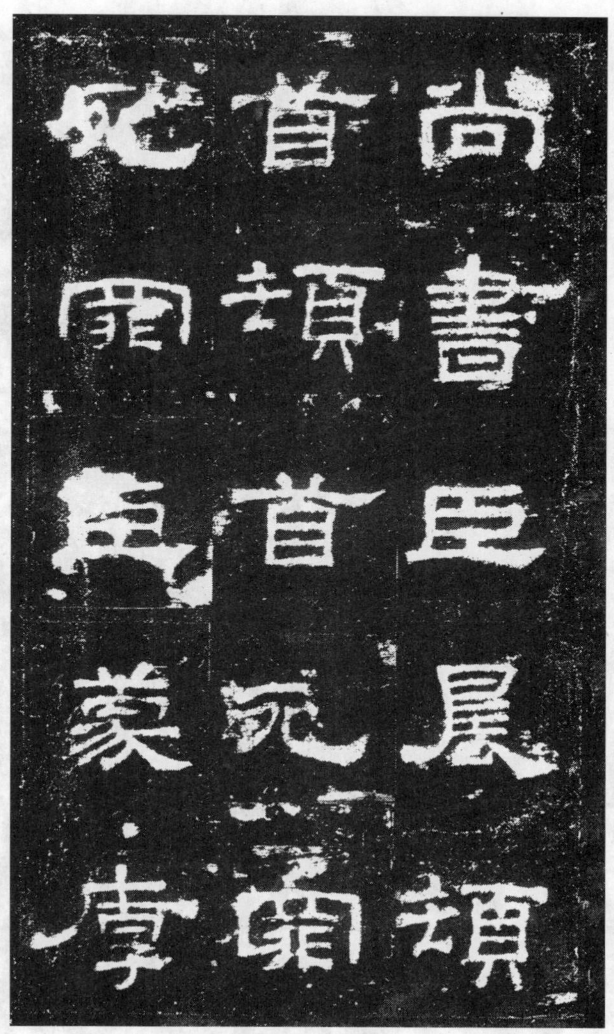

图 7　汉隶《史晨碑》

　　汉隶是在秦隶的基础上演变出来的，被称为今隶。汉隶是汉代通行的字体。从秦隶到汉隶的转变大约完成于距今 2100 年的西汉年间。这个转变在汉字发展史上又是一次传大的变革，它使汉字基本上摆脱了象形的形态，把小篆圆转弧形的笔画变成了方折平直的笔画。汉隶的字形跟今天的楷书已经很接近了。

（3）楷书

　　楷书又名真书、正书(图 8)。"楷"是规矩整齐、可为楷模的意思。

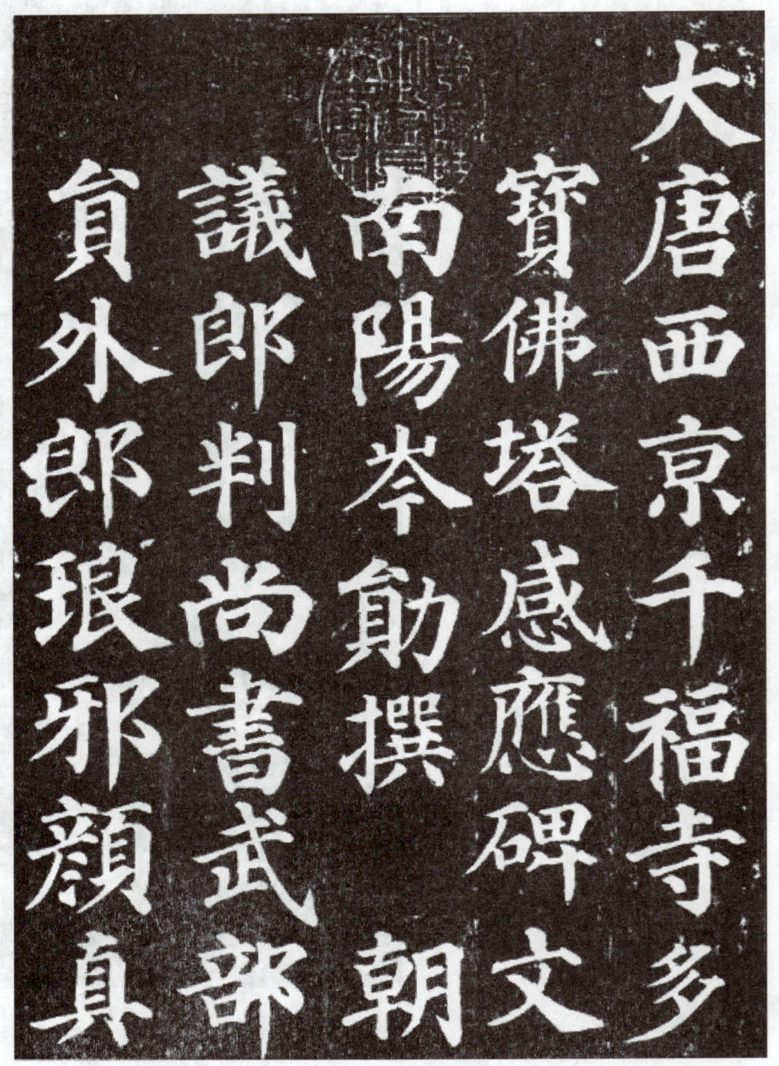

图 8　楷书 颜真卿《多宝塔碑》

Han Li evolved from Qin Li, and was also called Jin Li. Han Li was a commonly used script in the Han dynasty. Qin Li's evolution to Han Li was completed in the Xi Han dynasty approximately 2100 years ago. This transformation essentially removed modern day Chinese characters from ancient Chinese picture characters. It used square and straight lines instead of circular and round strokes of the Xiaozhuan scripts.　Han Li is quite close to the appearance of today's Kaishu script.

(3) Kaishu (standard script)

Kaishu, the standard script also named Zhenshu or Zhengshu. (Figure 8) Kai means orderly and evenly in appearance. Kaishu can be used as template in writing practices.

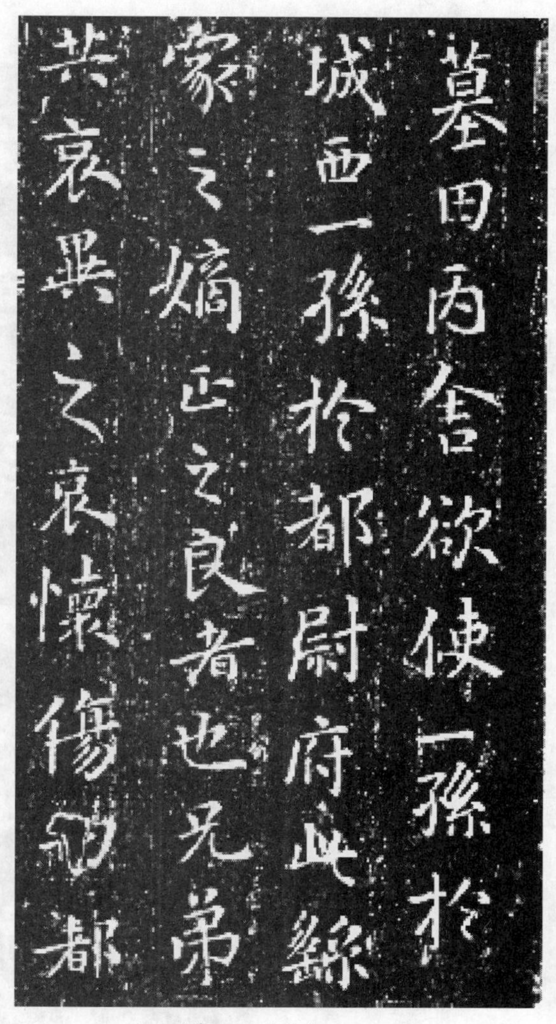

*《墓田丙舍帖》

西汉(公元前 206—公元 8 年)以前没有楷书;楷书是在隶书方正的基础上变化而来的,起始于东汉(25—220)末年,兴盛于魏(220—265)晋(265—420),距今约有 1800 年。楷书沿用至今,是通用时间最长的标准字体。

南北朝(420—589)时,书法艺术有很大的发展。尤其是北魏王朝(建于公元 424 年),在少数民族与汉民族的大融合中,出现了中国书法上瑰丽的魏碑(图 9)。魏碑是楷书中的奇丽作品。

隋(589—617)、唐(618—907)之际楷书发展到成熟的阶段,尤其是唐代,出现了一大批著名的楷书家和楷书作品。

北魏和唐代都是楷书高度发展的时期。对于这两个时期的楷书作品,史称魏碑和唐碑(也称唐楷,见图 8)。

如果把魏碑比喻为楷书的青少年时期,它还没有摆脱隶书的体势,还多少带有一些天真和稚气,那么,唐代的楷书就已经进入了壮年时期,也可以说是到达了鼎盛时期,笔画的个性特征十分鲜明,风格多样,充满创新意识。一千多年来,唐楷始终处在楷书的正统地位。直到今天,习楷书的人也多以唐楷作为学习的范本。

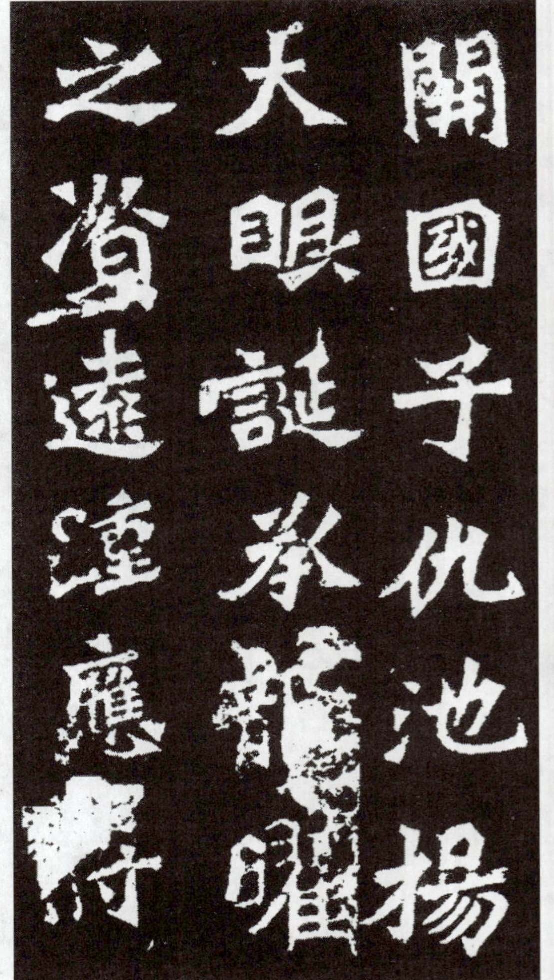

图 9　魏碑《杨大眼造像题记》

There was no Kaishu prior to the Western Han dynasty,　(206—8 BC).　The evolution of Kaishu from the square styled Lishu began in the last years of the Eastern Han dynasty (25—220 AD). This new writing style largely blossomed during the Wei dynasty (220—265 AD) and the Jin dynasty (265—420 AD), about 1800 years ago. Today, Kaishu is still a commonly used writing style, a very long and enduring Chinese writing script indeed.

In the Southern and Northern dynasties (420—589 AD), China had a major development in calligraphy art. During the Northern Wei dynasty, (founded in 424 AD), China fused many minority nations with the majority Han people; the excellent writing style of Northern Wei Bei appeared. (Figure 9). The beautiful Northern Wei Bei writing style is often called a jewel of the Kai script writing.

During the Sui dynasty (589—617 AD) and the Tang dynasty (618—907 AD), the Kaishu script reached its maturity. This was particularly obvious during the Tang dynasty. At that time a large volume created by Kaishu artists appeared.

The Northern Wei and Tang dynasties represent the peak of Kaishu calligraphy writing.　The calligraphy created during that period was called Wei Bei, Tang Bei (also called Tang Kai, Figure 8).

If one were to use the analogy of youth to represent Wei Bei, it would be because the writing of Wei Bei script retained some of the residual style of Lishu. Wei Bei, the new style was still innocent and youthful. On the other hand, Tang Kai was in the adult age where it reached its peak development. The unique strokes in Tang Kai were clear, clean and showed a variety of changes;　it was full of the expression of newer concepts. For over 1000 years, even to-day, Tang Kai retains its authoritative position in traditional calligraphy writings; all calligraphy learners used Tang Kai templates to begin their learning of Kaishu.

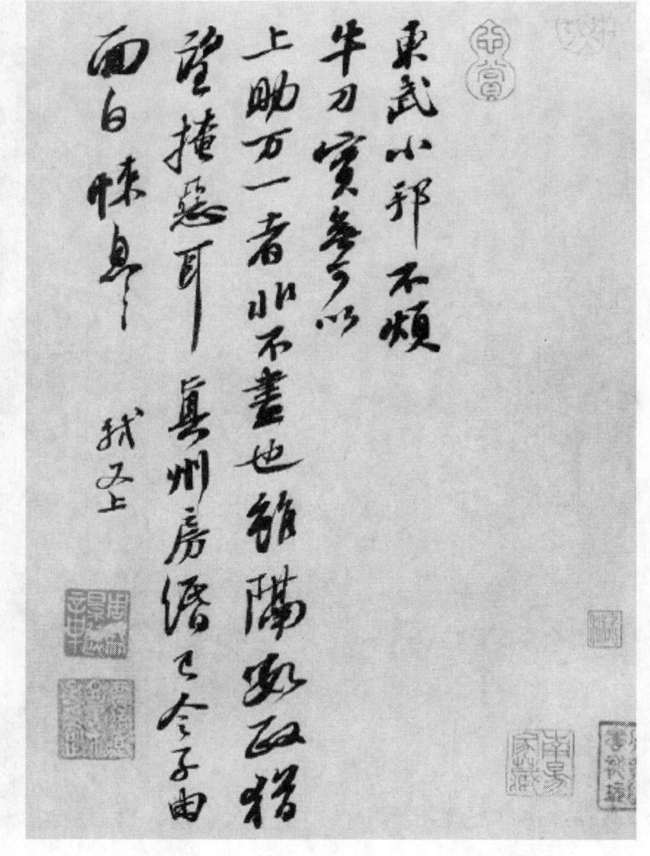

*《东武帖》

(4) 行书

行书(图 10)产生于东汉末年,是一种介于楷书和草书之间的字体。行书的特点是连笔很多,但行笔比较规矩,字迹也清楚易认,实用价值很高,既便于书写,又很美观。行书有两种:一种是接近楷书的,称真行,一种是接近草书的,称行草。无论真行或行草,都只具有相对的意义,有时很难分得很清楚。

(5) 草书

草书的产生跟行书差不多同时。草书有三种:章草(图 11)、今草(图 12)、狂草(图 13)。

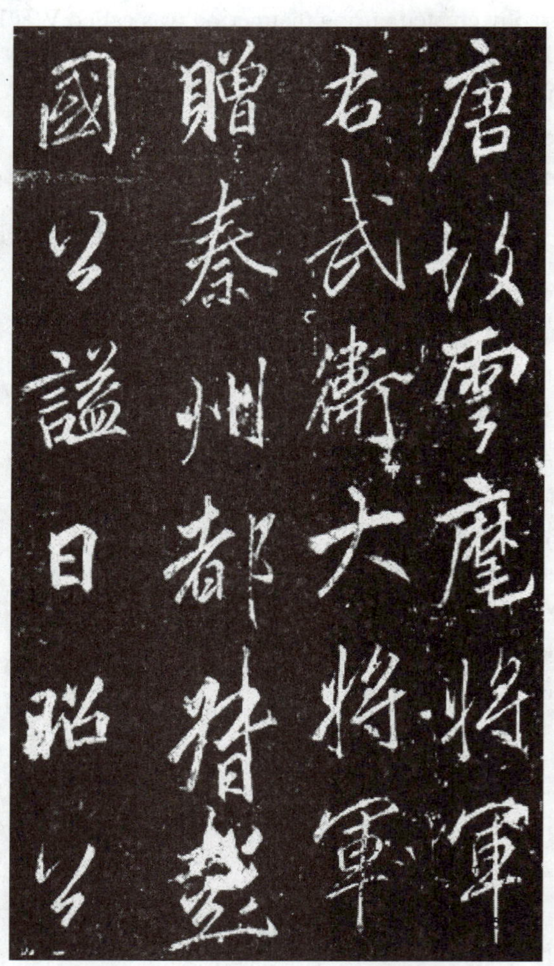

图 10　行书《李邕书云麾李思训碑》

(4) Xingshu (running script)

Xingshu (Figure 10) or "running script" appeared in the last years of the Eastern Han dynasty. It was a writing form in between Kaishu and Caoshu, in style. The unique characteristic of Xingshu is its use of multiple connecting strokes in the writing of each character though their strokes remain orderly and each character recognizable. Xingshu has a high practical value because it is easier to write, whilst retaining an artistic appearance. There are two kinds of Xingshu: one kind which is closer to the Kaishu style is called Zhenxing, the second kind which is closer to the Caoshu is called Caoxing. Irrespective of Zhenxing or Xingcao, they only give a meaning in relative terms; sometimes, they are difficult to distinguish.

(5) Caoshu (cursive script)

Caoshu appeared at about the same time as Xingshu. There are three kinds of Caoshu: Zhang Cao (Figure 11), Jin Cao (Figure 12), and Kuang Cao (Figure 13).

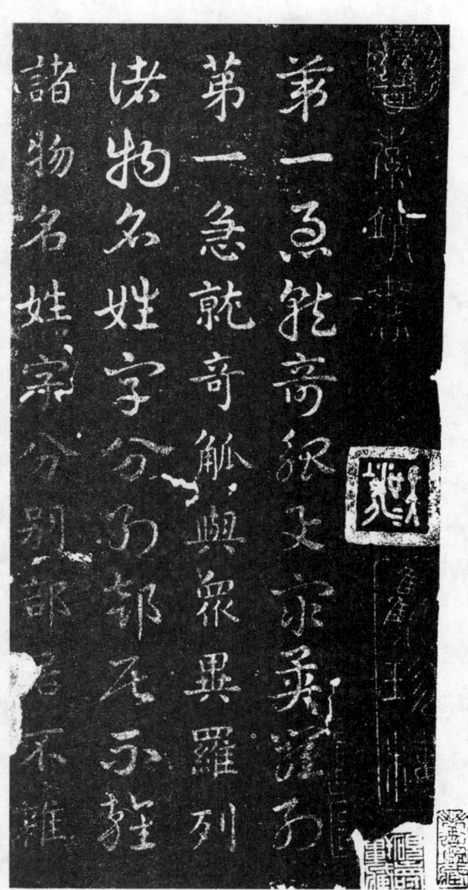

图 11　章草 史游《急就章》

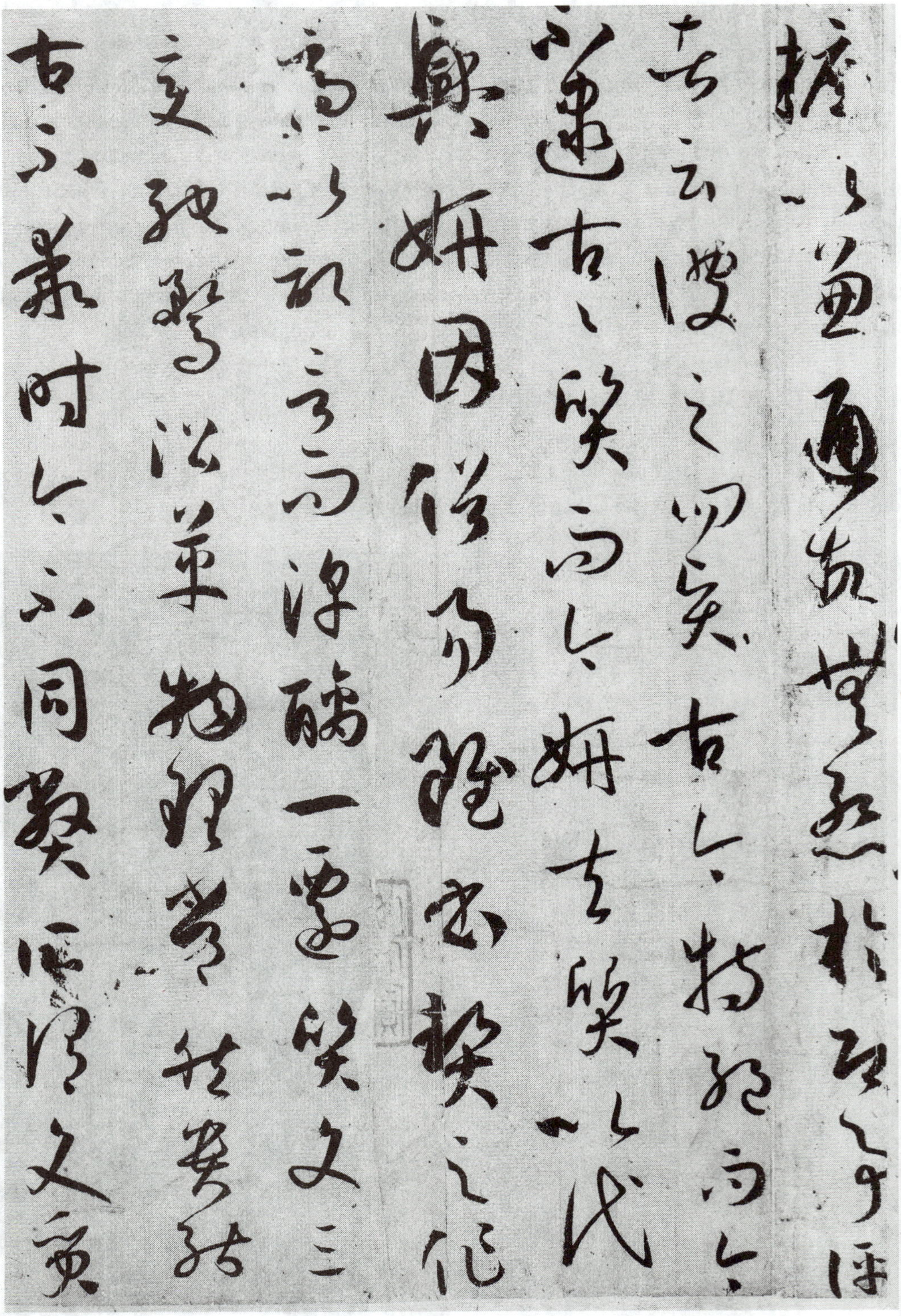

图 12　狂草 唐·怀素《自叙帖》

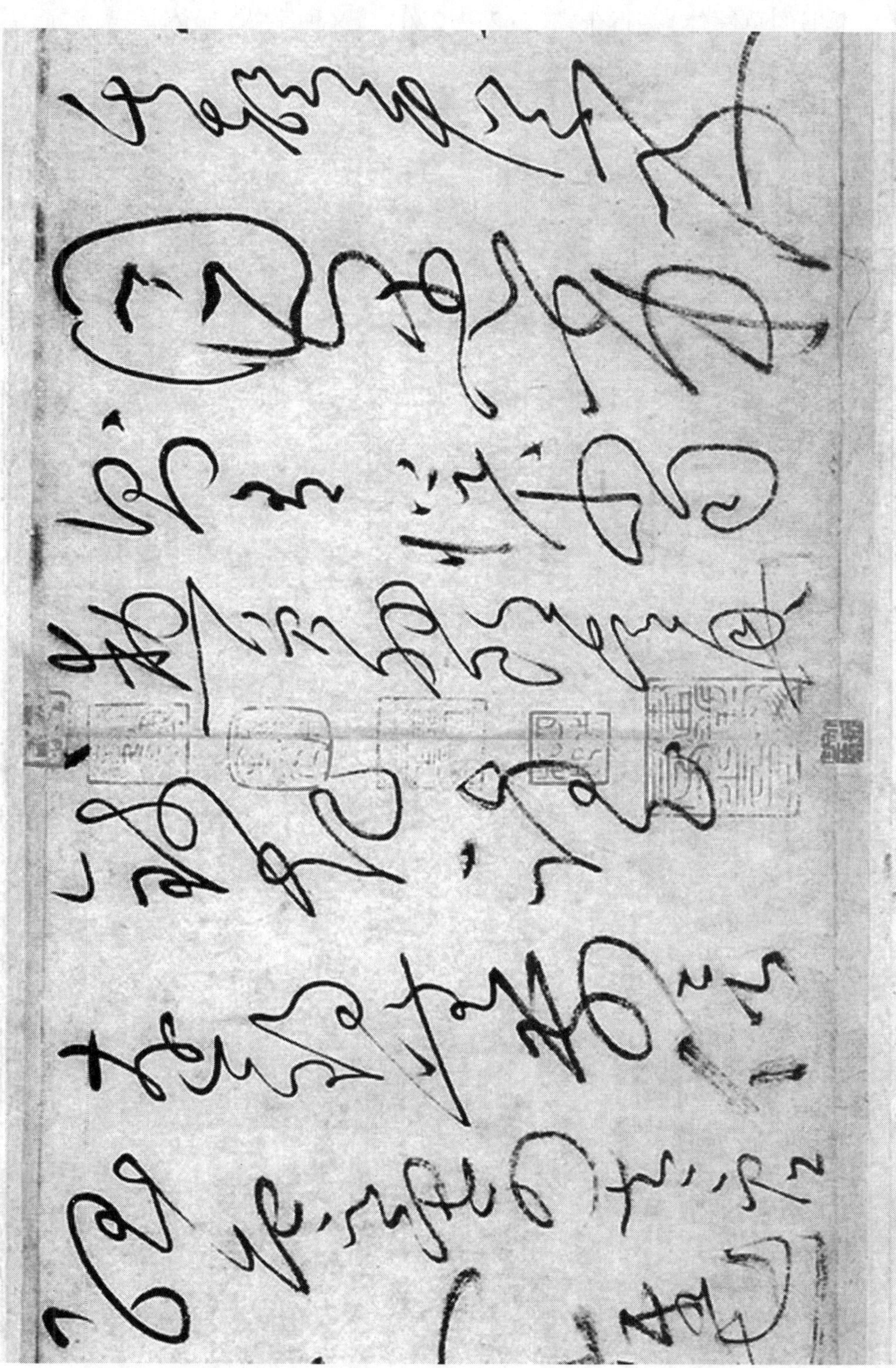

图 13　今草 唐·孙过庭《书谱》

　　章草是隶书的草写体,盛行于东汉(25—220)。这种字体,形体是隶书,而笔画相连,字字独立,很有规则。

　　今草是从章草变化来的,也产生于东汉末年。今草形体连绵,写起来便捷快速,字的大小、粗细、正斜相互交替,从整体上看,非常活泼,但字形难于辨认。

　　狂草产生于唐代,它在今草的基础上向纵横奔放的方向发展,以气势取胜,点画狼藉,大起大落,字形极难辨认,艺术价值甚高,但不实用。

　　古人把楷书比喻为站立,把行书比喻为行走,把草书比喻为奔跑,这是十分确切、生动的。

　　楷书、行书、草书这三种字体都是在魏晋时代定型而且成熟起来的。

　　下面将篆、隶、楷、行、草五种字体加以比较。(图 14)

	horse	cart	fish
Orade Bone script 甲骨文(jiǎ gǔ wén)			
Bronze script 金文(jīn wén)			
Large Seal script 大篆(dà zhuàn)			
Small Seal script 小篆(xiǎo zhuàn)			
Clerical script 隶书(lì shū)			
Standard script 楷书(kǎi shū)			
Running script 行书(xíng shū)			
Grass script 草书(cǎo shū)			

图 14　篆、隶、楷、行、草图表

Zhang Cao is the cursive writing of Lishu.　It was popular during the time of the Eastern Han (25—220 AD).　Zhang Cao's structure is similar to Li Shu. In Zhang Cao, however, strokes are connected, yet each character is written independently and orderly.

Jin Cao was an evolution of Zhang Cao and was born during the last years of the Eastern Han dynasty. Jin Cao strokes connect one another in the writing of characters, so they offer the convenience of applying fast moving strokes. Although characters are written in large or small sizes, thick and thin strokes, with the crossover of straight and tilted characters, these give Jin Cao the overall piece movement and vitality. It is, however, difficult to recognize individual Jin Cao characters.

Kuang Cao was also created in the Tang dynasty. It took from the basic styles of Jin Cao but moved Jin Cao strokes across an unrestricted boundary. There is vigor and vitality in the writing of such style. Strokes used in characters can be directed up or down and in all possible directions. The recognition of characters thus became a great difficulty. For this unrestricted appearance, Kuang Cao has a high value as art, but not for practical usage in communication.

One traditional analogy used to describe the unique characteristics of the three Chinese writing scripts above is:　Kaishu is like a person in a standing position;　Xingshu is like a person walking; and Caoshu is like a person running.

The three scripts: Kaishu, Xingshu and Caoshu were formed and matured in the Wei and Jing dynasty.

These three Chinese writing scripts are compared in Figure 14.

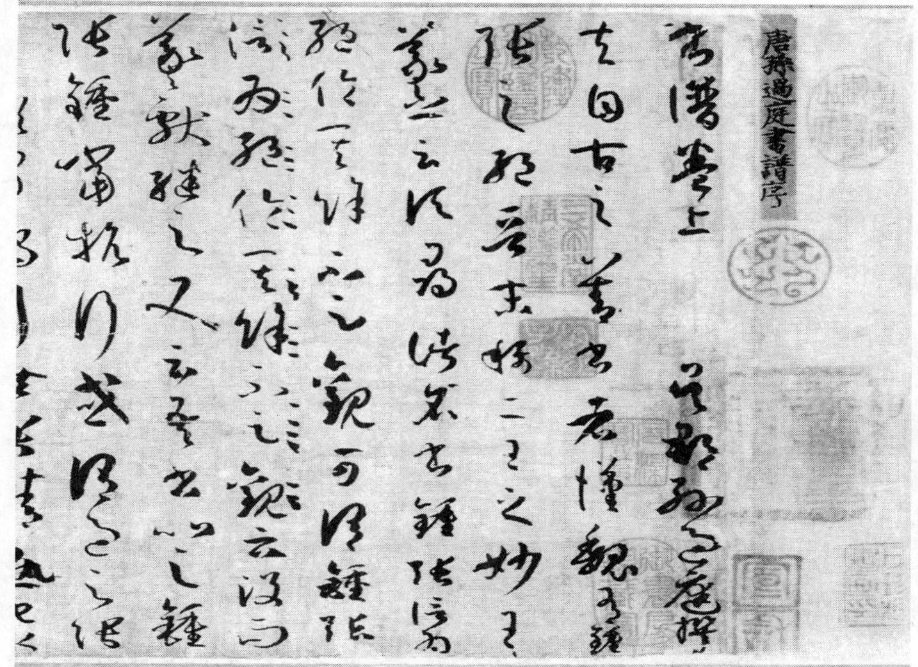

*《书谱》

第 三 章

Chapter 3

书 法 的 使 用 工 具

Tools for Chinese calligraphy

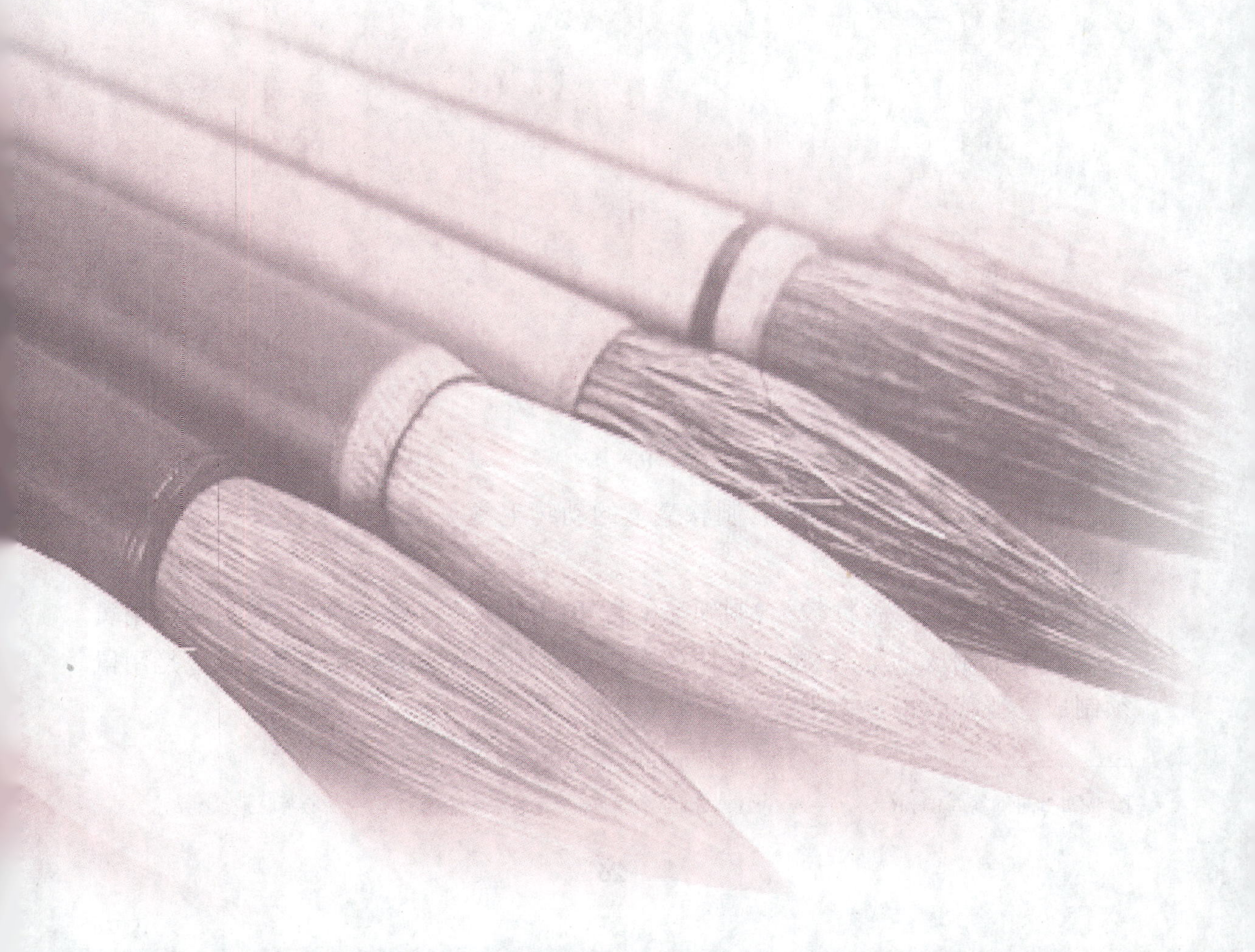

古代人书写汉字的工具主要是指笔、墨、纸、砚，也就是通常所说的文房四宝。古代称书房为文房，文房四宝就是书房里必备的四样用具。

(1) 笔

古代人写字使用的毛笔是中国人特有的书写工具。从考古的资料推断，毛笔的历史可追溯到约 6000 年前新石器时代的仰韶文化[1]时期。在仰韶文化遗址出土的彩陶上，我们看到描绘人、鱼等生物的生动形象和纵横交织的几何花纹，这显然是用毛笔所绘。

毛笔的种类很多。按毛笔的性能分，可分为软毫(图 15)、硬毫(图 16)、兼毫(图 17)三种。

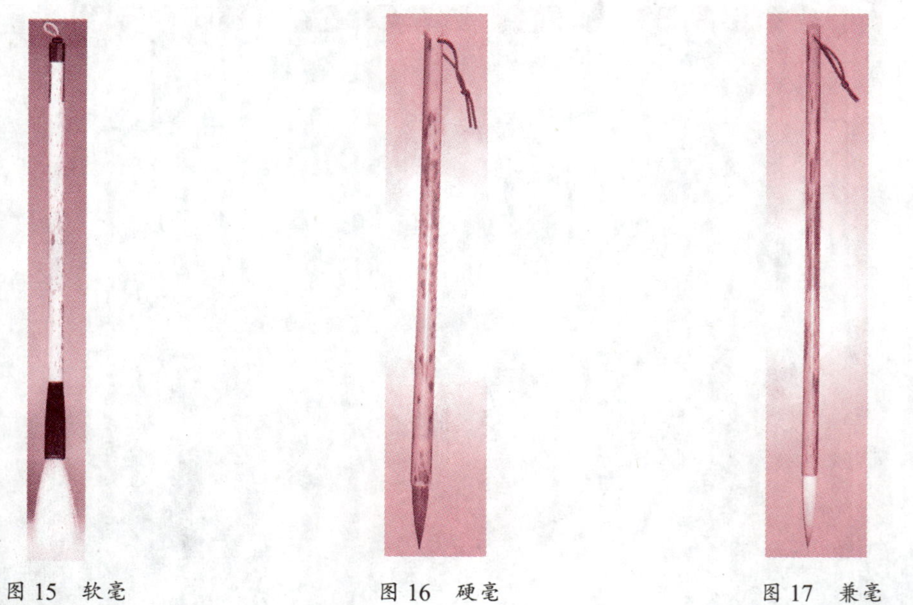

图 15　软毫　　　　　图 16　硬毫　　　　　图 17　兼毫

软毫，性柔软，弹性较弱，制软毫笔的动物毛常见的是羊毫，色白，也有用鸡毛制成的鸡毫笔。

硬毫，性刚硬，弹性较强，制硬毫笔常用的动物毛是狼毫。所谓狼毫是指用黄鼠狼的尾毛制成的笔，色黄。另外，硬毫中还有山兔毫、豹毫、鼠毫等。鼠毫是用鼠须制成。晋代大书法家王羲之喜用鼠须笔。

---

1 仰韶文化，中国新石器时代文化的一种，1921 年首次发现于河南渑池仰韶村，故名。生产工具以磨制的石器为主。

The principal tools for Chinese calligraphy are: Maobi or brush; Mo or ink; Zhi or paper; and Yan or ink-stone. The Chinese named them together as Wen Fang Si Bao. Wen Fang is the old term for a study. Si Bao means four treasures. The "four treasurers in the study" are the four essential tools for writing calligraphy in the study.

(1) Bi (brush)

The brush pen has a long history in China. It is unique to Chinese calligraphy. From archeological findings in China, the history of the brush may be traced back 6000 years ago to the New Stone Age of the Yang Shao Civilization[1]. Among unearthed ceramic fragments in the Yang Shao civilization, there were colorful paintings of people, fish, features of other living creatures, and crisscrossed geometric design patterns, all apparently drawn by brushes.

There are many types of calligraphy brushes. When brushes are classified according to the characteristics of their tips, there are Ruan Hao or "soft hair" (Figure 15), Ying Hao or "stiff hair brush" (Figure 16), and Jian Hao or "combination hair brush" (Figure 17).

The tips of Ruan Hao, or soft hair brushes are made of soft animal hair having a white color. These animal hairs have a weaker resilience. They are harvested from goats, or sometimes, from chicken feathers.

The tips of Ying Hao, or stiff hair brushes are made of stiffer animal hairs, having a yellowish color and with greater resilience. The stiff animal hairs are harvested from skunk, hare, leopard, or even mice. The mouse hair used actually comes from mouse whiskers. The greatest calligrapher in the Jing dynasty, Wang Xizhi, was a well known user of brushes made from mouse whiskers.

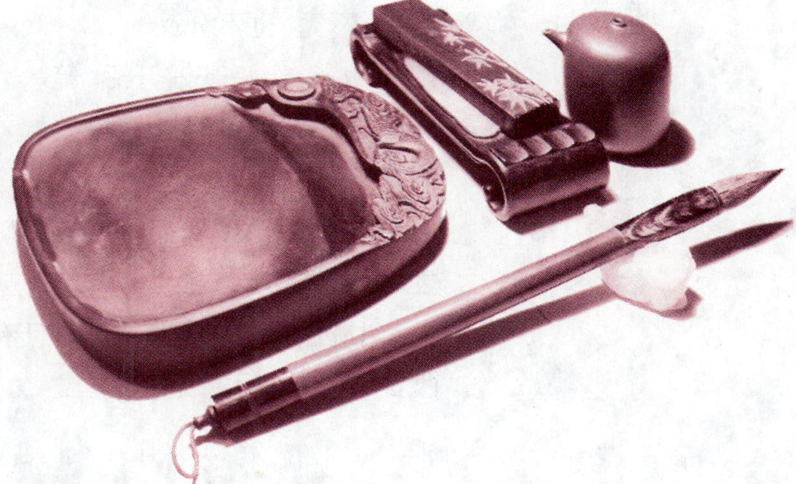

---

1 Yang Shao civilization. Chinese civilization in the New Stone Age (6000 years ago). It was so named because in 1921, the first archeological findings of the New Stone Age relics in China were unearthed in Henan province, Min Chi, Yang Shao Village. The main man-made instruments available in that civilization were polished sharp stones.

兼毫,刚柔和弹性介于软毫和硬毫之间,软硬适中,属中性,颜色呈灰色或杂色。常见的兼毫是山兔毫与羊毫合制成的紫羊毫笔,如七紫三羊(七成山兔毛、三成羊毛)、五紫五羊(五成山兔毛,五成羊毛)。羊毛的成分越多,笔性就越软。初学者常用的大白云、中白云就是羊狼兼毫。

无论软毫硬毫还是兼毫,书写者均可根据个人的习惯和爱好来选用。

按书写字体的大小来分,有小楷笔、中楷笔和大楷笔(图 18)。大楷笔指书写七公分左右大小见方字体的笔,中楷笔指写四五公分见方字体的笔,小楷笔指书写两公分以内见方字体的笔。

如要书写比大楷更大的字体,可用斗笔(图 19)。斗笔又称提笔,可书写三十多公分见方的字体,因字体状如斗方[1]而有斗笔之名。这种笔多用羊毫制成。

按毛锋的长短来分,可以分为长锋、短锋、中锋三类。长锋锋尖长,锋腹较柔,贮墨多,便于运转。短锋,锋尖短,锋腹较刚,贮墨少,宜于书写字体较小的字。中锋,锋尖介于长锋、短锋之间,宜于书写楷书体。

图 18　小楷笔、中楷笔、大楷笔

好的毛笔应具备以下四个条件：

a. 尖,笔毫聚合时,锋毛尖锐,不秃,也不分叉。

b. 齐,将笔毫铺开后,笔锋的毛平齐,没有长短参差的现象。

c. 圆,笔腹浑圆饱满,笔头呈圆锥形,没有凹凸不平之处。

d. 健,笔毫劲健有力,而且有弹性,笔毫展开之后能收拢,弯曲之后能挺直。

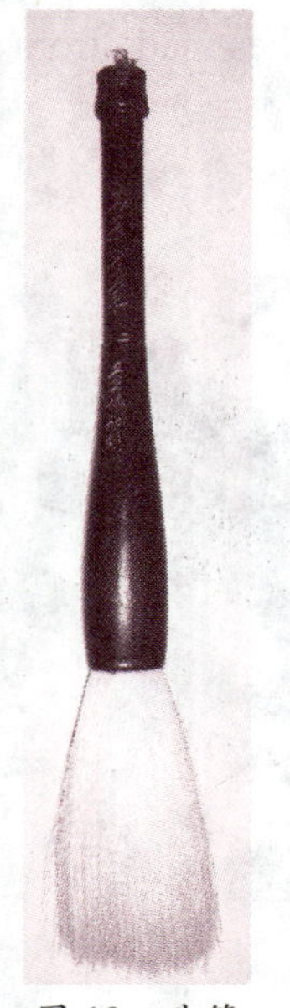

图 19　斗笔

---

1 斗方,30—70cm 的诗幅或书画页。

The tips of Jian Hao have a mixture of soft and stiff hairs. The color of this type of brush hair is often grey or a mixed color. The most common Jian Hao are made from combinations of hare hairs and goat hairs such as Zi Yang Hao bi. Specifically, there are 7 ZI 3 Yang (70 % hare hairs and 30 % goat hairs), or 5 ZI 5 Yang (50% hare hairs and 50% goat hairs).

When a higher percent of goat hair is used in Jian Hao Bi, the character of the brush is softer. The popular brushes Da Bai Yun and Zhong Bai Yun used by beginner calligraphers are made of a combination of goat hair and skunk hair. There are also Zi Lang Hao (a mixture of hare hairs and goat hairs) and Ji Lang Hao (a mixture of chicken hairs and skunk hairs). Although Zi Lang Hao is classified as a Jian Hao, it would more accurately be classified as a stiff hair brush. The latter Ji Lang Hao brush is on the soft side. Obviously, a calligrapher has the opportunity to select from a variety of combinations of brush characteristics to suit one's personal preference in stiffness and softness.

If one divides brushes according to the variation in sizes of intended writings, there are large brushes, medium-sized brushes, and small brushes. (Figure 18) The large brush is for writing characters one and a half inches to two inches square. The medium-sized brush is for writing characters one square inch in size. The small sized brush is for writing characters one tenth of an inch square in size.

If one intends to write characters even larger than a large sized brush can handle, there is Dou Bi (Figure 19). Dou Bi is also named Ti Bi and is suitable for writing one to two feet square sized characters. Because Dou Bi are shaped like a Dou Fang[1], the name of Dou Bi is therefore used. The brush of Dou Bi is often made of goat wool.

If one divides brushes according to variations in the lengths of the brush, there are Chang Feng (long tip), Duan Feng (short tip), and Zhong Feng (medium length tip). The tip of zhang feng is pointed and long. Its soft middle section can store more ink and the brush is easier to maneuver. The tip of Duan Feng is shorter. It has a stiffer middle section and thus carries less ink. It can be used to write smaller characters. The Zhong Feng is in between the two other sizes and is best for writing Kai Shu.

A high quality brush should possess the following four characteristics:
   a. Sharp point or tip. When in a folded position, the tip should stay together and be pointed. Any loose hairs or a partitioned tip are not acceptable.
   b. Uniform height. When the tip is placed in a flat position, all hair should be of the same length.
   c. Smooth. The middle section of the brush should be round and plump. The tip of the brush should be shaped like an inverted cone; and all the hair should be smooth.
   d. Resilience. Brush hair should have strength and resilience. Once a brush is open, the tip should collapse; once bent, the tip should bounce back.

---

1 Dou Fang, a piece of special calligraphy paper 30—70cm in size for the writing of poems or calligraphy.

（2）墨

墨是书写和绘画的黑色颜料。战国时期，墨已经得到比较广泛的应用。只是墨的制作并不固定，多数墨形同丸状，名为墨丸（图20）。

到了东汉，墨才逐渐制成墨锭而得以研磨。当时的制墨中心在陕西隃糜（今陕西千阳县东），人们就把"隃糜"作为墨的代称（图21）。从墨丸制成墨锭，在中国制墨史上是一件划时代的大事。

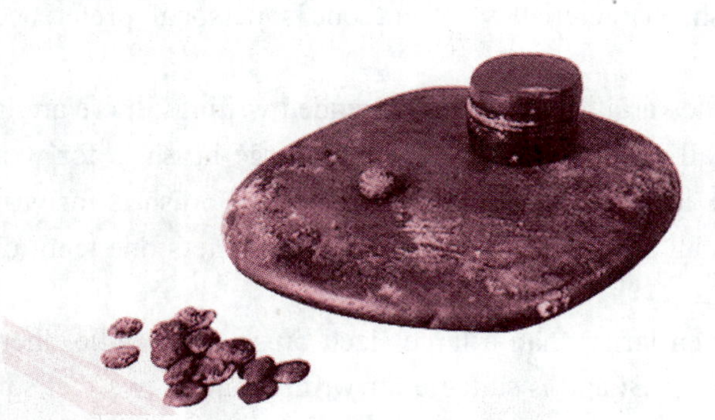

图20　墨丸

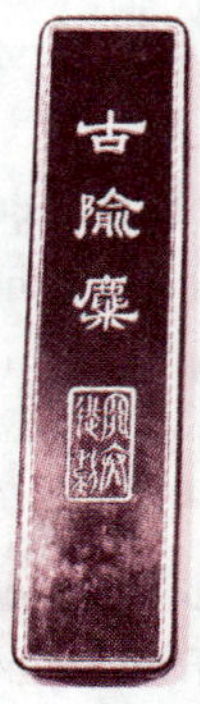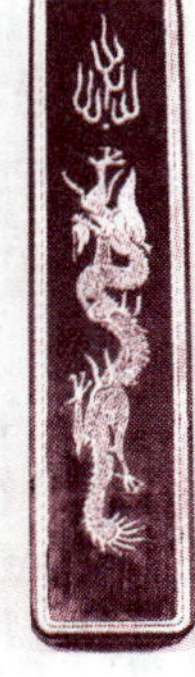

图21　隃糜墨

魏晋以后，墨的形状趋于规整，于是出现了很多制墨的名家。到了唐代末年，河北易县的制墨名家奚超、奚廷珪父子因为逃避战乱，从易县迁至歙州（今安徽歙县），奚超父子看见歙州多松，利于制墨，就定居下来。他们不断钻研制墨技术，大大提高了制墨工艺，名声大振。南唐后主李煜（公元961年）用了他们的墨以后，大为赏识，封奚超为墨官，并赏赐他们全家改姓国姓——李，于是奚超、奚廷珪便改成李超、李廷珪了。直到北宋时代（公元960—1127年），李超父子所制的墨依然盛名不衰，被誉为天下之冠。宋徽宗（公元1101—1125年）时，把李氏和其他名家所制的墨定为徽墨。

徽墨的特点是：色泽黑润，墨入纸后，久不褪色，香味浓郁，书写自如。

明（公元1368—1644年）清（公元1644—1911年）时期，徽墨的制作达到极高的境地。

墨的种类很多，从用料的不同可分为松烟墨、油烟墨、选烟墨三种。

松烟墨，以松枝烧烟为主要原料，加胶、药物、香料调制而成，这种墨质细色润，入水易化，不足之处是色黑少光泽。

(2) Mo (ink)

Mo is the black colored ink used for Chinese calligraphy and Chinese painting. During the Warring Period, Mo had already earned a broad public acceptance. Because the ink manufacturing process at that time was not uniform and stable, ink sticks were not made in the shape of a stick but rather a round shaped ball. (Figure 20)

During the Eastern Han Dynasty, Mo was truly made into sticks. It was found that this shape could be applied more conveniently by writers. The center of mo manufacturing was in Shan Xi Yu Mi (today's east of Qian Yang County in Shan Xi province), people have been using Yu Mi, the name of the town as an alternative name for ink stick. (Figure 21) The progression from making round shaped ink balls to the making of ink sticks was a major historical event in the Mo making history in China.

After the Wei Jing period, the shape of Mo became more standardized. Also, a number of famous manufacturers of ink sticks came into the market. In the final years of the Tang dynasty, the famous ink stick makers Xi Chao and his son Xi Tinggui in of province Yi county of Heibei province were forced to relocate their homes to She Zhou in order to avoid civil disturbances. Father and son both noticed the abundant amount of pine trees in She Zhou and decided to settle there in order to take advantage of the supply of this major ingredient for Mo manufacturing. Their continued research and improvement of manufacturing of Mo earned them great respect. King Li Yu of the reconstituted Nan Tang dynasty (961 AD) was so impressed by the Xi family and their Mo, he offered them his own last name, Li. Thus Xi Chao and Xi Tinggui became Li Chao and Li Tinggui. Their reputation in the manufacturing of high quality Mo lasted for many years until the Bei Song era (960 —1127 AD). King Song Hui Zong (1101—1125 AD) officially named Mo made by Li and others Hui Mo.

The unique character of Hui Mo is that it has an uniformly smooth black color. Once written on paper Hui Mo will not fade; and the fragrance in the ink will also last.

During the Ming Dynasty (1368—1644 AD) and the Qing Dynasty (1644—1911 AD), Hui Mo manufacture reached the pinnacle of its quality.

There are many kinds of Mo. Based on its ingredients they can be classified as Song Yan Mo or Pine Ash Mo, You Yan Mo or Oil Ash Mo, and Xuan Yan Mo or Xuan Smoke Mo.

The basic ingredient of Song Yan Mo is the ashes of pine wood.

In addition to the ash, glue, fragrance, other chemicals are added. Song Yan Mo is smooth and soft in its black color. It dissolves easily in water, but its weakness is the lack of brightness.

油烟墨，主要用桐油、菜籽油、麻籽油、猪油中的一种或兼用其中的二三种燃炼成烟，加胶、药物、香料调制而成。墨色黝黑透紫，不足之处是胶性较重。

选烟墨，用工业炭墨加胶和香料制成，价格低廉，不足之处亦是色黑少光泽。

好墨要具备以下几个条件：

质细，墨磨出后没有渣滓，书写时流畅、润滑。

胶轻，墨中配制的胶少，磨出的墨汁虽浓，但不涩笔。

色黑，指墨色黑而有神采，写在纸上的墨迹，经阳光照射，以泛紫光者为最佳，黑中泛绿或蓝光的也是好墨。

声轻，研墨时，或扣击墨块时，发出的声音轻脆，而不是粗浊。

现在为了省时省事，常用墨汁代替墨锭。常见的好墨汁有"一得阁墨汁"、"中华墨汁"、"书画墨汁"（图22）等。

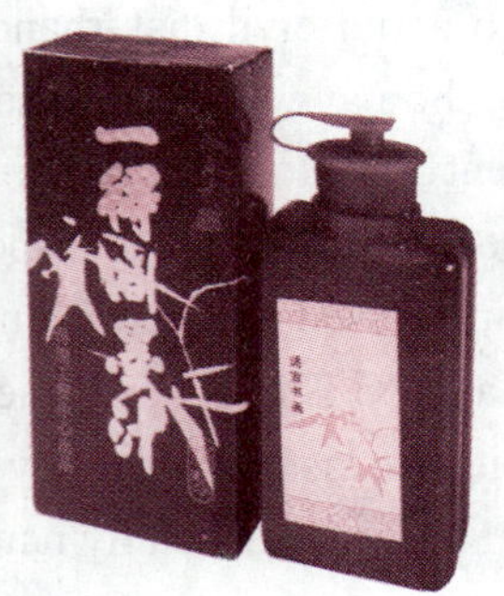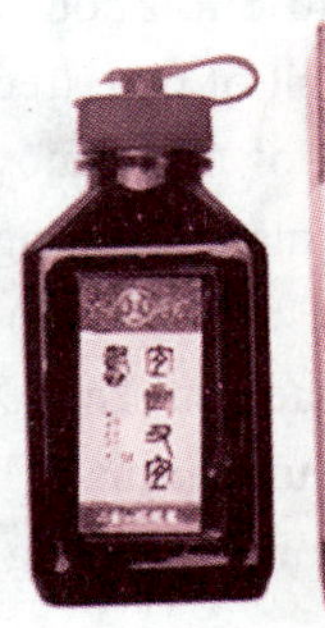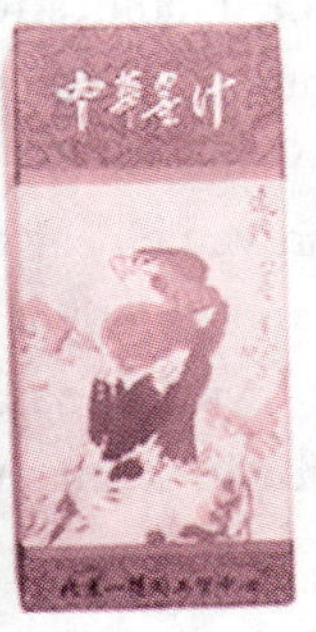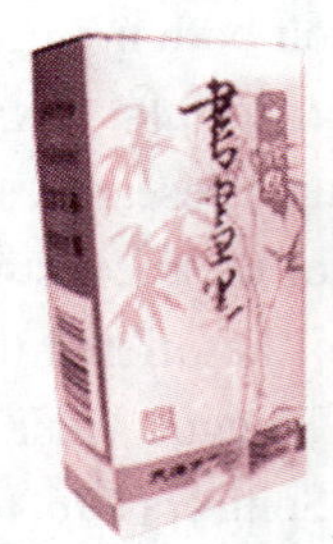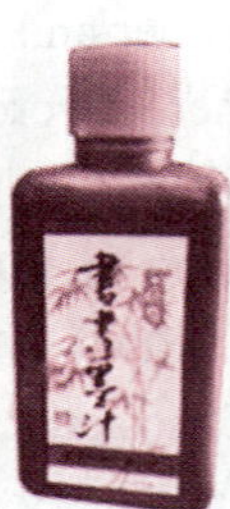

图22　一得阁墨汁、中华墨汁、书画墨汁

（3）纸

早在西汉时期，中国已经有了植物纤维纸的制作。1957年8月8日在陕西西安东郊灞桥古墓出土的灞桥纸是世界上最早的植物纤维纸，这些纸是用麻制成的。

纸号称中国的四大发明[1]之一。在中国的历史上，向来有蔡伦造纸的传说。

---

1 四大发明，纸、印刷术、指南针和火药，都由中国人发明，然后相继传入世界各地。

You Yan Mo uses ashes from burning linseed oil, vegetable seed oil, and lard either alone or in combination. Added to the ashes are glue, fragrance and other chemicals. The black color of the You Yan Mo has a touch of purple. Its weakness is the thickness of the glue.

Xuan Yan Mo uses ashes from burning industrial material. Added to it are glue and fragrance. It is economical to manufacture, but its weakness is a lack of luster in the black ink.

High quality Mo has the following characteristics:

Smooth ink. There should be no residue left in the ink stone. When applied in writing, the brush should move freely and fluidly.

Light glue. There should not be any excessive amount of glue in the ink. Although the ink is thick, it should not give the brush a stiff or immobile feeling.

Black and glittering color. The color of black ink should be dark black and glittering. When strokes are drawn on paper and sunlight radiates on the calligraphy,　a dark purple reflection from the writings is preferable.　A dark green or blue colored reflection is also acceptable.

Quiet sound. When the fine Mo is tapped on the ink stone, it should make a crisp rather than a dull sound.

Today, for the sake of convenience and time, many people use ready-made liquid black ink instead of ink sticks. High quality liquid black inks include: Yi-De-Ge Mo Zhi, Zhong Hua Mo Zhi, Shu Hua Mo Zhi (Figure 22) etc.

(3)　Zhi (paper)

As early as the Western Han era, China invented a paper making process using vegetable fibers. On August 8, 1957, in the unearthed Ba Qiao Zhi, an ancient tomb in the east suburb of Xian An City, the world's oldest fiber material paper was found. This paper was made from linen.

China claims paper as one of her four greatest inventions. [1] In Chinese history, Cai Lun is

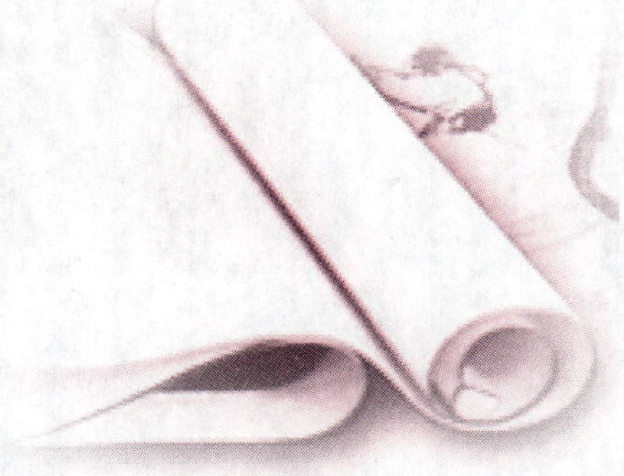

---

1 The four greatest inventions of China are paper, the printing process, the compass, and gun powder. They were invented in China and spread to other parts of the world.

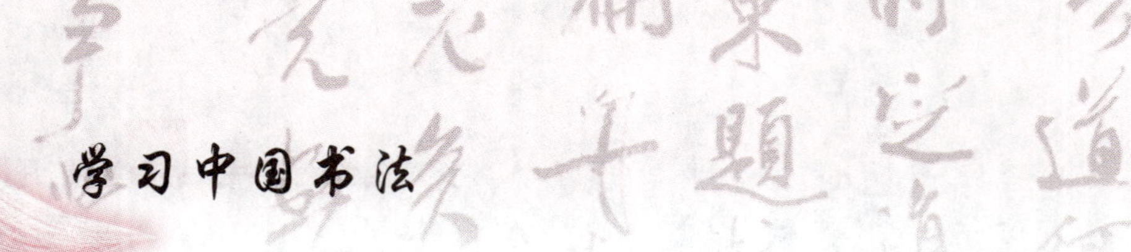

蔡伦是东汉时人,公元 105 年,蔡伦把造纸工艺上奏朝廷,得到了汉和帝的充分肯定,后来他所造的纸就风行天下了,被称为蔡侯纸[1]。然而,准确地说,蔡伦之前,也就是西汉年间,已有了植物纤维纸的存在,所以,蔡伦是总结西汉以来麻质纤维的造纸经验,改进了造纸技术,才使纸的制造工艺进入了一个崭新的阶段。在中国造纸史上,蔡伦的确是有伟大贡献的。

魏晋以后,造纸原料逐步扩大到树皮、藤、草、竹各类,纸的品种就越来越多了。

隋唐时期是造纸的全盛时期,纸的质量和产量都较魏晋时期有很大的提高。特别是有"纸中之王"美誉的宣纸(图 23)是这一时期最有名的产品。宣纸因产于安徽宣城而得名,它的实际产地是安徽泾县。

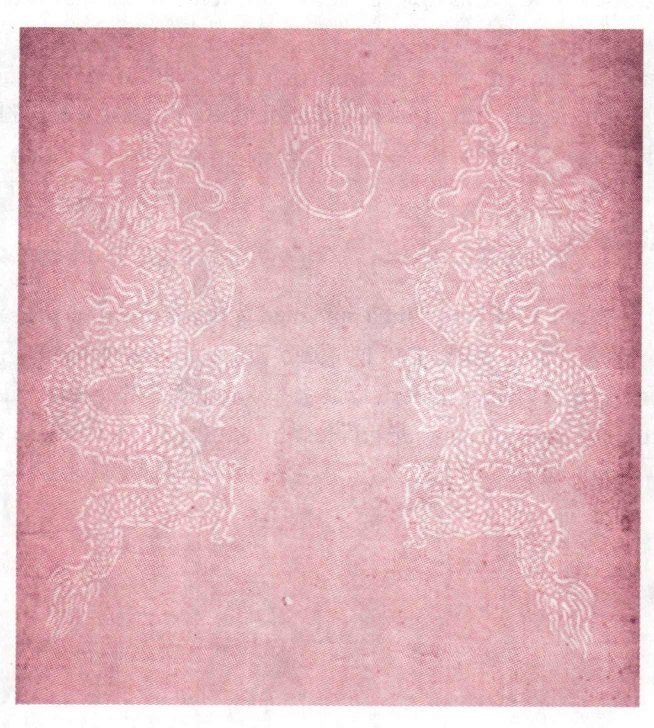

图 23　宣纸

---

1 蔡侯纸,蔡伦(? —121),字敬仲,桂阳(今湖南郴州市)人,封龙亭侯,发明了用树皮、麻头、破布、旧渔网为原料制成的纸。

recorded as the inventor of paper. Cai Lun, a person from the Eastern Han era, submitted his paper making invention to the King in 105 AD and received official recognition from Han Wu Di. Paper made by its inventor later became available throughout the entire country. It was called Cai Lun paper[1]. Earlier in the Western Han era, the use of fibers for making paper was already known. It was not until Cai Lun, however, that linen materials were used to make paper. Cai Lun also improved the manufacturing process, elevating the paper manufacturing to a higher level. In the Chinese history of paper making, Cai Lun made many important contributions.

After Wei Jin era, raw materials used in paper making broadened to include tree bark, vines, grasses, bamboo and other different vegetable fibers. The types of paper were also broadened.

The Sui Tang era was the peak of paper manufacturing in China. At that time, the quality and quantity of paper were much improved compared to that of the previous Wei Jin era, especially, Xuan Zhi (the king of papers) (Figure 23), a very high quality paper came into being at this time.

Xuan Zhi was so named because it was thought to be a product of Anhui Xuan City. In reality, Xuan Zhi is actually a product of Anhui Jing County.

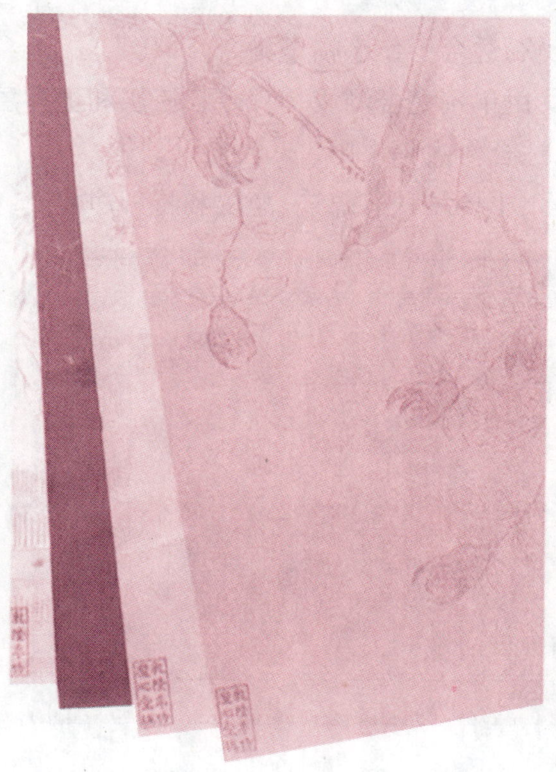

---

1 Cao Hou Zhi , Cai Lun (?-121AD) also named Jing Zhong , of Gua Yang (today's Hunan Province Zhen Zhou County). He was honored with the rank of Duke of Long Ting. He was also credited for the invention of using tree bark, linen, salvaged clothing materials, and old fish nets to make paper.

　　宣纸的主要成分是檀树皮和稻草。檀树皮决定纸的韧性和拉力，稻草决定纸的绵软性，两者掺用呈现一种独特的润墨性能。

　　按宣纸的性质可分为生宣、熟宣、半熟宣三种。

　　生宣，是直接从纸槽中抄出后经过烘干而不做加工处理的宣纸，特点是受墨后易渗化洇散，主要用于书法和大写意画[1]。

　　熟宣，是生宣纸加明矾、骨胶等制成，特点是不易受墨，也不渗化，主要用于画工笔画[2]，亦可用于写楷书、隶书。

　　半熟宣，是用生宣浸以各种植物液而成的加工纸，特点是比熟宣容易吸墨，又不像生宣那样容易渗化洇散，主要用于书写小幅屏条、册页和画小写意[3]。

　　按宣纸的大小分，纸的长度有三尺、四尺、五尺、六尺、八尺等，宽度为长度之半，也有长至一丈二、一丈六的。

按宣纸的厚薄分有单宣、夹宣两种。

　　单宣，纸薄而轻软，适合于作小幅书画。

　　夹宣，纸层较厚，由单宣叠合制成，有两层、三层和更多层的夹宣。纸厚必粗，不像单宣那样细腻，适合作大幅书画。

　　宣纸的品种很多，主要品种有绵连、净皮和特种净皮。

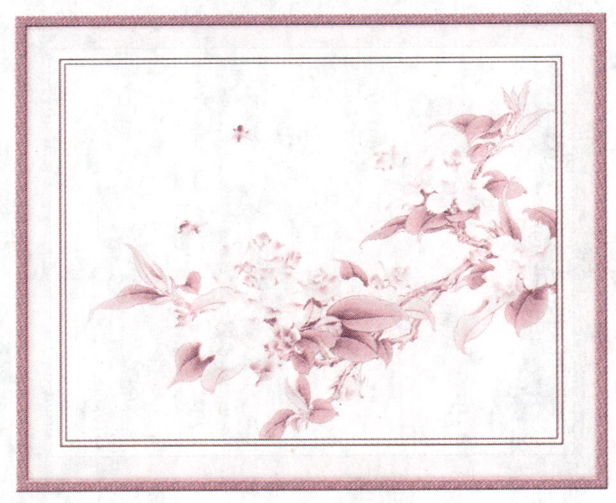

---

[1] 大写意画，中国画中属纵放一类的画法，要求通过简洁的笔墨，写出物象的形神，来表达作者的意向。

[2] 工笔画，中国画中属工整细致一类的画法。

[3] 小写意，画法不及大写意奔放，多为小幅作品。

The principal raw material used for the making of Xuan Zhi is sandalwood tree bark and rice stalks. Sandalwood tree bark determines the strength and elasticity of the paper; and rice stalk determines the softness of the paper. The combination of these two fiber materials gave the Xuan Zhi a special capability for ink absorption.

Xuan Zhi may be divided into Sheng Xuan (raw Xuan paper), Shu Xuan (baked xuan paper) and Ban Shu Xuan (half baked Xuan paper).

In the manufacture of Sheng Xuan, raw pulp is taken out of the Xuan Zhi from its mixing bin to dry without any additives. Its special quality is in the spreading of ink once applied on paper. The principal use of Sheng Xuan is for writing calligraphy and Da Xie Yi Hua (wash painting).[1]

Shu Xuan or baked Xuan is made by adding alum, animal glue, etc to the Xuan paper pulp. Its special quality is that it does not easily smear upon the application of ink (or water). The main use of Shu Xuan is in Gong Bi Hua (or detailed stroke painting) [2] and the writing of Kai Shu and Li Shu.

The process for making half baked Xuan paper is to soak raw Xuan paper with different kinds of vegetable juices in the raw ingredients. Its unique character is its absorption rate: faster than baked Xuan paper but not as quickly and freely as the raw Xuan paper. The main use of half baked Xuan paper is in the calligraphy writing that appears on small scrolls, pamphlets and painting of Xiao Xie Yi Hua (a moderately free-expressional painting) [3].

Today, Xuan Zhi comes in different sizes: 3 feet, 4 feet, 5 feet, 6 feet and 8 feet in length having widths half of the length. There are also extra large size Xuan Zhi paper as long as 14 feet or 18 feet.

Classifying Xuan Zhi according to its thickness, there are Dan Xuan and Jia Xuan .

Dan Xuan paper is thin, light, and soft. It is most suitable for small size painting or calligraphy.

Jia Xuan is a thick Xuan paper composed of multiple layers of Dan Xuan paper. Because this paper is thick, it is coarse and heavy rather than smooth and soft. Jia Xuan is suitable for large size calligraphy and painting.

There are many types of Xuan Zhi, such as Mian Lian, Jing Pi and Te Zhong Jing Pi.

---

1 Da Xie Yi Hua, A style of Chinese painting using simple strokes and applying different shades of black ink to express the essence of objects.

2 Gong Bi Hua, A kind of Chinese painting technique using detailed strokes to express objects in a picture.

3 Xiao Xie Yi, An impression drawing done in a smaller sized picture.

绵连是一种用坚韧柔软的茎皮制作的纸张，最早多用桑树皮制作，因为皮料坚固，纸纹扯断像棉丝一样，所以称绵连。现在的绵连多用檀树皮制作，适合于写楷书和中、小行书字。

净皮是一种质量很好的最薄宣纸，檀树皮的皮料较绵连为多，适合于写草书和大、中行书字。

特种净皮是皮料经过特别加工制作的宣纸，皮料较净皮为多，适合于书法中使用浓墨、斗笔，也适合于绘画中的泼墨、重彩之作。

在生宣中，绵连、净皮、特种净皮都是宣纸中的上品，宜书宜画，尤其是特种净皮，更是宣纸中的精品。

安徽泾县是宣纸的主要产地，泾县生产的宣纸，质量在全国书画纸中是最好的。一千多年来，代代相传，在国内外享有极高的声誉。

宣纸名贵，售价较高，初学写字的人可以用竹纤维制成的元书纸、毛边纸练习，既经济，又实惠。

（4）砚

砚的本意是"研"，就是供磨墨的意思。砚，亦称砚台、砚池、墨海。按原料的不同，砚可分为石砚、陶砚、砖砚、瓦砚、瓷砚、玉砚等等。石砚最为普通，砖砚、瓦砚易伤毛笔，最好不用。

20 世纪 50 年代在西安半坡仰韶文化遗址发掘出一种供研磨用的石磨盘（图 24），说明距今约六七千年前的新石器时代就已出现石砚了，但那时的石砚只是供彩绘用的。

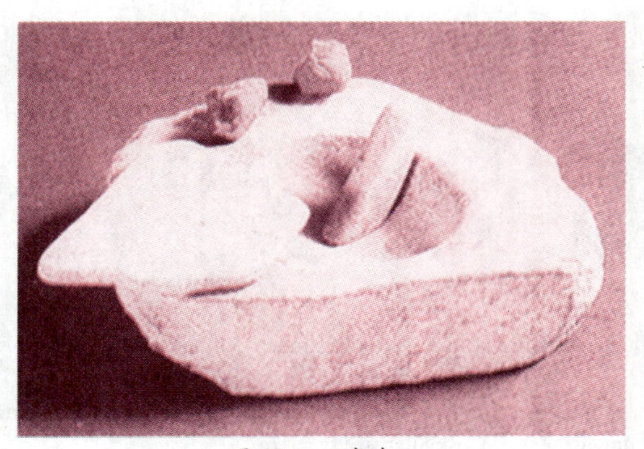

图 24　石磨盘

Mian Lian paper is made from strong and flexible fibre pulp. In earlier time, its pulp was made of mulberry tree bark. Because its toughness, shreded paper has the appearance of silk, so the paper was named Mian Lian. Today, Mian Lian paper uses mostly cedar tree bark as its raw pulp material and the tree bark represent 40% of its total raw pulp material. Mian Lian paper is most suitable for writing Kai Shu; medium and small sized Xing Shu.

Jing Pi is a thin but high quality Xuan Zhi. Its pulp is made of sandalwood tree bark and the tree bark represents 60% of its total raw pulp material. Jing Pi paper is most suitable for writing cursive style of large and medium sized running script characters.

Te Zhong Jing Pi uses a special process to treat tree barks for the making of its pulp. It has a higher percentage of wood bark and the paper is stronger and has more strength. When there is more water in the ink, or more ink in a larger sized brush pen, the ink does not smear easily on the paper. Te Zhong Jing Pi is most suitable for the using of thick ink or Dou Bi. It is also suitable for wash painting or heavily colored water painting.

Shen Xuan, Mian Lian, Jing Pi, and Te Zhong Jing Pi are all high quality Xuan Zhi. These papers are suitable for calligraphy writing or water color painting. In particular, Te Zhong Jing Pi is considered the best of all Xuan papers.

Jing County in An Hui province is the center of Xuan Zhi manufacturing in China. After over a thousand years of experience in making paper, Xuan Zhi made in Jing County has earned a world wide reputation for high quality.

Xuan Zhi is a relatively expensive paper. Beginners at calligraphy should consider using Yuan Shu Zhi and Mao Bian Zhi which are made from bamboo fiber and thus are cheaper.

(4) Yan (ink stone)

Yan is a hard top stone platform used for rubbing or mixing mo and water together to make ink. Yan is also named Yan Tai; Yan Chi; and Mo Hai. Yan is usually divided into Shi Yan, Tao Yan, Zhuan Yan, Wa Yan, Ci Yan, and Yu Yan, etc. Shi Yan is the most popular. Zhuan Yan and Wa Yan have rough surfaces which can harm brush tips.

Among the archeological findings in the 1950's of Xi'an, Ban Po Yang Shao, there was a stone plate (Figure 24) for rubbing Mo and painting colors. It indicated that during the New Stone Age, approximately 6000 to 7000 years ago, in China, Yan was already known and used.

　　1975 年在湖北云梦县出土了秦代的鹅卵石石砚，与此同时，还发现了与墨丸配套使用的研石。这种研石是压住墨丸来使用的，说明秦汉时期砚的作用已经从调色为主转为磨墨为主了。

　　唐代以后，石砚最有名的品种是端砚（图 25）和歙砚（图 26）。

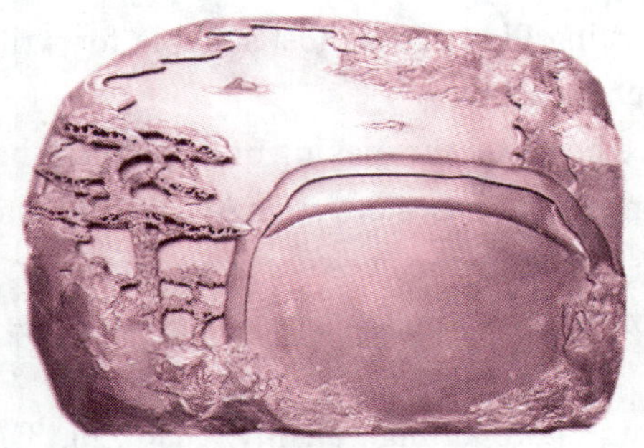

图 25　端砚

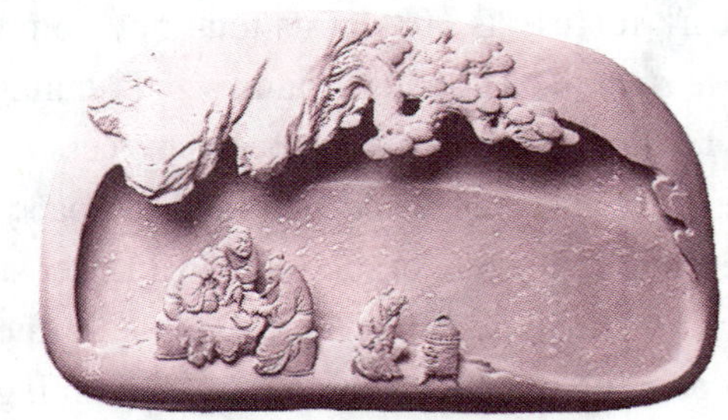

图 26　歙砚

　　端砚产于广东肇庆的端溪，距今有 1300 年的历史。就石质来说，端砚肌肤细密，质地坚实，摸上去稚嫩而湿润，墨光莹澈，捺笔时不伤笔毛，的确是砚中珍品。

　　端砚的另一突出特点是石的品种多而且美。有的端砚浸在水中可以看到有如"微尘""鹅毛"状的青色花纹夹在几点较大的玫瑰紫中间，这就是最为名贵的青花紫石砚。

　　歙砚，产于歙州府的婺源县（今属江西省），距今有 1200 多年的历史。歙砚又名婺源砚、龙尾砚，呈青灰色，比端砚质嫩，因为石纹多彩，所以品种也很繁多。歙砚的生产很重视雕刻的技艺，因此观赏价值极高。

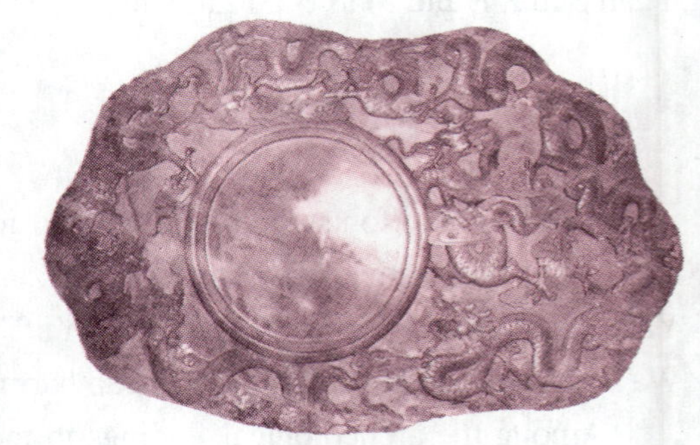

图 27　鲁砚

　　中国有四大名砚。除端砚、歙砚外，还有三种砚台也很有名。一种是山东的鲁砚（图 27）。鲁砚的特点是：纹理丰富多样，石色五彩缤纷，发墨如油。鲁砚中最有名的是石砚中满布红丝纹理的红丝石砚，乃鲁砚中的极品。

　　第二种是产于甘肃洮州（今甘肃省甘南自治州临潭县一带）的洮砚（图 28），质地细润如玉，以绿色的洮砚最为名贵。

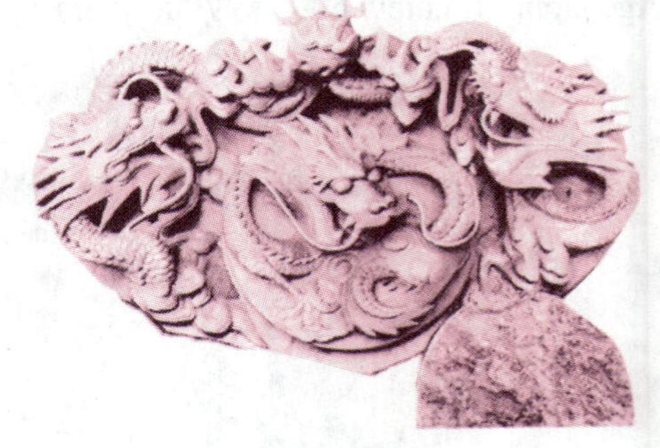

图 28　洮砚

In Yun Meng county of Hubei province in 1975 an E Luan Shi (cobblestone) Yan was unearthed. At that time, also discovered in the site was Yan Shi. Yan Shi was used to press on Mo Qiu while rubbing the ink. These ancient products indicated the availability of Yan for use in ancient artistic work and that it was used for the main purpose of rubbing ink.

Since the Tang dynasty, the most reputable Yan have been Duan Yan (Figure 25) and She Yan (Figure 26).

Duan Yan is a product of Guangdong, Zhao Qing Duan Qi. It has been used for about 1300 years. The Duan Yan stone is smooth and firm. Upon touching, the stone feels soft and damp. It reflects the ink with a glittering blackness. The softness of the stone does not do harm to the brush. As a result, it is considered a truly high quality Yan.

The other special feature of Duan Yan is its variety of color and beautiful grain. Some Duan Yan are found in fresh water, in rivers such as Wei Chen, or E Mao where one can see shaped green color grain mixed in with larger purple colored rose petals. The most expensive Yan are those made of purple stone with green grain flower petals in the stone.

She Yan is a product of She Zhou、 Wu Yuan County. It has been around for about 1200 years. She Yan is also known as Wu Yuan Yan, or Long Wei Yan. The stone is dark grey and green in color. She Yan is a softer material than Duan Yan. Because the stone has a multi-colored grain, it can be made into many more varieties of Yan. She Yan manufacturers emphasize their carving skill, thus, She Yan is considered to have a higher artistic value.

Other than the above two kinds of famous Yan, there are three other varieties of Yan, considered reputable. One noted example is the Lu Yan of Shangdong. (Figure 27) Lu Yan stone also has multi-colored grain.

The second is a product found in Tao Zhou, Gan Su province. Tao Yan (Figure 28) stone has a smooth quality. The most elegant Tao Yan is green in color.

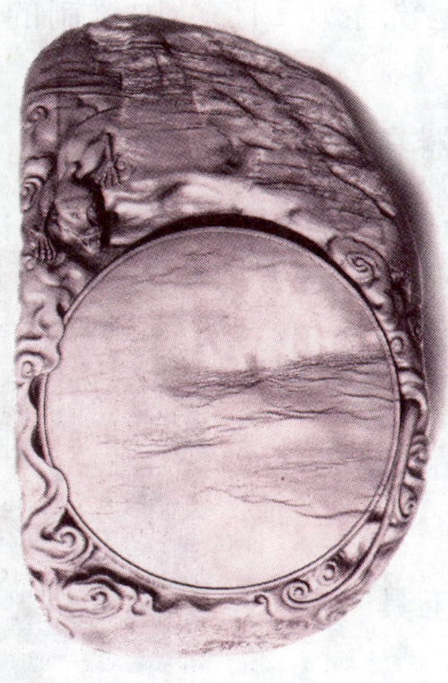

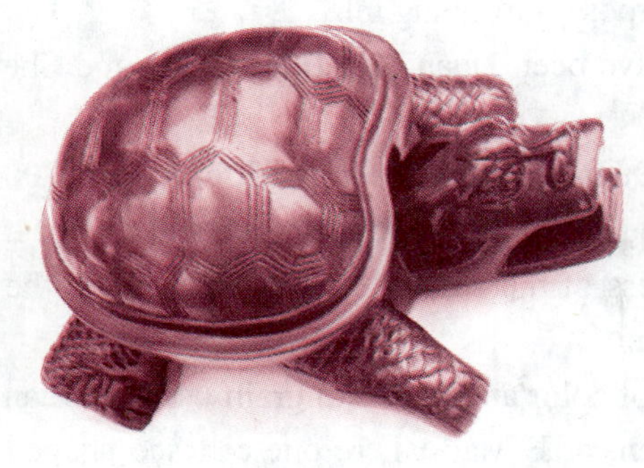
图 29　澄泥砚

还有一种澄泥砚(图 29),产于山西绛州(今山西绛县)。这种澄泥砚与以上四种石砚不同之处是:四种石砚是自然天成的,澄泥砚是人工制作的。夏天发大水的时候,工人在汾河中,滤取泥沙,经过捏塑,烧制而成。

在古代文献中,有的把端砚、歙砚、鲁砚、澄泥砚称为四大名砚,也有的把端砚、歙砚、洮砚、澄泥砚称为四大名砚。

好的砚台具有细、腻的特点。细,指不粗糙,不含杂质;腻,指容易下墨,磨出的墨汁润滑,有光泽。名砚都具有细、腻的特点。

(5) 其他工具

除笔、墨、纸、砚外,还有其他一些书写使用的工具,例如:

笔筒:用于装毛笔,用时将笔杆置于筒内,笔毛向上。

笔架:用于搁毛笔,样子像笔山。

笔挂:用于挂笔,多用木制。

笔帘:写完字后,将毛笔洗净、晾干,可用竹制的细帘将笔卷起,便于存放、携带。

笔洗:用于洗涮毛笔的器具。

水盂:磨墨时盛清水的器皿。

墨盒:盛放墨汁的器具,内放丝绵,浇上墨汁,随时备毛笔蘸用,便于学生携带。

毡垫:写字时压在宣纸下面,它的作用是吸墨而不沾墨。

镇尺:写字时压纸用的工具。

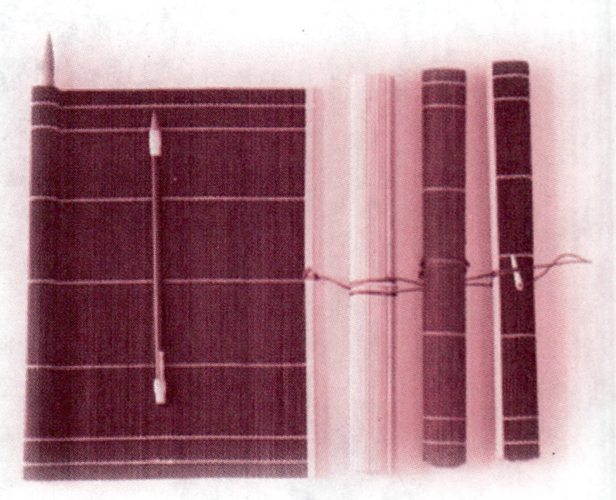

The third other kind of reputable Yan is Cheng Ni Yan, a product of Shan Xi Jiang County, The uniqueness of Cheng Ni Yan is in the stone. The four kinds of Yan discussed above are all made of stones gathered from nature. In contrast, Cheng Ni is a manmade hard surface. During flood seasons in the summer, workers gather mud from Fen River. The mud is filtered, kneaded, formed and fired in urns to form the Yan.

In Classical Chinese literature, some named Duan Yan, She Yan, Lu Yan and Cheng Ni Yan, the four famous Yan; but some named Duan Yan, She Yan, Tao Yan, Cheng Ni Yan as the four famous Yan.

In summary, a high quality Yan should have a smooth and oily stone quality. Smoothness indicates that the stone is fine, rather than coarse, and that it does not contain impurities. Oiliness indicates that it is easy for the Mo to grip the stone. The ink rubbed off from the ink stick should be shiny, and smooth.

(5) Others

Bi tong (vase): A container to place the Mo Bi with the brush tips facing upwards.

Bi Jia (shelf): A shelf to lay Mao Bi sidewise. The shelf takes the shape of a group of hills.

Bi Gua (hanger): A hanger for Mo Bi. It is usually made of wood.

Bi Lian (brush screen): After using a brush, it should be washed, cleaned, and dried. Mo Bi may be wrapped in a Bi Lian to store or to carry.

Bi Xi (an urn): It is used for washing the Mo Bi.

Sui Yu (water container): This is a container to keep clean water on hand.

Mo He (ink box): A box used to hold and carry Mo having silk cotton placed inside. When Mo is added to the silk cotton, the Mo will not spill.

Zhan Dian (felt blanket): A felt blanket for placing under the paper to absorb excess ink and preventing the ink from sticking or smearing.

Zhen Chi (weight); A weight to keep the paper stationary.

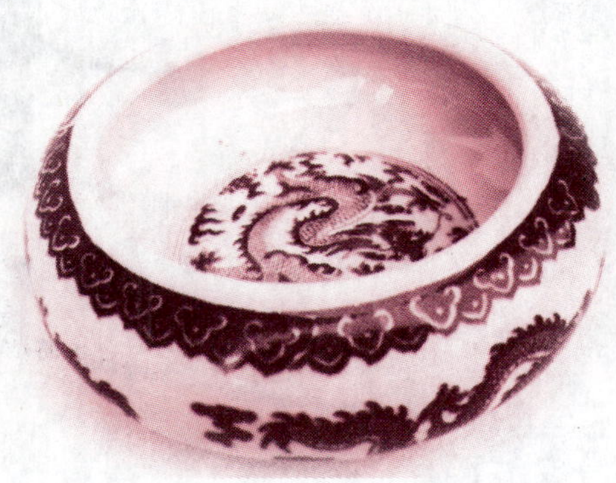

使用书写工具时应注意的事项：

　　使用新毛笔时，要将笔头放在冷水或温水中浸泡一段时间，待笔毛的胶溶化和笔毛软化后，再开始蘸墨书写。千万不要用开水泡笔，以免烫曲笔毛，降低弹性。也不要用肥皂、洗衣粉等洗笔，因为笔毛受碱会变脆易折。写大字时，笔头可全部泡开，写小字时，笔头泡开一半或三分之二就可以了。用完笔后一定要用清水将笔头上的墨汁洗净，洗净后不要上下左右抡甩，要慢慢将笔毛上的水搌干，理顺笔毛，将笔挂在笔挂上，或平放在阴凉处晾干，笔尖不可高于笔杆，以免笔杆因注水而破裂，尽量不要使用笔帽套笔，避免损伤笔毛。

　　使用墨汁时，用多少倒多少，不要一次倒很多。如墨汁过浓时，可加少许清水调拌。少用积墨，多用新墨。写完字后，要将墨汁洗净或擦净。

　　使用宣纸时，要注意宣纸的保存。最好将宣纸卷起来存放，或将宣纸摞成一摞，避免将宣纸压成许多皱折，影响书写的流畅。要防潮湿以免变形变色，也要防日晒，以免纸质变脆。

　　使用石砚时，要保持砚内的清洁。砚内不能有油渍，也不要有积墨的渣滓。有了渣滓时，要用冷水洗净后再使用。如积墨粘在砚面上，不可用力扳敲，以免损伤砚面。使用墨盒时，盒中的丝绵容易干涸，可以放一些冷水，使丝绵湿润后使用。

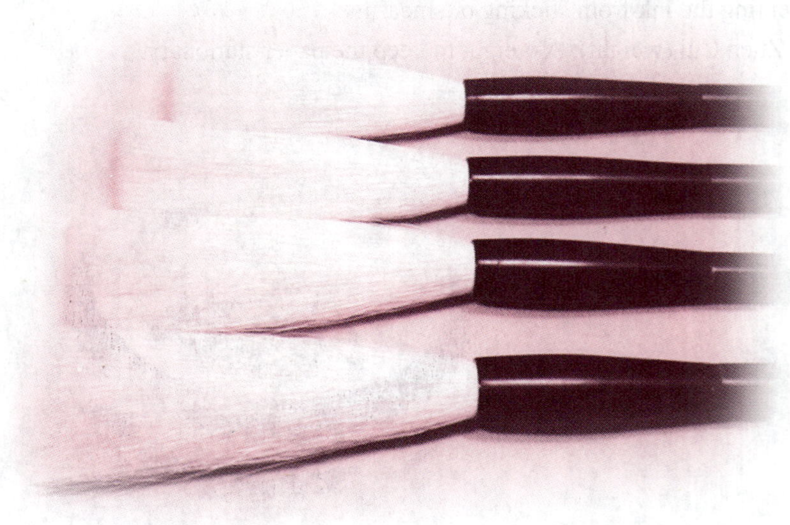

The proper way to break in a new Mao Bi is to soak the brush in cold water (or luke-warm water) to dissolve the glue in the brush. One should never use boiling hot water to soak a new brush as hot temperatures will damage the resilience of the brush. Also, do not use soap or cleaning chemical to soak the brush, as it will also damage the quality of the brush.

When using a Mao Bi to write big characters, the brush tip should be completely opened up. When using a Mao Bi to write small characters, the brush should only be opened up 1/2 or 2/3 of the way. It is important to wash Mo completely off the brush. It is also important not to swing off water in the brush. It is better to absorb the water off the brush, straighten the hairs, and then hang the Mo Bi on a Bi Gua to dry. Or, lay flat the Mo Bi in a shady, cool place to dry. When laying flat a brush to dry, do not leave the brush hair higher than its bamboo handle, as the water will cause a crack in the bamboo when dried. Do not attempt to replace the cap of the Mo Bi when the brush is still wet as it is likely to damage the brush tip.

When using a ready made Mo or black ink, do not pour out too much Mo from the bottle. If the ink becames too thick, just add a little bit of clean water. It is best not to use left over Mo. After each use of Yan, one must wash off or soak up any left over ink in the Yan.

When using Xuan Zhi for calligraphy, it is important to be aware of the safe storage of Xuan Zhi: the paper should be rolled up for storage and direct sunlight and a damp environment should be avoided.

Yan should be kept clean, having no foreign oil, or left-over Mo sledge. The Mo sledge should be washed off in cold water, but scraping with a metal knife should be avoided.

When using a Mo He, if the silk cotton is already dried, adding some cold water will extend the useful life of the Mo He.

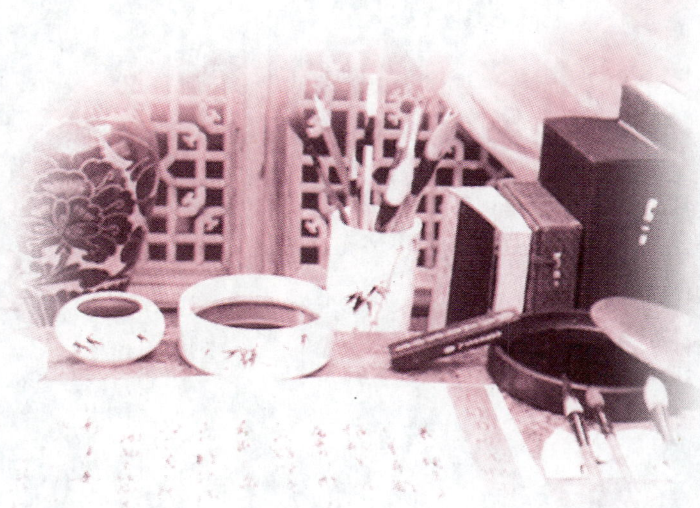

第 四 章

Chapter 4

执 笔 和 书 写 的 正 确 姿 势

The proper way of holding a brush and the correct posture for writing Chinese calligraphy

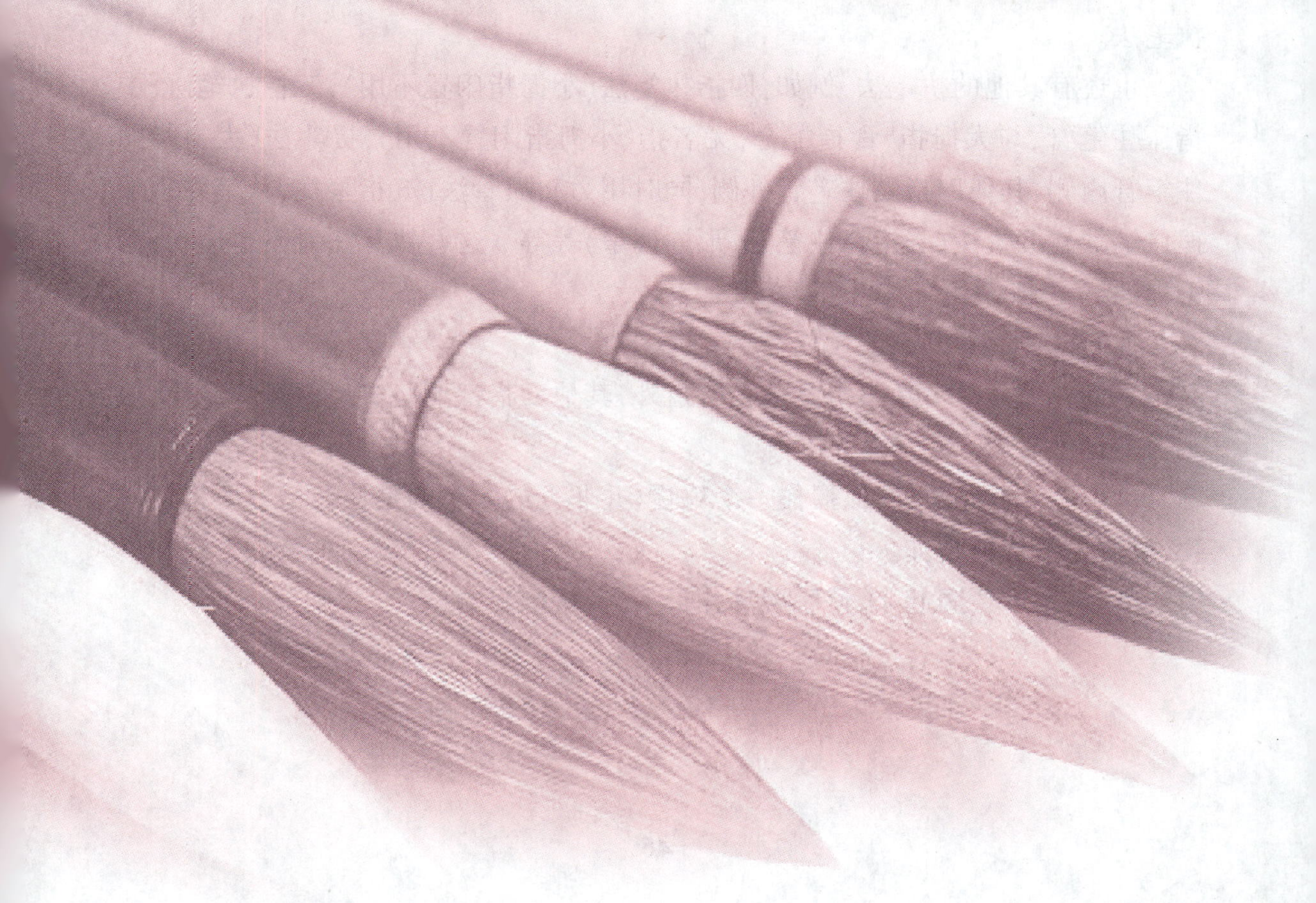

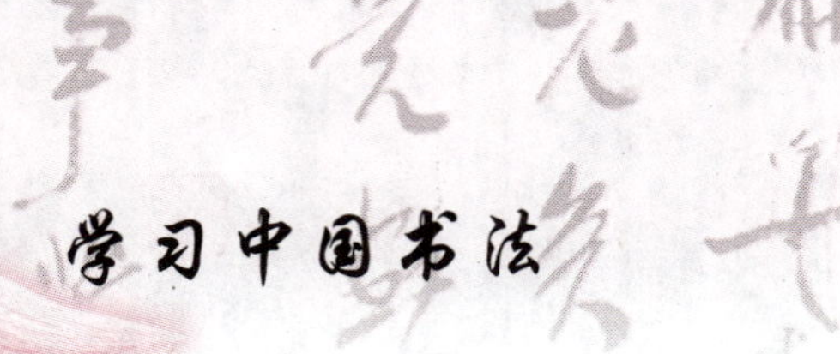

古人非常注意毛笔的执笔法，毛笔的执笔法与硬笔斜捏笔管的执笔法是很不相同的。唐代书法家陆希声总结前人的经验，提出了五指执笔法(图30)。

擫(yè)：按，大拇指前端稍斜而上仰，紧贴笔管内侧出力，力量方向是由内向外。

押(yā)：压，食指第一节斜而向下贴在笔管外侧，力量方向是由外向内。大拇指由内向外推，食指由外向内推，内外配合，捏住笔管。

钩：中指第一节与第二节弯曲如钩，从笔管外侧钩住笔管，力量方向由外向内，这样使笔管的按、压形成坚实的力量。

格：顶，无名指指甲根部紧贴笔管右侧，由内向外顶，力量方向由右内向左外推出。

抵：托，小拇指垫在无名指下，起辅助作用。

五指执笔法是常见的执笔法，直到今天，当代人用毛笔写字依然遵循这样的执笔法。

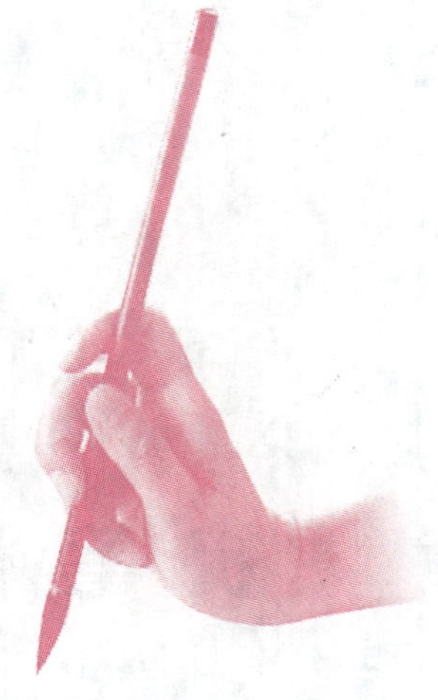

图30　五指执笔法

也还有其他的执笔法，例如：四指执笔法(小拇指闲置不用)，三指执笔法(中指压住笔管，与大拇指、食指配合，无名指、小拇指闲置不用)，提斗法(大拇指贴住笔管内侧，其他四指贴住笔管外侧，同时用力)，撮管法(五指聚拢，从笔管顶端捏住笔管)，握管法(五指抓住笔管，形同握拳)等等。这些执笔法并不普遍，我们不提倡练习者采用。

执笔时要注意几个要领：

指实：五个指头除小指紧贴无名指外，其他四指都要坚实地把笔约束住，做到握管稳健有力。

掌虚：掌心要虚，好似握住一个鸡蛋(并非真的)，目的是使四指不要捏得过死，以便笔管运转自如。

掌竖：手掌要竖起来，使手腕动作灵活，保持笔锋端正。

Calligraphy students in the China of the past were always reminded of the proper way to hold their brushes. The traditional way of holding a brush was summarized by the Master Calligrapher Lu Xisheng of the Tang Dynasty as follows: (Figure 30)

1. "Ye"—Place front section of the thumb facing upward and tilting. The front section of the thumb touches the inside of the brush handle, while force is applied always in an outward direction.

2. "Ya"—Place the top of the pointer finger on the right-exterior side of the brush handle. The force in the pointer finger is applied from outside to inside while the thumb pushes the brush handle from inside to outside; a balance of forces is reached in this grasp on the handle.

3. "Gou"—Bend the first section and second section of the middle finger into a hook position. Use this hook to hold the exterior side of the brush handle. The applied force should come from the outside of the brush handle toward the inside of the brush handle in order to keep a solid control in making a Ye, or Ya.

4. "Ge" or "Ding"—Touch the bottom part of the fingernail on the ring finger against the right side of the brush handle. The force applied from the ring finger to the brush handle should come from its inside and push towards its outside.

5. "Di" or "tou"—Place the pinky finger under the ring finger to creat a cushion or auxiliary support.

From the Tang dynasty—time of Master Lu Xisheng—to the modern day, Calligraphy students have followed closely this traditional way of holding brushes. There are, however, recorded exceptions such as using four fingers, or three fingers instead of five fingers to hold a brush. These practices are not recommended to students. In addition, another Chinese tradition is discouraging using the left hand to write.

A few key points on how to hold the brush are summarized below:

1. "Zhi Shi"—Using five fingers to hold the brush.

Except for the pinky finger which should be placed closely with the ring finger and functioning only as a supporter, other fingers are used to give a solid control of the brush.

2. "Zhang Xu"—Letting loose of the palm.

The center of the palm should be kept free and forming a hollow pocket. The purpose is to maintain a complete control of the brush-handle while utilizing the full range of free movement. The brush handle should be held firmly with four fingers but must never be held overly tight.

3. "Zhang Shu"—Keeping the palm in an upright position.

The palm is held up in a vertical position in relation to one's forearm. This posture allows the brush handle to be held in a vertical position against the writing paper and it also allows the wrist to perform a complete flexible movement

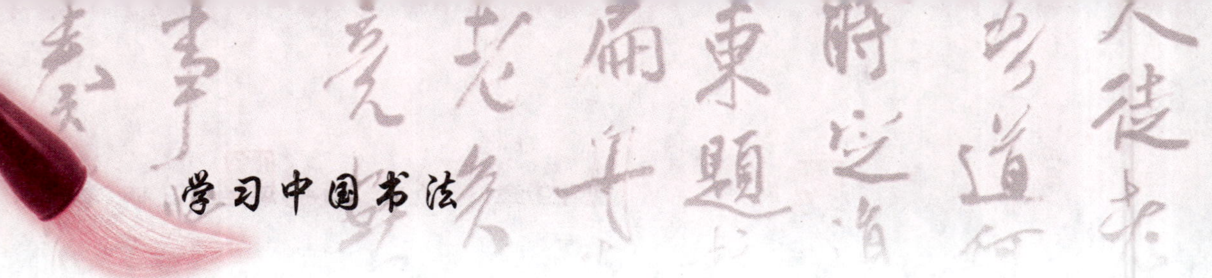

　　腕平：手腕尽量与桌面平行，这样写出字来不致歪斜。

　　写小楷字时，可将手腕贴在桌面上，但贴时不要过紧，以免手腕不灵活而影响写字，这叫枕腕。

　　写中楷字时，应将手腕提起而将臂肘轻放在桌面上，这样做可使运笔灵活，摆脱手指的僵硬状态，这叫悬腕，或提腕。

　　写较大字体的正楷或行、草书时，应使腕与肘同时离开桌面，用肩胛牵动肘、腕在运笔时作大幅度的运转，这叫悬肘。

写字时的姿势也很重要。如果是坐着写，那就要做到：

　　头正：不可左右歪斜，也不可把头伏在桌面上；

　　身直：身子要坐正，微微向前倾，但不要将胸部贴紧桌子；

　　臂张：两臂自然撑开，使左右均衡，挥洒自如；

　　足安：两脚自然地平放在地面上，既不要并拢，也不要岔开，更不可翘起或蹬在别处，保持两足的自然状态。

如果写较大的字，需站起身来，那就要做到：

　　头俯：把头俯向桌子，与纸面保持一尺多的距离；

　　身躬：身子略向前弯曲，腰部不要挺得太直；

　　臂悬：腕、肘和臂都要悬起，以便甩动；

　　足开：两脚自然分开，略如肩宽，右手写字时，为便于用力，可使左脚稍前。

　　为了把字写好，执笔和书写时掌握正确的姿势，养成良好的习惯，是首先要注意的问题。

4. "Wan Ping"—Keeping the wrist in a parallel position with the table top. This posture will avoid making the appearance of a written character tilted.

"Zhen Wan"—When writing small sized characters, the wrist could be pressed lightly against the table top. This wrist position is called a "pillow wrist."

When one is writing a medium sized character (size of character is above one inch and below 3 inches), one should raise the wrist and place the elbow gently on the table. This position gives a greater mobility to the brush, also eliminate the stiffness of the fingers. This is called Ti Wan or Xuan Wan.

When writing a larger sized characters (size of a character is above three inches), regardless of the script used is regular mode; is running mode; or is cursive mode, the elbow and wrist should both be held above the table top. This wrist posture is called "Xuan Wan". This posture allows the shoulder blade to provide a control of elbow and wrist in intended free movements.

It is also important to maintain a proper body posture in writing calligraphy. A few key points for calligraphy students to maintain a proper body posture are:
1. "Tou Zheng"—Maintain the head in a straight and forward position; do not tilt the head to the left nor to the right while writing. One should never drop down one's head near the table.
2. "Shen Zhi"—Both arms should be kept in neutral positions and a body balance should be maintained between left side and right side.
3. "Bi Zhang"—Both arms should be kept in natural position; and a body balance should be maintained between left side and right side.
4. "Zhu An"—Both feet should be kept side by side in their natural positions on the ground. Do not split, raise or step either one or both feet away from their natural standing positions.

If one is writing larger sized characters, one needs to write them in a standing up position. To do that, one should:
1. "Tou Fu"—Bow the head slightly towards the writing table; and keep it about a foot from the surface of the paper.
2. "Shen Gong"—bend forward the body; but do not keep the waist in a stiff position.
3. "Bi Xuan"—Arms should be kept hanging loose along with the forearms and wrists.
4. "Zu Kai"—Feet should be kept apart at approximately the same width as one's shoulders.
Once again, to produce a beautiful piece of calligraphy, the first priority is to remember the proper posture in the holding of a Mo Bi.

第五章

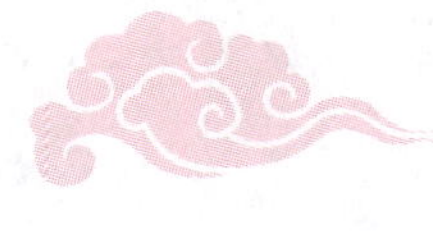

Chapter 5

汉字的基本笔画

The basic strokes

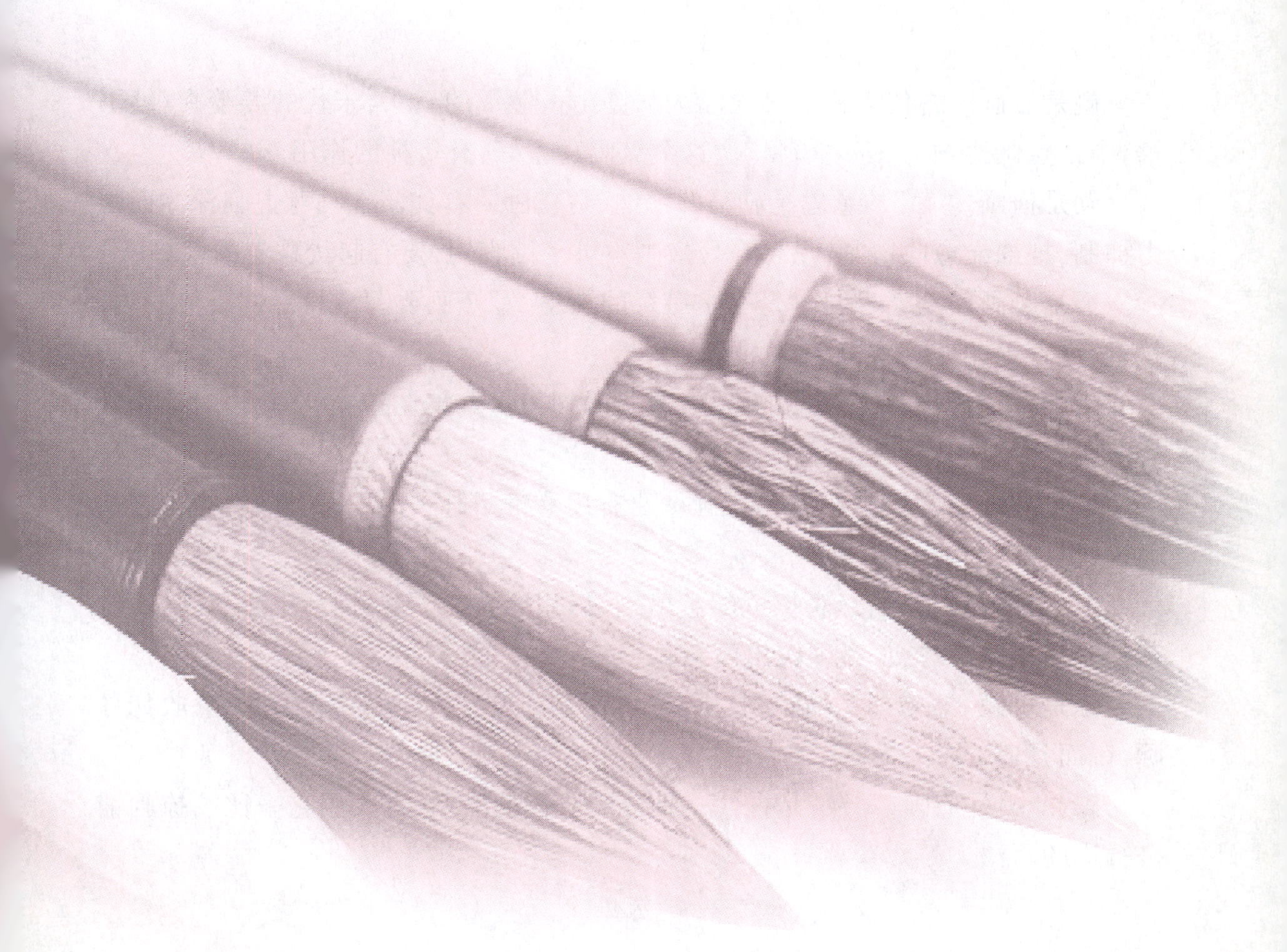

汉字的基本笔画有八种。古人借用"永"字形象地说明这八种笔画,称为"永字八法"(图 31)。

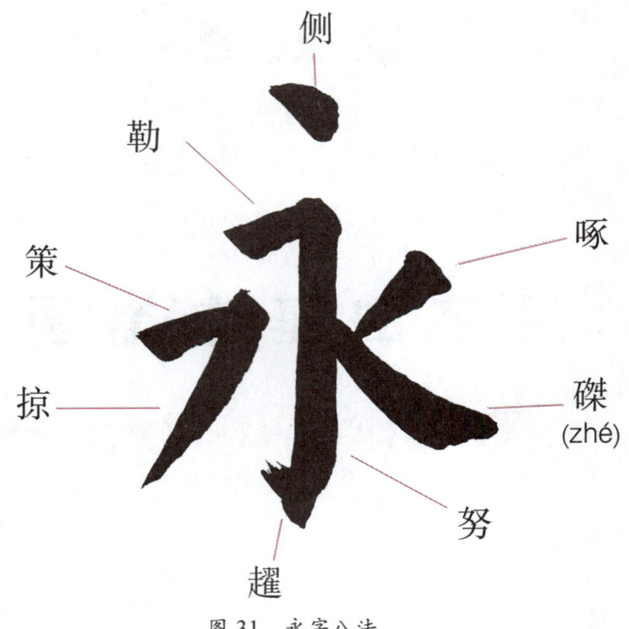

图 31　永字八法

侧是点画。古代人把点画比喻为从高山上坠下的石头,宋代的姜夔在《续书谱》中把点画比喻为"字之眉目"。这个点画写得好,有传神的作用。

勒是横画。"勒"的意思是勒马的缰绳,写横画时有如骑在马背上临深渊而强力抑制,把缰绳愈收愈紧,意思是写横画不可平铺直泻,要有起伏跌宕的气势。

努是竖画。"努"又写作"弩",是弓弩的意思。写竖画要写成拉弓的姿势,不可过直,过直则无力,要在直中见曲。

趯(tì)是钩画。"趯"是踢的意思,起脚时把力量聚集在脚尖上,踢出时动作既要沉实有力,又要急收。

策是挑画。策是马鞭子。写挑画就要有用马鞭子赶马的姿态,仰笔铺毫,轻抬而进,柔中带刚。

掠是长撇。"掠"是轻轻擦过的意思。长撇用笔初时须缓,而后铺毫急行,斩钉截铁。从整体来看,长撇须缓出而急收。

啄是短撇。短撇如鸟嘴啄物,所以用"啄"来形容。行笔时初缓,然后急收如鸟啄,锐而且速。

磔(zhé)是捺画。"磔"是古代一种分裂肢体的酷刑,古人用它来比喻捺画铺毫行进的写法。

Chinese people traditionally use the character "Yong" to describe eight basic strokes in Chinese square characters. This is commonly known as the "Yong Zi Ba Fa" (Figure 31):

1. "Ce" (Ce is a dot stroke). Ancient Chinese used the description of, "a falling stone from high mountain" to illustrate the proper way of writing a dot stroke. Also described the stroke during the Song Dynasty by "Jiang Kui". In his famous book *Calligraphy Continued*, he proclaimed, "a dot stroke is like one's eye-brows." If the dot stroke is drawn well, it induces the spirit to radiate from the written characters.

2. " Le " (Le is a horizontal line stroke). The meaning of "Le" is similar to the horse's bridle. Drawing a horizontal line stroke is like pulling back tightly on a bridle in order to stop a running horse that is fast approaching a falling cliff. Chinese calligraphers in ancient times also described the method of drawing a horizontal line as analogous to, "fish scale and horse bridle." When drawing a line horizontally, one should avoid making a flat straight line, but rather, include some uneven up and down streaks in drawing the line.

3. "Nu" (Nu is a vertical stroke). It can also be written as a character Nu which means bow and arrow. Drawing a vertical line stroke well is analogous to the pulling of a bow. One should avoid drawing of an overly straight line as an overly straight line expresses no strength. A line needs curvature to express a vertical straight line.

4. " Ti " (Ti is a hook stroke; and Ti means kicking). When the foot is raised to kick a ball, force is concentrated in the front part of that foot. The kicking motion must be fast, solid and ready to be withdrawn after kicking.

5. " Ce" (Ce is a rising stroke). This means using a horse's whip to motivate the running horse going faster.) The first "Ce" indicates a whip; the second "Ce" means to rush the horse. The writing of a rising stroke is as if one is using a whip to rush the horse, with the brush rising slightly upward; burying inner strength in a soft touch.

6. "Lüe" (Lüe is a long diagonal left-falling stroke.means to brush over lightly.) A long diagonal stroke moves the brush slowly in the beginning of this stroke. Then, one uses a quick tempo in the end to conclude the stroke.

7. " Zhuo" (Zhuo is a short diagonal left-falling stroke). A short falling stroke may be illustrated by the analogy of a bird's pecking on the ground. Again, the brush begins to move slowly in a diagonal left-falling stroke, and concludes sharply and quickly (like a bird pecking on the ground).

8. "Zhe" (Zhe or Na is a diagonal right-falling stroke). Zhe originally meant a motion derived from cruel torture wherein a person's limb was split from their body. The Chinese calligraphy masters use "Zhe" to illustrate the "Na" stroke movement: "Begin to move the brush downward moderately slow and towards right direction, gradually exert pressure on the brush to make the stroke thicker and thicker. At the end of the thick stroke, give the brush a pause and then move right with a pick. "

我们仔细观察"永"字的八种笔画，发现它还不能代表汉字笔画的全部。所谓"永"字的八种笔画，其实只有七种笔画，"掠"和"啄"都是撇，不过是长撇和短撇的差别罢了，这里还缺少一个"折"的笔画。于是我们暂时抛开"永字八法"，用现代人的观点看看汉字的基本笔画究竟是哪几种。概括起来，汉字的基本笔画仍是八种，只是与"永字八法"稍有不同而已。

（一）横画

（二）竖画

（三）点画

（四）撇画

（五）捺画

（六）钩画

（七）挑画

（八）折画

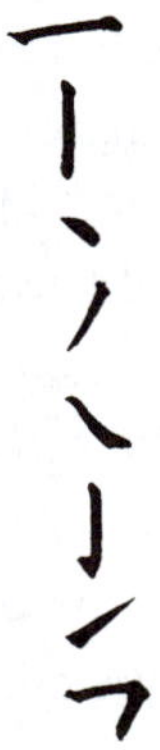

具体分析起来，这八种笔画还包括更细致的内容。试看下面的表格。

名　称		笔　画	例　字	
横画	（长横）	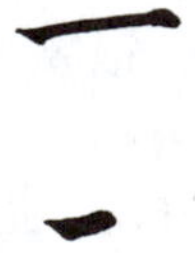 一	一	五
	（短横）	一	三	上
竖画	（垂露竖）	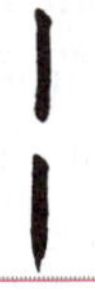 丨	卜	中
	（悬针竖）	丨	千	升
点画	（右侧点）	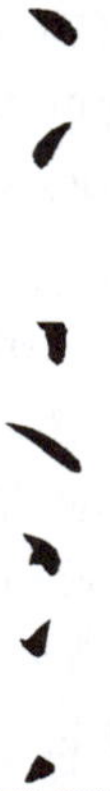 丶	下	寸
	（左侧点）	丶	京	宋
	（竖点）	丶	宫	室
	（长点）	丶	公	凶
	（出锋点）	丶	小	河
	（提点）		冷	清
	（撇点）		火	羊

When observed closely, the eight strokes of "Yong" really do not represent all possible strokes used in writing Chinese square characters. Actually, "Yong" has only seven different strokes, the "Lüe" and "Zhuo" are both falling strokes but different only in their length of slanting (one is a long falling stroke, while the other is a short falling stroke). The omitted stroke is a Zhe stroke; Zhe is a different Chinese character but has the same pronunciation as (Zhe). In summary, we shall put aside the "older" "Eight Strokes of Yong ", and follow a modern day version of "Eight Strokes of Yong"—an even finer stroke classification as shown in Figure 32.

Stroke Names	Strokes	Examples
"Heng hua", horizontal stroke		"Chang heng", long horizontal stroke
		"Duan heng", short horizontal stroke
"Shu hua", verical stroke		"Chui lu shu", dropping deer vertical
		"Xuan zhen shu" hanging needle vertical
"Dian Hua", dot stroke		"You che dian", right-side dot
		"Zuo che dian", left-sided dot
		"Shu dian", vertical dot
		"Chang dian", long dot
		"Chu feng dian", right- slanted dot
		"Ti dian", up dot
		"Pie dian", slant dot

*《前赤壁赋》

笔画	名称	笔形	例字	例字
撇画	（斜　撇） （竖　撇） （平　撇） （横折撇）	ノ　丿　フ　乀	刀　川　瓜　又	八　月　香　癸
捺画	（斜　捺） （平　捺）	乀　乁	人　之	入　道
钩画	（竖　钩） （横钩，或称俯钩） （斜钩，或称戈钩） （反钩，或称右上钩） （竖弯钩） （背抛钩） （横折弯钩，或称浮鹅钩） （横弯钩） （耳　钩）	亅　㇇　乚　乙　）　マ　ろ	丁　久　成　比　屯　風　乙　心　即　陽	寺　子　式　良　北　氣　几　少　却　部
挑画	（斜　挑） （平　挑）	㇀　丿	拾　地	折　疏
折画	（横　折） （竖　折） （斜　折） （撇　折）	フ　ㄴ　乚　く	已　匹　玄　女	里　罒　紅　巡

"Pi hua", left-down slanting

"Xie pie", slant
"Shu pie", vertical slant
"Ping pie", horizontal pie
"Heng zhe pie", horizontal turn slant

"Na hua", right-down slanting

"Xie na", slant
"Ping na", horizonatl right slant

"Gou hua" hook

"Shu gou", vertical hook
"Heng gou", horizontal hook
"Xie gou", slanted hook
"Fang gou", right-upward hook
"Shu wang gou", vertical turn hook
"Bei pao gou", right slanted upward hook
"Heng zhe wang gou", horizontal turn slanted hook
"Heng wang gou", horizontal turn hook
"Er gou", ear shaped hook

"Tiao hua", right upward stroke

"Xie tiao" , slanted right upward
"ping tiao", horizontal right upward stroke

"Zhe hua", turn or a bend

"Heng zhe" horizontal bend
"Shu zhe", vertical bend
"Xie zhe", slanted bend
"Pie zhe", turn and bend

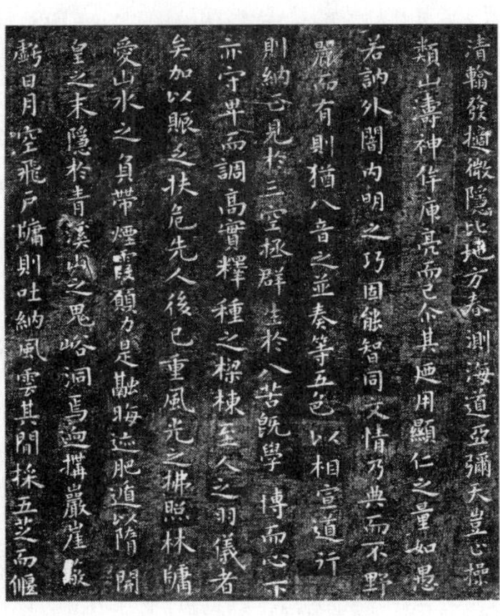

*《破邪论序》

第 六 章

Chapter 6

笔 顺

Bishun (the stroke orders)

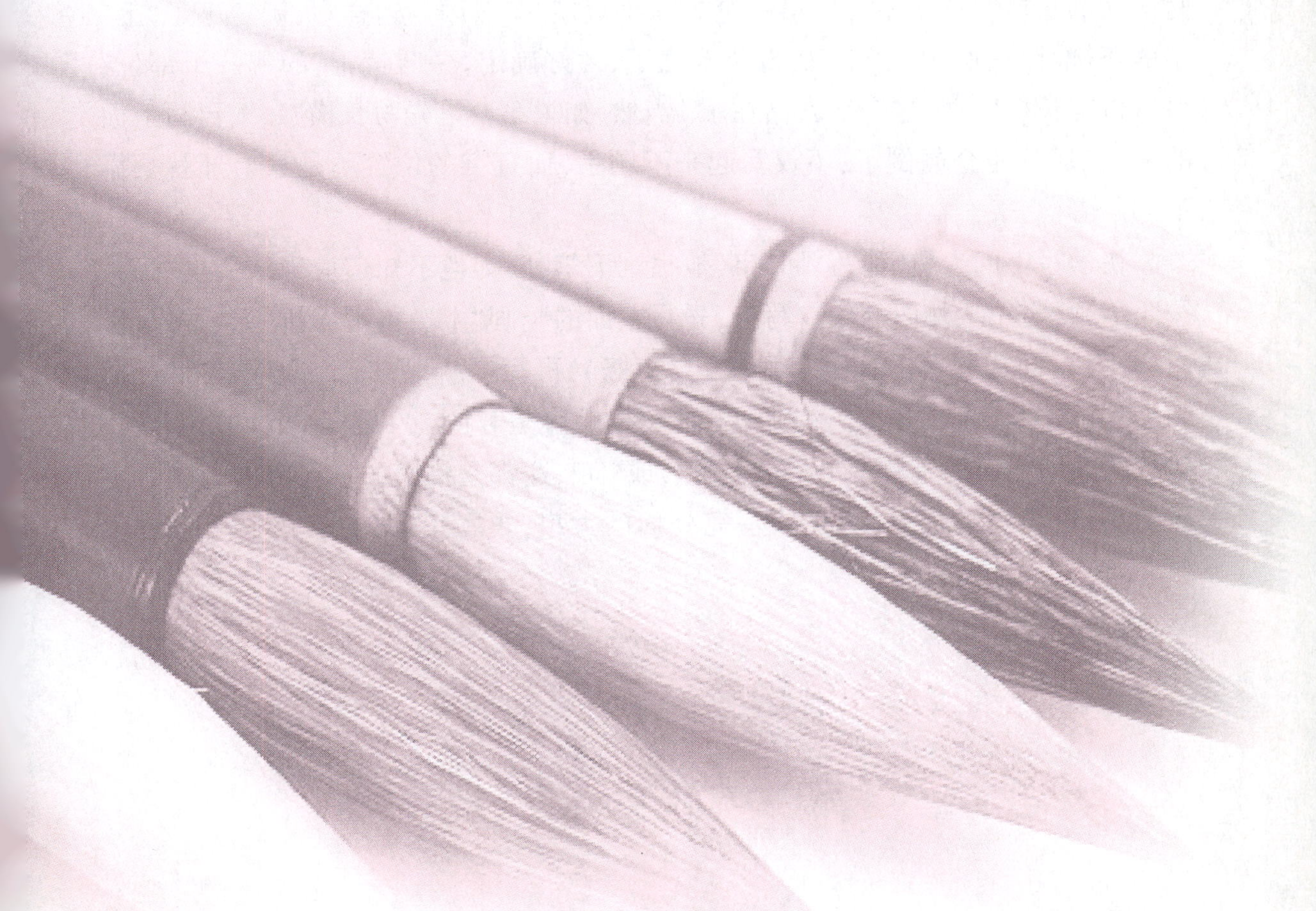

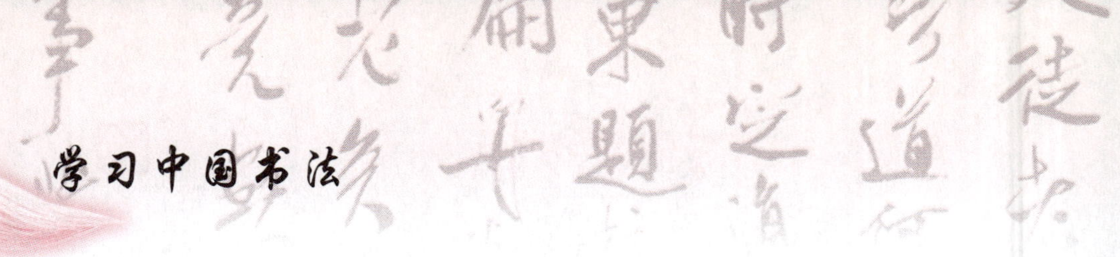

什么是笔顺？笔顺就是笔画的先后次序。

为什么写汉字一定要根据笔顺？因为，第一，按笔顺写字，就写得顺手，而且美观，不按笔顺写，就会很别扭，而且难看。第二，按笔顺写字，容易使上下左右的部位搭配匀称，让人感到平稳得当；反之，会令人产生建筑倒塌的感觉。第三，按笔顺写字，可以提高书写的速度。

中国的小孩子学写汉字，教科书上总要教他笔顺。对于习惯写拼音文字的人来说，认识方块字的笔顺会有一些困难。在他们的眼里，汉字好像一幅幅图案，要把图案画好，横要绝对地平，竖要绝对地直，为了把横、竖画得标准，甚至可以照着米尺来划，至于这个笔画，是从左到右划，还是从右到左划，似乎都无关紧要。举例来说，如果写一个"十"字，不懂得汉字笔顺的人，他可能先写"丨"，再写"一"；写横的时候，他可能从右往左画。然而，这样做，是不符合中国人的书写习惯的。中国人写"十"字，必须先写"一"，从左到右，然后再写"丨"，从上到下。

又比如，写"上"字时，按照笔顺，应先写"丨"，再写竖旁的小短横"一"，最后写下面的长横"一"。不可以第一笔先写小短横"一"，因为这样写，确定不了"上"字的正确部位，必须把"丨"的部位确立了，才好确定"一"在"丨"的哪一个部位，最后再写长横"一"，这个字就站住了。当然，如果第一笔先写长横"一"，再写上面的两画，那就完全颠倒了，不仅写起来不顺手，而且字的位置不是靠上部就是靠下部。

初学写字的人，让他写"回"字，他很难下笔，因为他不知道应当从哪里下手。按照笔顺，应先从外面的大口写起，先写左面的竖画"丨"，再写横折"┐"，再写里面的小口，同样先写左面的竖画"丨"（短竖），再写横折"┐"，最后两笔，用短横"一"先收小口，再用横画"一"收大口，整个顺序是丨、冂、冂、囬、囬、回，共六画。但有的人用下面的笔顺写"回"字：回，或回，这都是错误的。还有的人先写里面的小口，再写外面的大口，或写完外面的大口，再写里面的小口，这也是错误的。

What is "Bishun"? Bishun is the fixed order in which Chinese characters are written. Why one must follow the Bishun to write Chinese characters?

There are three reasons:

1. When Bishun is followed, the writing produced is smoother.

2. When Bishun is observed, it facilitates the proper arrangement of component strokes in a character. This proper arrangement gives each character a feeling of balance; conversely, if Bishun was not followed, a character would present a sense as if a tower is tilted and falling apart.

3. When Bishun is used, it increases the speed of writing.

Chinese children learn Bishun in school. It might be difficulty, for people who use alphabetical languages, to understand the need for Bishun in the writing of square characters. Seen from their perspective, Chinese characters might appear more like geometric patterns. To draw a good geometric pattern, the horizontal lines must be perfectly level; and the vertical lines must be perfectly straight. In order to draw a perfectly level or straight line, a ruler is used to guide the drawing. It does not matter whether the drawing of a line is done from right to left or from left to right. Specifically, to write the Chinese character "十", a person who does not know Chinese Bishun might draw the vertical line " | " first and followed by writing the horizontal line "一". Then, this person might draw the horizontal line from right to left. On the other hand, a Chinese writer who uses the correct Bishun in forming their characters "十", will first draw a horizontal line from left to right, and followed by drawing a vertical line from top down.

To use another example, according to Bishun, in the writing of the character "上" one needs to draw first the vertical line, followed by drawing a short horizontal line adjacent to the vertical line, and finally, to draw the longer horizontal line below. It would be incorrect Bishun to draw the short horizontal line first because to do so one would lose the opportunity to anchor the exact position of the whole character "上". Once the vertical long line is placed in a fixed position, it would be easy to place the short horizontal line correctly in relation to the vertical long line. The final horizontal line below will guide the character "上" in a stand up position. Naturally, if one insists on writing the long horizontal line in below first, and then follow by drawing the two strokes above. This reverse step in Bishun makes the positioning of the character depending on an inappropriate component.

For beginners, writing of the character "回" is often difficult to execute . She or he would not know exactly which stroke in the character is to initiate first. According to rules of Bishun, one would start with the big "口" outside. That is first to write the vertical stroke on left, and followed by a Heng zhe. In writing of the small "口" inside, also write the vertical stroke first on left, and followed by a heng zhe. Finally, use a short heng hua to conclude the inside small 口 and then followed by a short "heng hua" to conclude the larger "口" outside. .The complete sequence to write (Hui) has six strokes. They are: (1) shu hua, (2) heng zhe , (3) shu hua, (4) heng zhe, (5) a short heng hua for the inside "口", and (6) another short heng hua for the outside "口". Any other sequence used will be wrong according to Bishun.

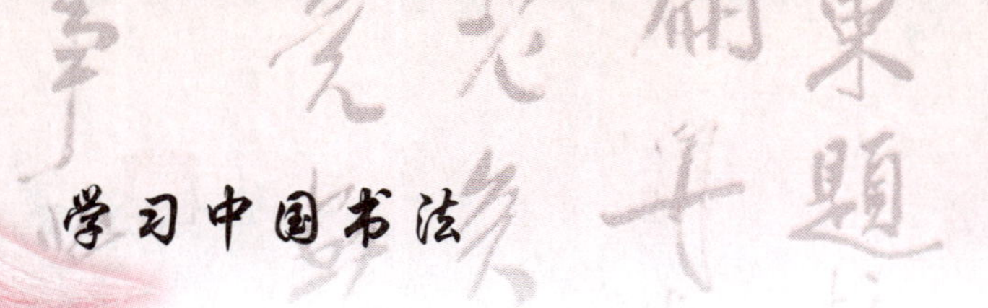

笔顺是有规律的，一般的规则是：

① 先横后竖，如"十、下、井"。

② 先撇后捺，如"人、八、全"。

③ 从上到下，如"三、立、空"。

④ 从左到右，如"江、以、行"。

⑤ 从外到内，如"月、向、风"。

⑥ 从内到外，如"还、建、函"。

⑦ 从外到内，后封口，如"回、田、国"。

⑧ 先中间，后两边，如"小、业、承"。

另外，有几种笔顺的情况，在书写时也常遇到，可以作为补充的规则。

点画在左上时先写点，如"为"字的笔顺是丶、丿、为、为，与此相同的有"斗、头"等字。

点画在右上时后写点，如"戈"字的笔顺是：一 弋 戋 戈，与此相同的有"我、武"等字。

点画在里面时后写点，如"瓦"字的笔顺是：一、丁、瓦、瓦，与此相同的有"叉、义"等字。

横画、撇画交叉使用时，要先横后撇，如"左"字的笔顺是：一、ナ、广、左、左，与此相同的有"在、存"等字。

有些形体怪异、笔画曲折的字，要注意它们的特殊笔顺，如"凸"字的笔顺是：丨、冖、冖、冂、凸，"凹"字的笔顺是丨、冖、冖、冂、凹。

有些字的笔顺与一般规则相反，如"中"，不是"先中间，后两边"，而是"先两边，后中间"：丨、冂、口、中，与此相同的有"申、串"。

"女"字先写撇折"乚"，最后写横画"一"，笔顺是：乚、女、女，也与一般规则相反。

还有些字，笔顺有争议，如"万"，第一笔写"一"，没问题，第二笔先写"丁"，还是先写"丿"，意见不一致，这也没关系，两种写法都可以。又如"母"，开始的笔顺是：乚、口，后三笔是母、母、母，还是母、母、母，看法不一致，这也不要紧，两种写法均可保留。

以上讲的是楷书的笔顺。行书、草书由于行笔的需要，笔顺与楷书不同，这里就不叙述了。

There are fixed rules in Bishun. General rules applying to Bishun are summarized below:

1. The horizontal before vertical rule: i.e. in characters 十、下、井, a horizontal stroke is placed before the writing of a vertical stroke.
2. The Pie Hua before Na Hua rule, i.e. in characters "人、八 and 全," a Pie Hua stroke is placed before the writing of a Na Hua.
3. The from above to below rule, i.e. in characters "三、立 and 空," a stroke from the top position in a character is placed first.
4. The from left to right rule, i.e. in characters "江、以 and 行," the first stroke begins from the left side.
5. The outside component before inside component rule, i.e. in characters "月、向 and 凤," outside strokes are placed before any inside strokes.
6. The inside component before outside component rule, i.e. in characters "还、建 and 函," strokes of inside component are placed before strokes of outside components.
7. The outside before inside rule, then close up, i.e. three outside strokes in characters "回、田 and 国" are placed before writing inside strokes and the enclosing strokes are last.
8. The middle before outside rule, i.e. in characters "小、业 and 承," middle strokes are placed first.

Unfortunately, even with eight fixed rules to apply in Bishun, there are still more exceptions than fixed rules! We only encourage a student to learn Bishun by paying attention to their teacher's writings, rather than trying to memorize all rules and exceptions. In due time, you will accumulate enough experience on Bishun.

In addition, some supplementary rules are needed in several situations:

When a dot stroke is found in the left top of a character, write the dot first. For example, in the character "为", its stroke order is: 丶、丿、力、为 Also, apply this rule in examples "斗", and "头", etc.

When a dot is found in the right top of a character, write the dot stroke last. For example, in the characters "戈": its stroke order is: 一、弋、戈、戈. Also, apply this rule in examples "我", and "武", etc.

When a dot is found inside of a character, write it last. For example, in the character "瓦". Also, apply this rule to "叉", "义", etc.

When the usage of a Heng Hua and the usage of a Pi Hua meet together in a character, write the Heng Hua before the Pi Hua. For example, in the character "左", its stroke order is:. Also in characters "在" and "存".

In some exceptionally strange and crooked characters, one must pay special attention to Bishun or stroke order. For example, in the character "凸", its correct stroke order is: 丨、乚、凵、冂、凸; in the character, "凹", its correct stroke order is: 丨、𠃌、凵、凵、凹.

In some characters, Bishun or stroke order is applied in reverse order to this rule. For example, in the character "中", the correct stroke order is to write the two side strokes first and then the central stroke. This rule is also applied to characters "申", and "串".

In another character "女", its correct stroke order is: 𡿨、女、女.

In our discussion, it should also be obvious that these Bishun rules are limited to the writing of Kaishu script Chinese or Standard Script Chinese. Because, in the writing of Running Script and Cursive Script, many strokes are connected through brush movement, the Bishun for Standard Script is no longer applicable to them.

第七章

Chapter 7

运笔方法

Yunbi (brush movement)

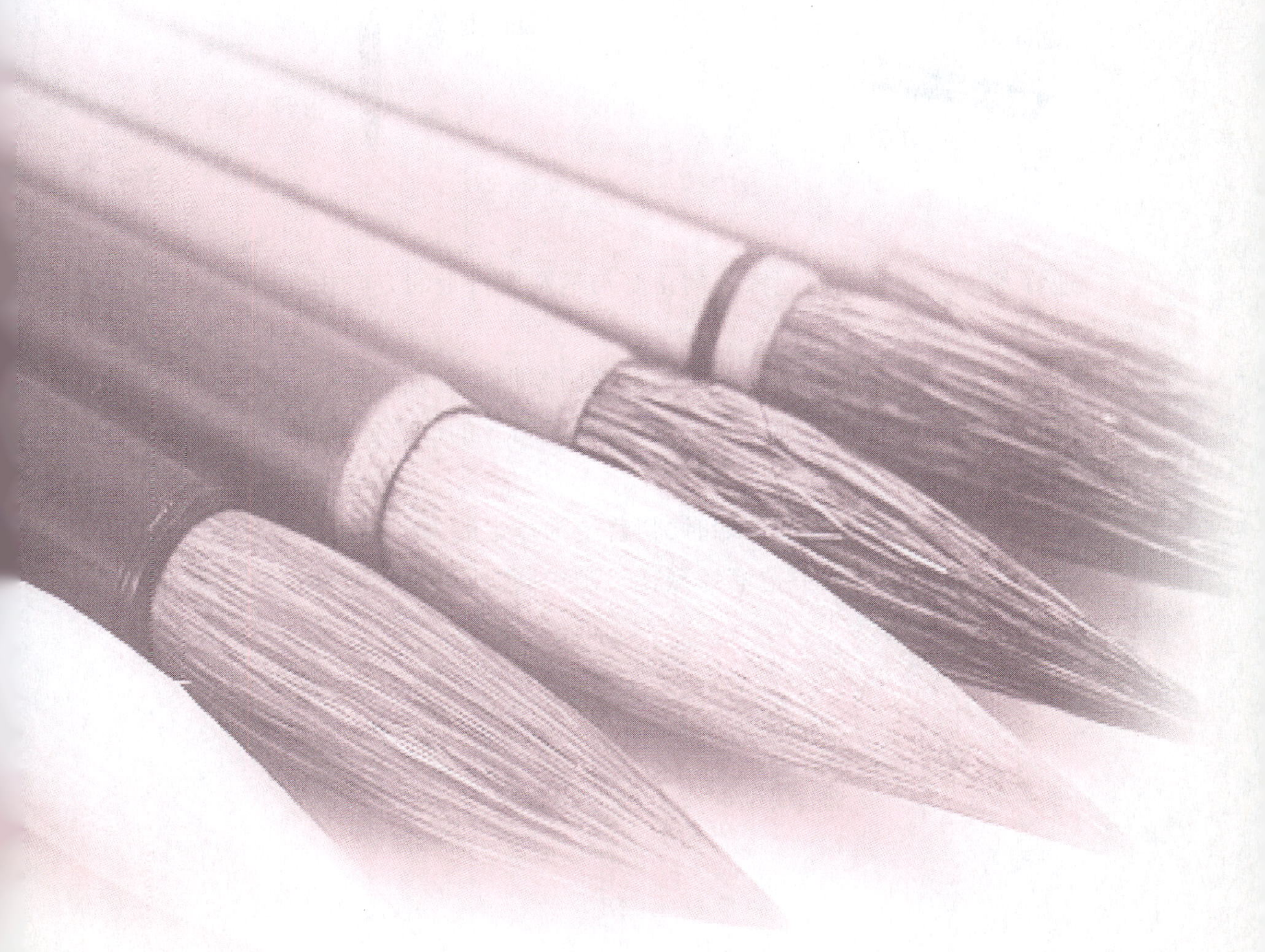

　　笔画是组成汉字的基本部件,部件的质量决定字的质量。不要把一点一画看成简单的事,运笔的学问很大。汉字千姿百态,都是由运笔方法不同和结构方式不同产生出来的形状,而运笔方法更为基本。

　　运笔方法,即笔法,亦称用笔。

　　历代书法家都把运笔方法当成写好汉字的最重要的条件。

　　运笔方法包含哪些内容?当我们写汉字的基本笔画时,我们要考虑如何起笔,如何行笔,何时该轻提,何时该着力,如何转动笔锋,如何收笔等等。把这些步骤都圆满完成了,这个笔画也就有力量了。这些步骤综合起来,就是运笔方法。

　　为了把这个问题说得更清楚,我们把运笔方法概括为下列各项加以介绍。

(1) 起笔、收笔

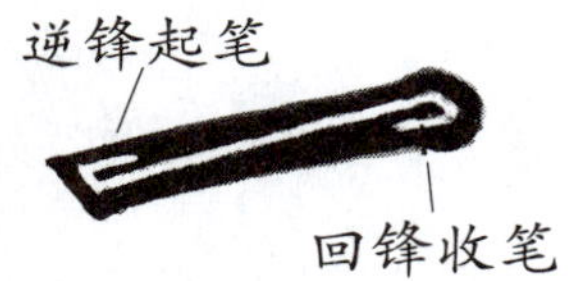

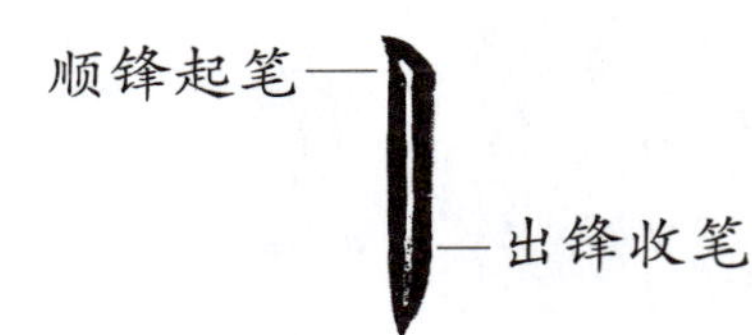

图 33　逆锋、顺锋、回锋、出锋

　　逆锋起笔——起笔时笔锋方向正好与笔画要行走的方向相反。逆锋起笔,使写出的笔画丰满有力。

　　顺锋起笔——起笔时笔锋的方向与笔画要行走的方向相同。

　　回锋收笔——写到笔画末端时,朝着行笔路线的反方向收笔,目的是使书写的笔画沉着有力。

　　出锋收笔——写到笔画末端时,朝着笔画行走的方向直出收笔。

　　逆锋、回锋因在书写中把笔锋藏在笔画中间,所以又称藏锋;顺锋、出锋因笔锋外露,所以又称露锋。

A proper application of "Yunbi", the proper sequence of brush movement for making strokes in calligraphy writing, is the basic factor in writing better Chinese characters. The quality of the parts determines the quality of the whole; and the aesthetics writing of each component in a character determines the aesthetics quality of the whole character. Thus, one should never too casual about the writing of a single stroke. The beauty of Chinese writing is created through different approaches to Yunbi and using different structure for a character. Yunbi is considered to be the fundamental contributor to a fine writing.

"Yunbi" or Brush Movement is sometimes called also "Yongbi", the technique by which to use brush properly.

The famous calligraphy theoretician held that the foremost criterion for creating a good piece of calligraphy stems from brush movement.

What are the ingredients of "Yunbi"? When one writes a character, one should consider how to begin the stroke; how to move the brush; when to lightly lift up the brush; when to press the brush down; how to twist the brush tip; and how to complete a stroke. When each and every stroke is meticulously written, the whole character will show "power". The complete brush movement process is called Yunbi.

The following descriptions are used to facilitate the general explanation of Yunbi.

(1) Qibi, shoubi

1. "Nifeng qibi": In the beginning of a stroke, tip of the brush is moving towards the opposite direction of the stroke intended to be.
2. "Shunfeng qibi": At the beginning of a stroke, the tip of the brush is moving in the same direction as the stroke intended to move.
3. "Huifeng shoubi": At the end of a stroke, the brush moves in the opposite direction of the stroke was intended to be.
4. "Chufeng shoubi": At the end of a stroke, the brush moves in the same direction as the stroke intended to move.

Nifeng and Huifeng are also called "Cangfeng". Cangfeng is to hide the brush tip inside a stroke; Shunfeng and Chufeng are also called "Loufeng". Loufeng is to show the brush tip inside a stroke.

（2）提笔、按笔

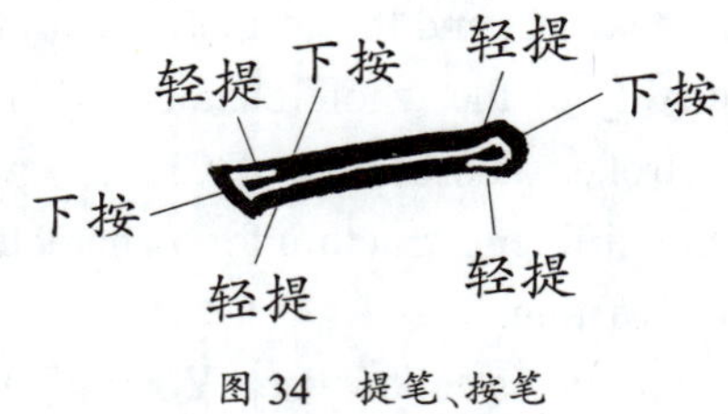

图 34　提笔、按笔

提笔（图 34）——行笔时将笔稍稍提起，但不离纸面，使笔画轻细些。

按笔（图 34）——在笔画下落时将锋按下，使笔画粗壮些。

写字的过程就是毛笔在纸上运行时提按交替的过程。

按笔又可分为顿笔、蹲笔、驻笔、挫笔四种笔法（图 35）。

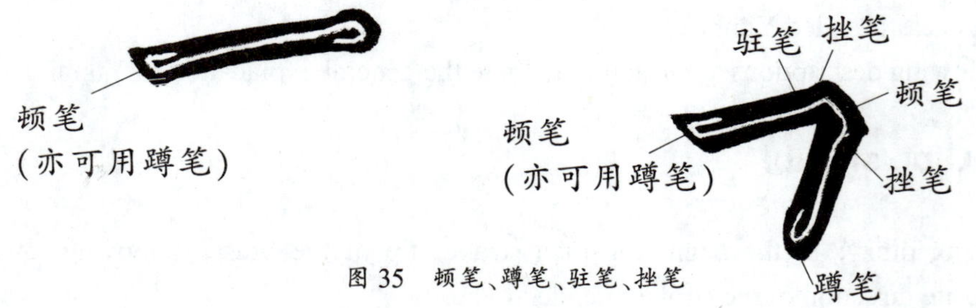

图 35　顿笔、蹲笔、驻笔、挫笔

顿笔——将毛笔向下重按，并作短暂停留。顿笔时，水墨下注，使笔画粗肥，多用于楷书的笔锋转换之处。

蹲笔——用笔如顿，但按笔较顿笔为轻，多用于行、草书中笔锋转换之处。

驻笔——笔锋行至一定的地方，稍作停留，安排好部位，为下一步作准备，多用于笔锋将要变换方向的时候。

挫笔——转折时，顿笔前后，将笔略提，使笔锋转动，多用于钩画、提笔及转角处。

（3）转锋、折锋

转锋（图 36）——笔锋变换方向时转以成圆。

折锋（图 36）——笔锋变换方向时折以成方。

(2) Tibi, anbi

"Tibi" (Figure 34)—Slightly lift up the brush while a stroke is in progress. (tip of the brush should still be touching the paper)

"Anbi" (Figure 34)—Push down the brush a little bit while a stroke is in progress. (this action produces a heavier and thicker stroke)

The method of writing is to use alternately "lifting up the brush" and "pushing down the brush".

"Anbi" can be divided further into "Dunbi"、"Dunbi"、"Zhubi" and "Cuobi". (Figure 35)

"Dunbi"—Push down the brush heavily; and stop momentarily while the stroke is in progress.

"Dunbi"—This stroke is similar to the Dunbi technique indicated above but one should press down the brush slightly than in Dunbi.

"Zhubi"—While the brush tip is moving to a certain desired position, stop it momentarily.

"Cuobi"—After apply a Dunbi turning, lift up the brush tip a little bit and then make a slightly twisting motion.

(3) Zhuanfeng, zhefeng

"Zhuanfeng" (Figure 36)—Making a circular motion of the brush tip while changing direction simultaneously.

"Zhefeng" (Figure 36)—Folding the brush tip in a square movement while changing it to a different direction simultaneously.

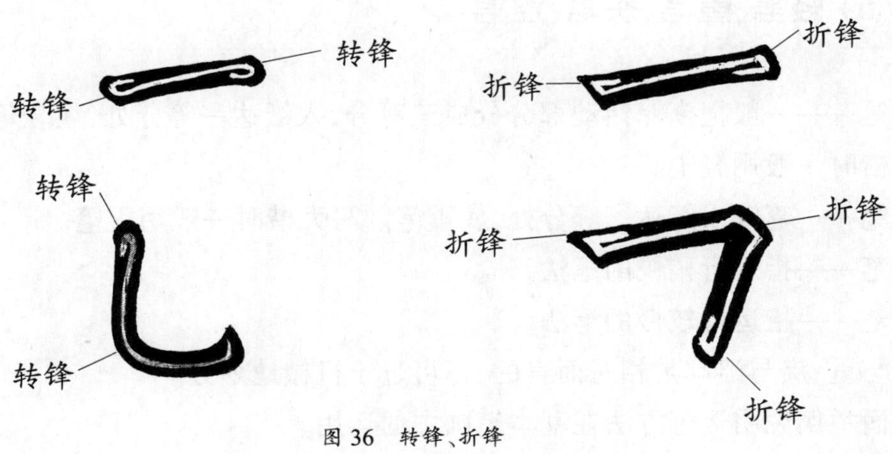

图 36　转锋、折锋

(4) 中锋、侧锋

中锋(图37)——亦称正锋,行笔时笔头的中心锋芒在笔画的中心移动。

侧锋(图37)——亦称偏锋,行笔时笔头的中心锋芒在笔画的一侧移动,也可以说是笔锋的重心落在笔画的一侧。

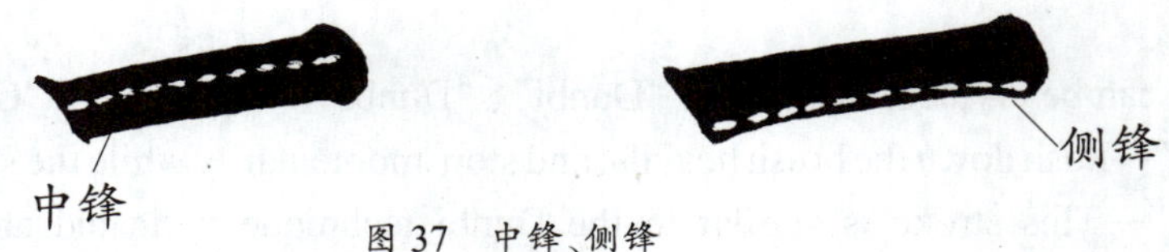

图37　中锋、侧锋

(5) 衄(nǜ)笔

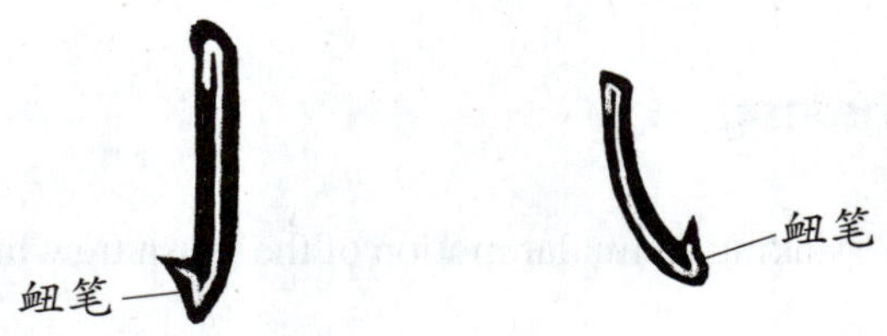

图38　衄笔

衄笔(图38)——"衄"是退缩的意思,笔锋去后,由原路退回,有似蜗牛退回壳内。

(6) 轻笔、重笔、疾笔、涩笔

轻笔——一般把毫锋活动部分分成三等分,入纸达一等分处,属轻笔。写提笔和小楷时一般用轻笔。

重笔——笔锋入纸达三等分处,属重笔。写大楷时一般用重笔。

疾笔——指运行稍快的笔法。

涩笔——指运行较慢的笔法。

轻与重、疾与涩都是相对而言的,不可过于机械地划分。

下面举例说明运笔方法在基本笔画中的运用。

(4) Zhongfeng, cefeng

"Zhongfeng" (Figure 37) —It is also called " Zhengfeng". Place the movement of the brush tip in the middle of a stroke.

"Cefeng"—It is also called " Pianfeng". Place the movement of the Brush tip on one side of the stroke.

(5) Nübi

"Nübi" (Figure 38)—Nü means to pull back. When the motion of the brush tip is stopped; the backward motion of the brush is like a snail retreating into its shell.

(6) Qingbi, zhongbi, jibi, sebi

"Qingbi"—In general, one can divide the press- down motion of a brush tip into three parts. When the brush tip is said to be pressed down by one part, it represents a light pressure on the page. Qingbi is most often applied in Tibi and writing of small characters.

"Zhongbi"—When the brush tip is said to be pressed down by three parts, it represents a heavier pressure on the paper. Zhongbi is most often used in writing of larger characters.

"Jibi"—The rapid movement of a brush.

"Sebi"—The slow movement of a brush.

The instructions "A light press-down" and "a heavy press—down" of the brush tip are used as relative terms; one should not make a mechanical interpretation in their respective applications.

The following examples are used to illustrate how Yunbi is applied in basic strokes.

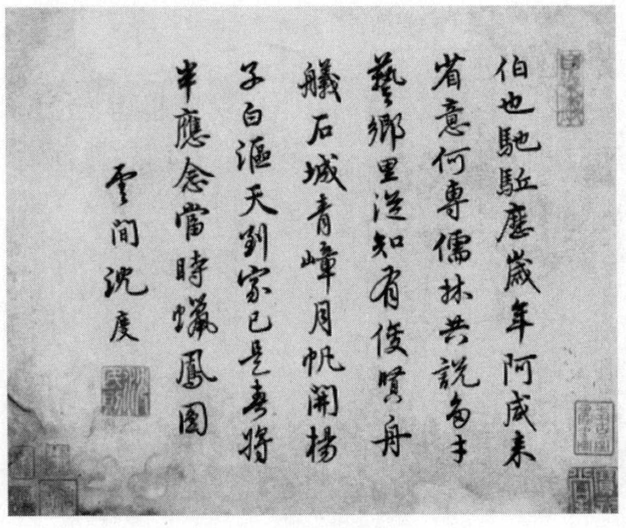

*《行书七律诗》

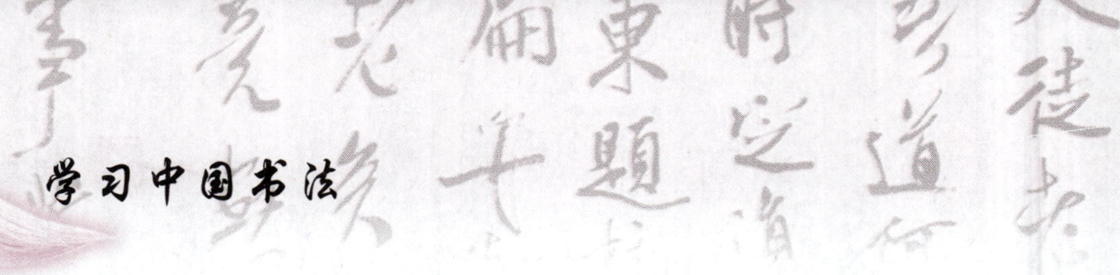

横画(图 39)

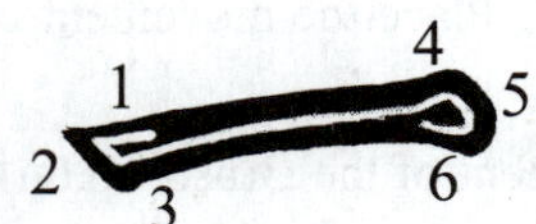
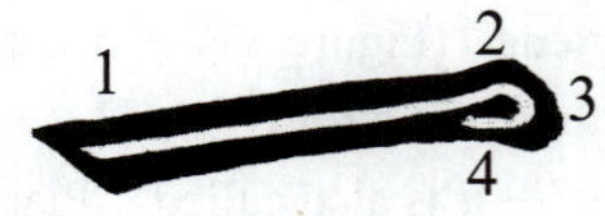

图 39　横画的运笔方法

① 逆锋起笔。

② 转锋(或折锋)向右下方顿笔成点。

③ 轻提笔向右上缓行。

④ 在右上稍作驻、挫。

⑤ 转(或折)笔重顿。

⑥ 在笔画内回锋紧收。

① 顺锋起笔,由轻渐重,向右上方缓行。

② 稍作驻、挫。

③ 转(或折)笔重顿。

④ 回锋紧收。

竖画(图 40)

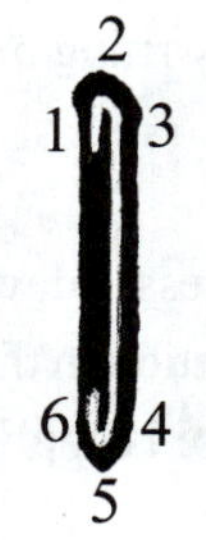
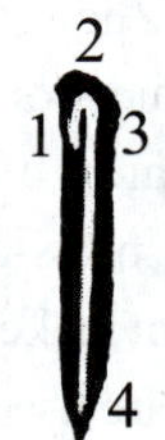

图 40　竖画的运笔方法

① 逆锋起笔。

② 转(或折)笔向右下方顿笔成点。

③ 提笔正锋下行。

④ 稍驻。

⑤ 轻顿成圆角形。

⑥ 转(或折)笔回锋。

① 逆锋起笔。

② 转(或折)笔向右下方顿笔成点。

③ 提笔正锋下行。

④ 涩笔出锋。

"Heng Hua" (Figure 39)

(left)

(1) Nifeng to begin a stroke.

(2) Zhuanfeng towards right-lower side and Dunbi to make a dot.

(3) Lightly lift the brush and move it slowly towards the right-above.

(4) Zhu, and Cuo the brush momentarily on right-above.

(5) Zhuanbi and make a heavy Dun.

(6) A quick and tight return of the brush tip.

(right)

(1) Shunfeng to begin the stroke. Use a light weight press down and then slowly increase the weight of this downward pressure;   moves the brush in a deliberate speed towards right-above.

(2) A light Zhu and Cuo.

(3) Zhuanbi and make a heavy Dun.

(4) A quick and tight return of the brush tip.

"Shu Hua" (Figure 40)

(left)

(1) Nifeng to begin a stroke.

(2) Zhuanbi and move the brush towards the right-lower side and then apply a Dunbi to make a dot.

(3) Tibi to move the brush tip downward.

(4) Apply a moment of stoppage.

(5) A lightdun to make a round-cone shape.

(6) Zhuanbi to make a return of the brush tip.

(1) Nifeng to begin a stroke.

(2) Zhuanbi and moves the brush towards the lower—right side and then apply a Dunbi to make a dot.

(3) Tibi to move the brush tip downward.

(4) Sebi Chufeng.

点画(图 41)

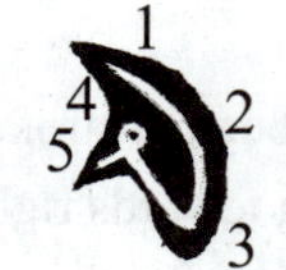

图 41　点画的运笔方法

① 顺锋起笔。

② 由轻而重,顿笔成圆。

③ 提笔转锋(或折锋)向上。

④ 回锋收笔。

① 顺锋起笔。

② 由轻而重,顿笔成圆。

③ 提笔转锋(或折锋)向上。

④ 稍驻,笔锋圆转向左。

⑤ 出锋疾收。

钩画(图 42)

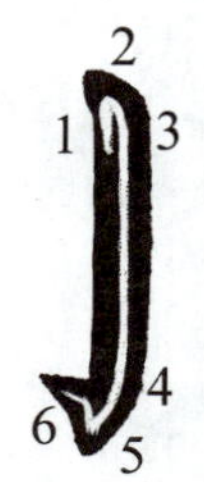
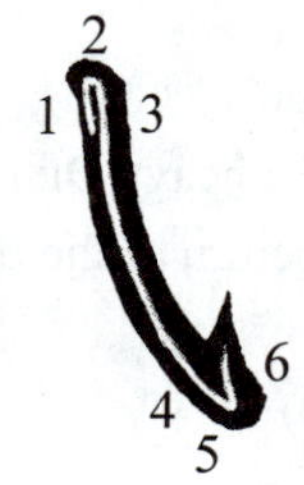

图 42　钩画的运笔方法

① 逆锋起笔。

② 转(或折)笔向右下方顿笔成点。

③ 提笔正锋下行。

④ 驻笔,稍向外挫。

⑤ 向左下重顿。

⑥ 转锋(或折锋)衄笔出锋(亦可于转锋后直接出锋)。

① 逆锋起笔。

② 转(或折)笔向右下方顿笔成点。

③ 提笔正锋向右下方缓行。

④ 稍驻。

⑤ 向右下重顿。

⑥ 转锋(或折锋)衄笔出锋(亦可于转锋后直接出锋)。

"Dian Hua" (Figure 41)

(left)

(1) ShunFeng to begin the stroke.

(2) Use Dunbi (from a light press—down to heavier press—down to make a round.)

(3) Tibi Zhuanfeng towards above.

(4) Huifeng to end the stroke.

(right)

(1) Shunfeng to begin the stroke.

(2) Use Dunbi (from a light press—down to a heavier press—down to make a round.)

(3) Tibi Zhuanfeng towards the top.

(4) Stop momentarily, then turn the brush tip with a left upward movement.

(5) Chufeng to end rapidly the stroke.

"Gou Hua" (Figure 42)

(left)

(1) Nifeng to begin the stroke.

(2) Zhuanbi towards right-below and apply Dun to make a dot.

(3) Tibi to draw the stroke straight downward.

(4) Apply Zhubi; also apply a little bit of Cuobi on the outside of the brush.

(5) Apply a heavy Dun towards the bottom left.

(6) After Zuangfeng; then apply Nübi to end the stroke.

(right)

(1) Nibi Qifeng to begin the stroke.

(2) Zuangbi towards right-below and apply Dunbi to make a dot.

(3) Tibi to draw the stroke towards right-below in a slow movement.

(4) Apply Zhubi.

(5) Apply a heavy Dun towards the lower-right.

(6) After Zuangbeng; apply Nübi to end the stroke.

撇画(图 43)

① 逆锋起笔。

② 转(或折)笔向右下方顿笔成点。

③ 提笔向左下方缓行。

④ 疾笔出锋。

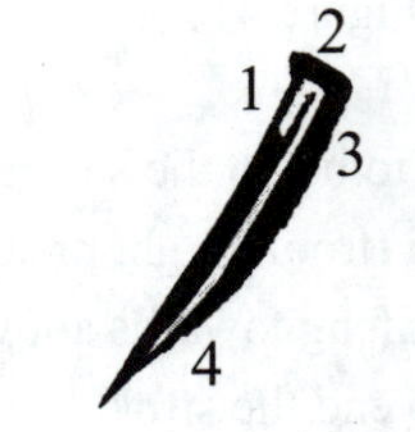

图 43　撇画的运笔方法

捺画(图 44)

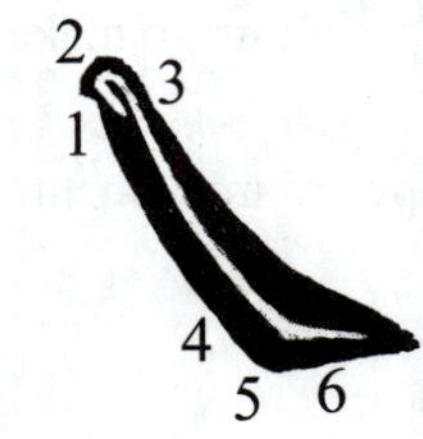

图 44　捺画的运笔方法

① 逆锋向左上落笔。

② 转(或折)笔向右下。

③ 提笔正锋向右下缓行。

④ 稍驻。

⑤ 重顿。

⑥ 轻提后涩笔向右出锋(亦可于重顿后稍作衄笔出锋)。

① 逆锋向左下落笔。

② 转(或折)笔向右上(写出捺画的头颈)。

③ 提笔正锋向右方(偏下)缓行。

④ 稍驻。

⑤ 重顿。

⑥ 轻提后涩笔向右(偏上)出锋(亦可于重顿后稍作衄笔出锋)。

挑画(图 45)

① 逆锋起笔。

② 转锋(或折锋)顿笔。

③ 轻提笔向右上缓行。

④ 疾笔出锋。

图 45　挑画的运笔方法

"Pie Hua" (Figure 43)

(1) Nifeng to begin the stroke.

(2) Zhuangbi towards the lower-right side; and apply Dunbi to make a dot.

(3) Tibi to draw the stroke towards the lower-left in a slow movement.

(4) Apply Jibi or a quick motion to end the stroke.

"Na Hua" (Figure 44)

(left)

(1) Nifeng to begin the stroke towards upper-left.

(2) Zuangbi towards lower-right.

(3) Tibi to draw the stroke towards the lower-right.

(4) Pause a moment.

(5) Apply a heavy Dun.

(6) After a light lift of the brush, apply Nübi to end the stroke.

(right)

(1) Nifeng to begin the stroke towards the lower-left.

(2) Zhuanbi towards the upper- right side (to draw the neck of the Na Hua).

(3) Tibi to draw the stroke towards lower-right; and in a slow movement.

(4) Pause a moment.

(5) Apply a heavy Dun.

(6) After a light lift of the brush, apply Nübi to end the stroke.

"Tiao Hua" (Figure 45)

(1) Nifeng to begin the stroke.

(2) Zhuanfeng; then make a Dunbi.

(3) Lift up the brush lightly and move it towards the upper-right.

(4) Apply a Jibi or a quick motion to end the stroke.

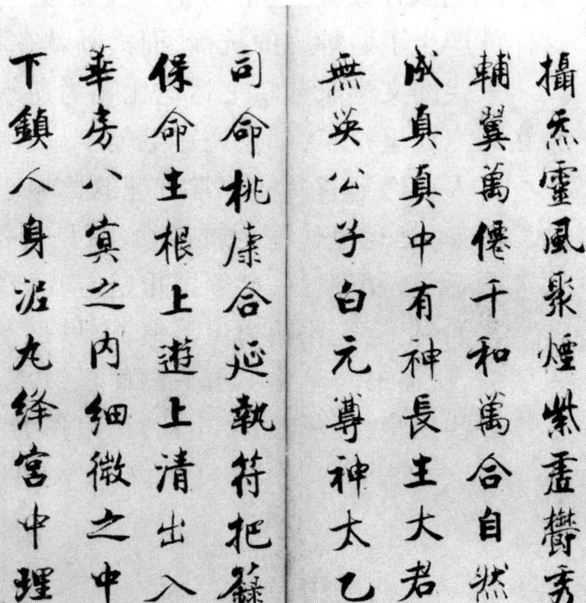

*楷书《度人经帖》

79

折画（图 46）

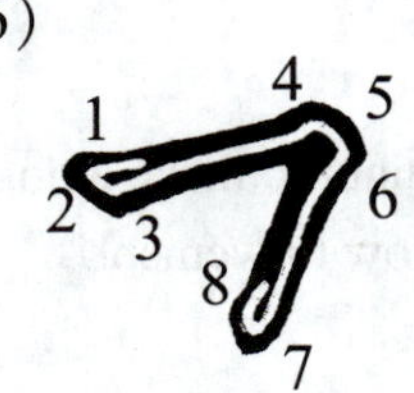 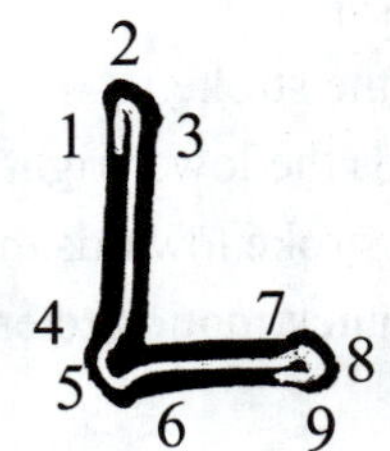

图 46　折画的运笔方法

① 逆锋起笔。

② 转锋（或折锋）向右下方顿笔成点。

③ 轻提笔向右上缓行。

④ 在右上稍作驻、挫。

⑤ 转（或折）笔重顿。

⑥ 稍作挫笔后下行。

⑦ 轻顿转锋（或折锋）向上。

⑧ 回锋收笔。

① 逆锋起笔。

② 转（或折）笔向右下方顿笔成点。

③ 提笔正锋下行。

④ 驻笔，稍向外挫。

⑤ 向右下重顿。

⑥ 轻提笔向右上缓行。

⑦ 驻后向上挫笔。

⑧ 顿笔。

⑨ 回锋收笔。

　　运笔的目的是要把每个笔画写得很有力度，比如写横画右行时，左边有一个力量把笔画往回拉，而右行的力要摆脱左边的力的牵掣，艰难地继续向右行驶，这样就产生了两种力的抗衡，而横画就在相抗衡的力中运行。

　　宋代的文学家苏轼把运笔比喻为逆水行舟，元代书法家鲜于枢把运笔比喻为在烂泥地里拉车，都是说写毛笔字只有在对抗的力中运行才是最有力量的。

　　古人对运笔有一些非常有趣的比喻。

　　例如，把运笔比喻为锥画沙，就是用锥子在沙土上画出一道深沟来，表现书写笔画不可轻滑而过，必须厚重坚定，沉着有力。

　　又如，把运笔比喻为屋漏痕，意思是下雨时，雨水自屋角沿墙壁下注，最后渗入墙内，比喻书写笔画不可一泻而下，须左右蜿蜒，顿挫行笔，使笔画圆活生动。

　　这些比喻，既形象，又生动，可以作为我们运笔的重要参考。

"Zhe Hua" (Figure 46)

(left)

(1) Nifeng to begin the stroke.

(2) Zhuanfeng and use Dunbi to make a dot towards the right-below.

(3) Lightly Tibi and slowly move it towards right-above.

(4) Apply a moment of Cuo at right-above.

(5) Zhuanbi to make a heavy Dun.

(6) Make a little Cuobi and move down the brush.

(7) Make a light Dun and Zhuanfeng towards above.

(8) Huifeng to end the stroke.

(right)

(1) Nifeng to begin the stroke.

(2) Zhuanbi and use Dunbi to make a dot towards the right-below.

(3) Tibi Zhengfeng moves the brush towards the right-below.

(5) Zhubi and then moves the brush towards above and Cuobi.

(6) Lightly lift up the brush and move towards right-above.

(7) After Zhubi; apply a Cuobi towards above.

(8) Apply a Dunbi.

(9) Huifeng to end the stroke.

The purpose of Yunbi is to show energy in each and every stroke. For instance, when one is writing a Heng Hua from left towards the right direction, one should feel there is a force in the opposite direction trying to pull back the brush.   The right moving force is trying to shake off this resistance. The Heng Hua is produced by the brush under these two opposing forces.

The Song dynasty calligrapher Master "Su Shi" used the analogy of peddling a river boat against the water current for Yunbi. Yuan dynasty calligraphy Master "Xianyu Shu" used the analogy of pulling a cart stuck in the soft mud for Yunbi.   These examples describe how the force of brush writing is coming from two opposite directions.

Ancient Chinese have many interesting descriptions to teach us the Yunbi. For example, to use a spade to dig across the beach means the spade should be making a deep groove in the sand. The stroke should not be just making a superficial dip. Another example for Yunbi is like the rain water is leaking down in a house.   The rain water does not usually pour down straight from the roof; but it penetrates from a corner of the house and then flow down the room in zig-zag stream. These images are vivid and lively examples that can help us to understand better the meaning of Yunbi.

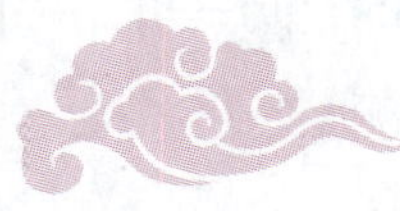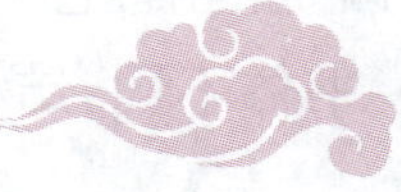

第 八 章

Chapter 8

结 构

Jiegou (structure)

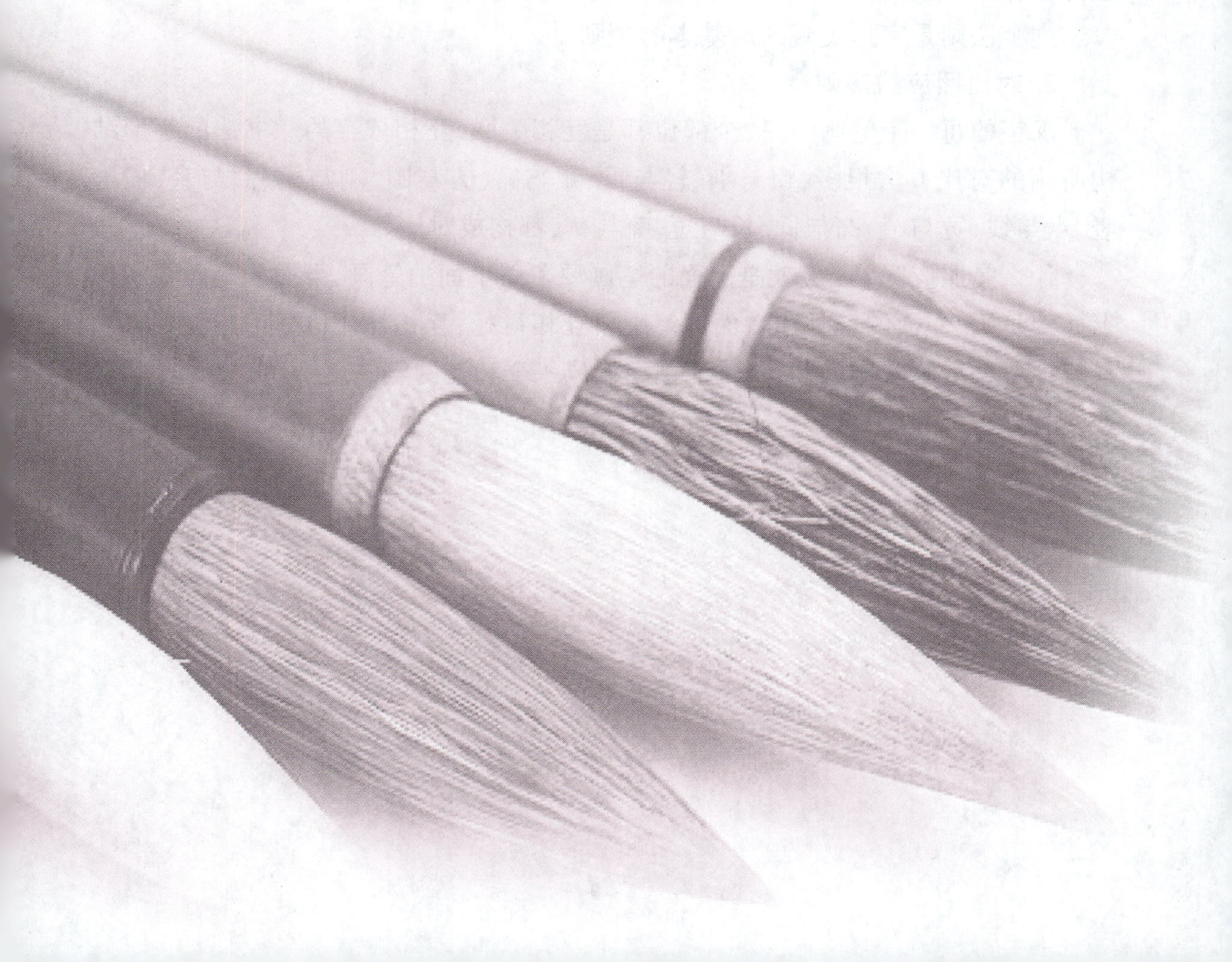

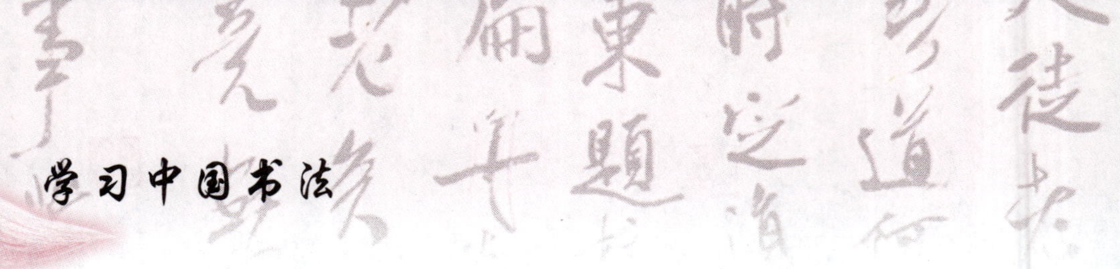

笔画的安排就是结构。结构又称结字、结体、间架。

运笔在书法中是占第一位的,结构的重要性仅次于运笔。

笔画是基础,它只有八种,而笔画的安排却是千变万化的。同一个字,因为书家不同,书体不同,结构不同,所以写出的字形不同,变幻莫测。

(1) 结构的基本法则

1. 平衡对称的法则:

在日常生活中,各种建筑、日用器皿和人体,如果各部位的安排平衡对称、比例协调的,就能美观生色;如果各个部位倾斜不安、杂乱无章,就会使人感到不美、失色。

字形结构的道理也一样,如果写字违反了平衡对称的原则,写出的字必然歪歪扭扭,非常难看。

这个法则是字形美观的最基本的法则。

2. 对比照应的法则:

汉字的每一个笔画、每一个部位都是互相关联、互相依存的。书法的字形结构所用的对比方法很多,粗与细、轻与重、藏与露、方与圆、刚与柔、曲与直、横与竖、点与线、宽与窄、高与低、长与短、疏与密,都构成对比。

什么是照应呢? 照应就是上面的笔画要覆盖下面的笔画,下面的笔画要承托上面的笔画,左面的笔画和右面的笔画要互相衬托,互相补让,这就是互相照应。只有把各种笔画安排妥贴了,才能把字构成一个和谐的整体。

The arrangement of strokes in Chinese is best translated by the word "structure". "Structure" is alternately called "Jie Zi", "Jie Ti", or "Jian Jia".

Yunbi remains the factor of foremost importance in writing Chinese. The importance of structure is second only to Yunbi.

Strokes are fundamental to Chinese; there are only eight types of such strokes. However, the arrangement of strokes has infinite varieties. The same character, if it is written by a different calligrapher, perhaps using a different script or structure, can produce a different appearance. As such, different writers, often produce characters with many different appearances.

(1) Basic rules of structure for Chinese characters

1. The rule of a balanced opposition arrangement:

There are many events in daily life that can be used as an illustration of this balanced opposition arrangement rule. For example, to install windows in a second floor room; when there are two windows placed on the east side and two windows placed on the west side of the room, it gives a sense of balanced opposition arrangement rule applies to the structure of writing Chinese characters. When characters are not written in accordance with the rule of balanced opposition, their overall appearance on a page may be tilted, uncoordinated, or unbalanced; which makes the piece of writing appear unsightly.

2. The rule of dependency and supplementary in opposition:

Every dot, line, and stroke in Chinese calligraphy must be properly placed in order to express a sense of mutual dependency. Their placements are also depended on other strokes to express their mutual dependent on other strokes interrelation.

In Chinese calligraphy, many structures are employed to accommodate the "opposite" conditions in their appearance. For instance, a fat line and a thin line, a lightly touched stroke and a heavily pressed stroke; a stroke from a slow brush movement and a stroke from a rapid brush movement; a stroke makes a square turn and a stroke makes a round corner turn; a harsh line stroke and a soft line stroke; a crooked line stroke and a straight line stroke; a horizontal line stroke and a vertical line stroke; a wide line stroke and a narrow line stroke; a dot in a high place and a dot in a lower place; a long line and a short line; a loosely placed group of characters and a densely placed group of characters.

What is coverage? Another important concept in calligraphy writing, coverage is the practice of depending upon the upper strokes in a character to cover up the strokes below. Conversely, the lower strokes of a character depend upon the strokes above to anchor them. Strokes on the left side and strokes on the right side must also function as mutually supportive. Only when all strokes possess a proper coverage arrangement, the character will be a harmonious unit.

3. 多样统一的法则：

多样而又统一的法则要求字既要平衡对称，又要避免平淡，力求结构有新颖的变化。多样统一的法则是一切美的事物的最高法则，也是字形美的最高法则。只有多样性而无统一性，会使人感到杂乱无秩序；只有统一性而无多样性，会使人感到机械、呆板。二者相辅相成，互为条件。

例如，在楷书中，同样写并列的四个点，但点画的安排很不相同。唐·颜真卿在《颜勤礼碑》中写的"马"(图47)字，四个点是向着一个方向点的；隋·智永在《真草千字文》中写的"鱼"(图48)字，四个点是向中心聚攒的；晋·王羲之在《兴福寺断碑》中写的"鸟"(图49)字，四个点是用横画代替的；唐·褚遂良在《孟法师碑》中写的"鸟"(图50)字，四个点有疏有密；唐·欧阳通在《道因法师碑》中写的"鱼"(图51)字，四个点写成"火"字。如此等等，都是多样统一的具体体现。

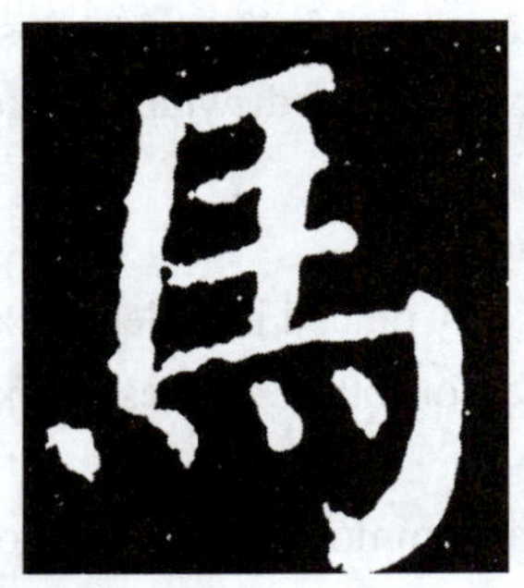
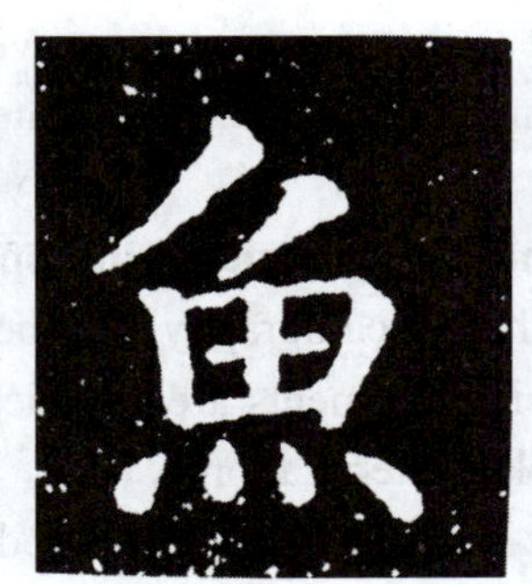
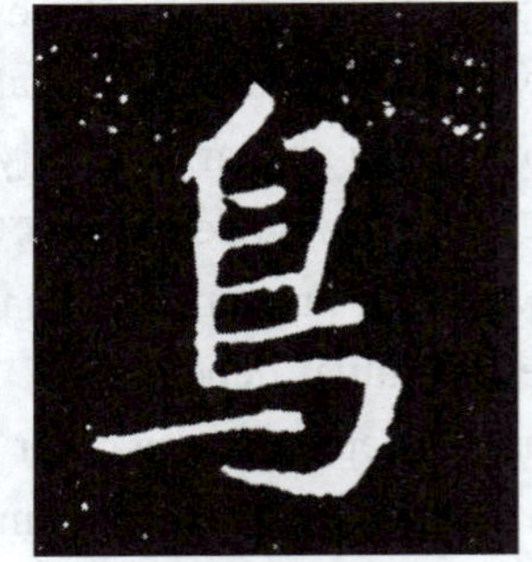

图47　唐·颜真卿《颜勤礼碑》　　图48　隋·智永《真草千字文》　　图49　晋·王羲之《兴福寺断碑》

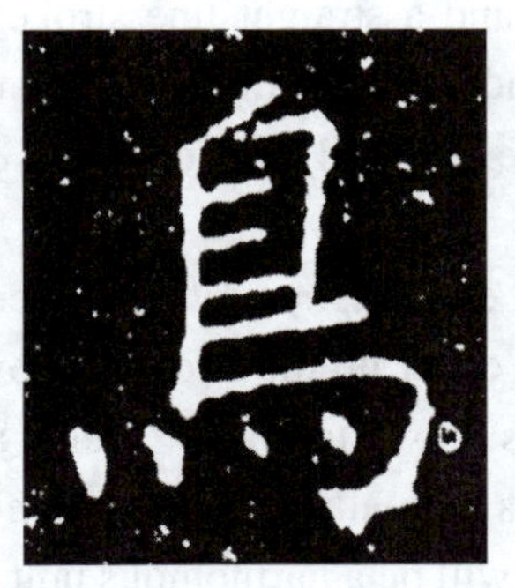
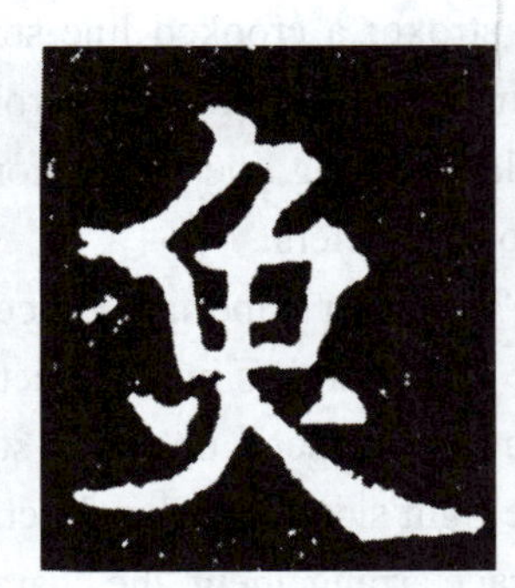

图50　唐·褚遂良《孟法师碑》　　图51　唐·欧阳通《道因法师碑》

3. The rule of multiple components:

This rule of multiple components calls for the exhibition of uniformity among multiple components. For example, when a page of calligraphy is written in different sizes, or each character is tilting towards a different direction, the page of calligraphy risks appearing to be merely ugly doodles. In general, when all characters written on a page are uniform in one size, the page of calligraphy will be more beautiful. However, this rule of uniformity must not be observed blindly, when all characters are written strictly with uniformity in mind, the page of calligraphy might appear dull and mechanical. To follow the spirit and intent of this rule and to avoid dullness, one requires a higher understanding of the rule of uniformity and the need to include a mutual support among different components.

To illustrate this rule in Kai style writing, the appearance of four dots in a character could have totally different appearance when written by different Calligraphy Masters. Tang dynasty *Calligraphy* Master Yan Zhenqing wrote the character Ma in *Yan Qin Li Bei* (Figure 47), his four dots were written pointing to the same direction. Sui dynasty Calligraphy Master Zhi Yong wrote the character "鱼" in the *Zhen Cao Qian Zhi Wen* (Figure 48), the four dots he wrote were crowded towards the center. Jing dynasty Calligraphy Master Wang Xizhi wrote the character "鸟" in the *Xing Fu Si Duan Bei* (Figure 49), the four dots he wrote were shown as a horizontal line. Tang dynasty Calligraphy Master Chu Suiliang wrote the character "鸟" in *Meng Fa Shi Bei* (Figure 50), the four dots he wrote were placed apart from one another without any regularity. Tang dynasty Calligraphy Master Ouyang Tong wrote the character "鱼" (Figure 51), in which the four dots were shown as the character "火". These are but some interesting examples of the rule of multiple components.

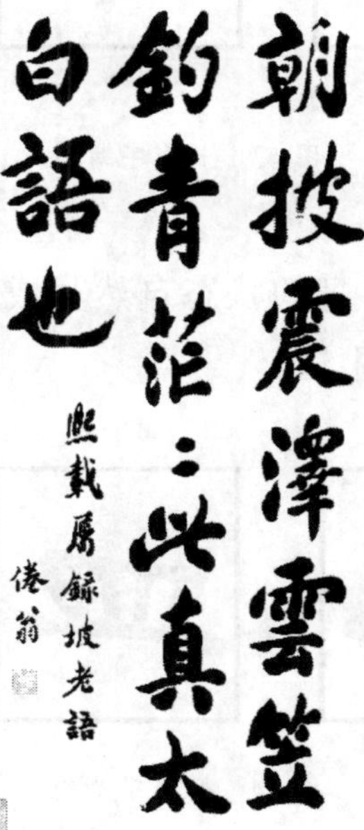

《楷书坡老语轴》

87

（2）结构的形式

汉字的结构分两大类：独体字和合体字。

1. 独体字：

独体字是由一些笔画直接组成的字，其中又分几种情况：

（1）平衡对称结构：书写时注意左右两边均衡。

　　　例：十、中、山、亦。（图 52）

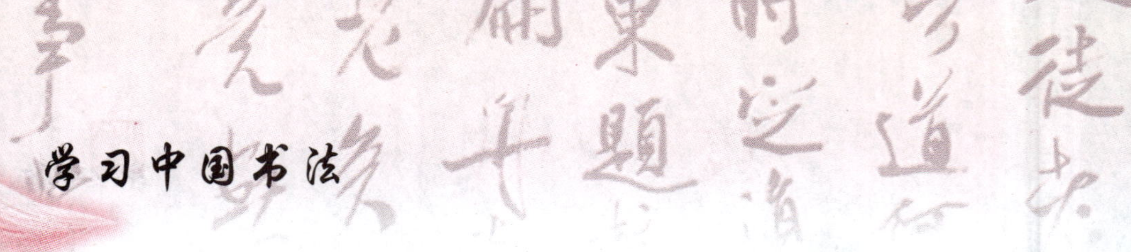

图 52　平衡对称结构

（2）长形字结构：书写时按字形本身的状态自然拉长。

　　　例：目、其、耳、身。（图 53）

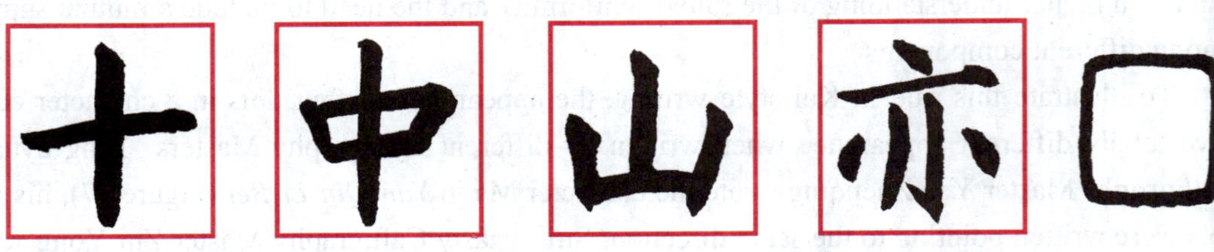

图 53　长形字结构

（3）短形字结构：按字形本身的状态自然写成扁形。

　　　例：曰、工、皿、而。（图 54）

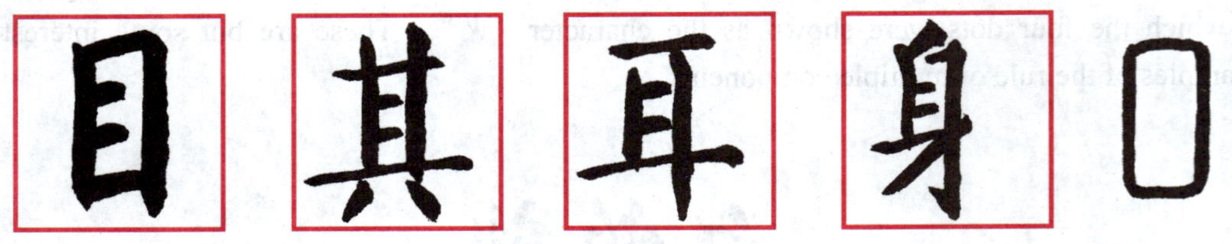

图 54　短形字结构

(2) Different types of structure for Chinese characters

Structure of Chinese characters can be divided into two groups: a single or unit character group and a combination character group.

1. A single or unit character group:

This group of characters is formed by individual strokes directly, but some characters in this group may be further divided into sub-groups.

(1) A balanced structure: The appearance of this group of characters requires a careful display of balance between the left side component and the right side component of the character. For example: 十、中、山、亦. (Figure 52)

(2) A tall main body structure: In writing a character that has a tall main body structure, it is natural to write it in a longer shape. For example: 目、其、耳、身. (Figure 53)

(3) A short main body structure: When writing a short main body character, it is natural to give a compressed appearance. For example: 曰、工、皿、而. (Figure 54)

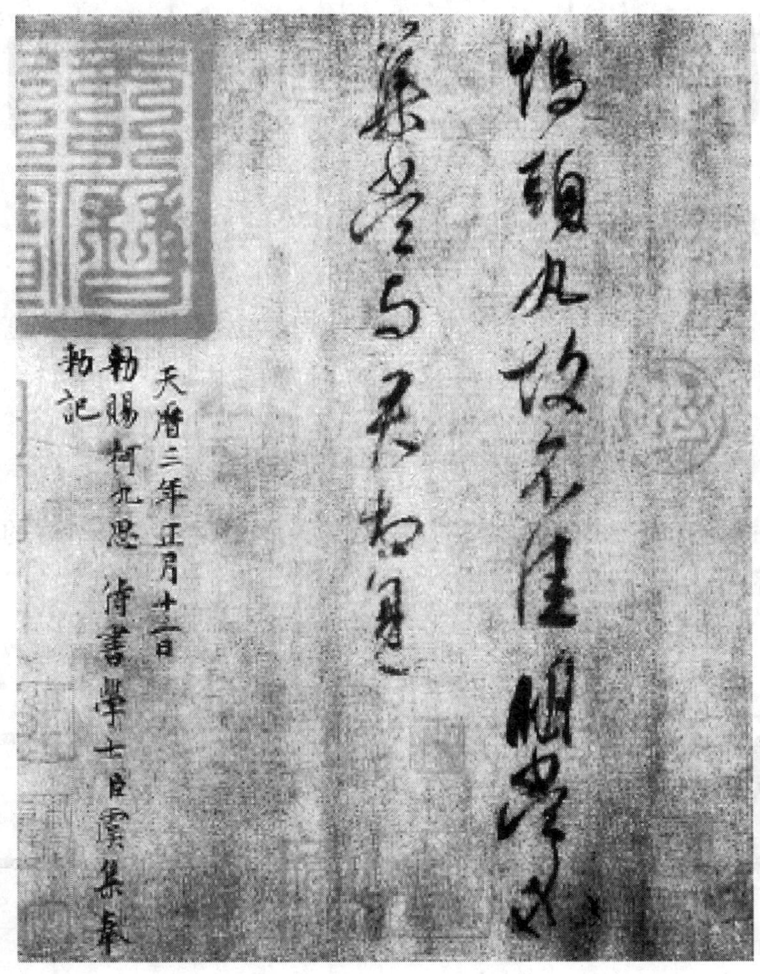

*《鸭头丸帖》

89

（4）斜体字结构：按字体本身的状态自然写成斜形，但要注意斜中取正。

　　例：母、勿、夕、戈。（图55）

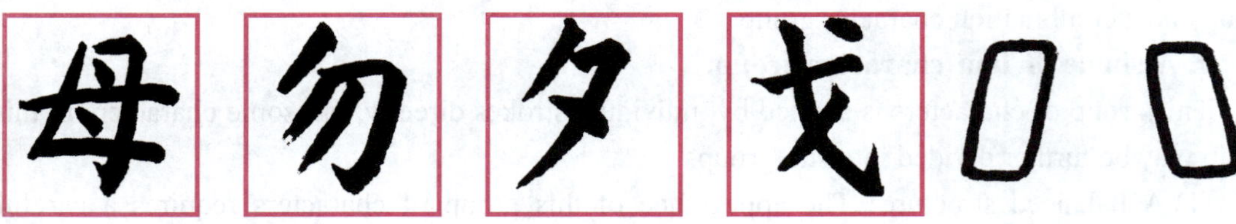

图55　斜形字结构

（5）形散意连结构：字的笔画虽是分散的，但笔意连贯，也就是笔画之间的
　　走向是衔接的。例：心、匕、之、州。（图56）

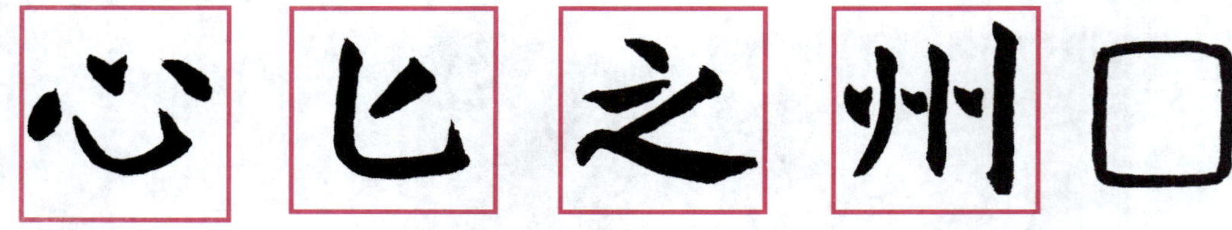

图56　形散意连结构

2. 合体字：

　　合体字是由两个或两个以上的偏旁部首和其它结构单位组合而成的，它的结构可归纳为以下六种形式：左右结构、左中右结构、上下结构、上中下结构、半包围结构、全包围结构。

（1）左右结构：

　　1）左轻右重字形结构：左边笔画相对少；右边笔画相对多，但左边的笔画不可草率。

　　　　例：信、情、渡、推。（图57）

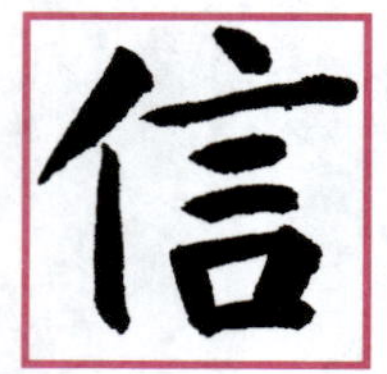

图57　左轻右重字形结构

(4) A tilted main body structure: When writing a tilted main body character, it is natural to give it a tilted appearance, but one must also be sure to keep it a "straight" appearance in the tilted shape. For example: 母、勿、夕、戈. (Figure 55)

(5) A divided structure yet the sense of strokes are linked together in unison. For example: 心、匕、之、州. (Figure 56)

2. Character that has multiple components.

This group of characters is made up by two or more than two distinguishable components. A character having this type of structure may be further classified into six different groups: a left and right structure; an upper and bottom structure; a left, center and right structure; a top, middle, and bottom structure; a semi-enclosed structure; and a totally enclosed structure.

(1) A left and right structure:

1) This group of characters has a structure that is lighter on its left side component and heavier on its right side component. In this type of structure, it would have lesser strokes (lighter) on the left side component; but more strokes (heavier) on the right side component. A word of caution, although there are lesser strokes in the left side, one should not casually write left side strokes. For example: 信、情、渡、推. (Figure 57)

*《周上卿墓志铭》

2) 左重右轻字形结构：左边笔画相对多，右边笔画相对少，但右边的笔力宜强。

　　例：刻、剑、乳、亂。（图 58）

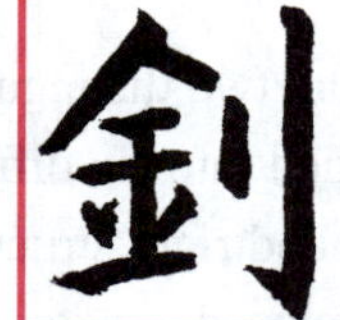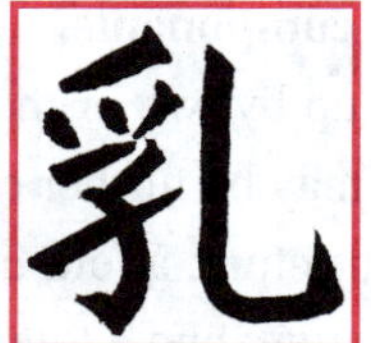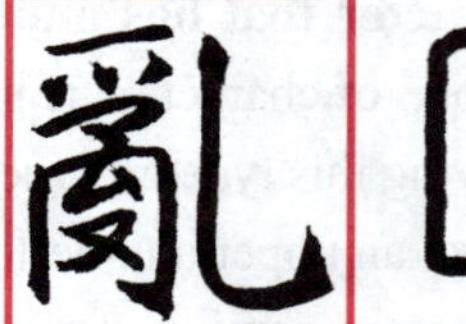

图 58　左重右轻字形结构

3) 平分字形结构：左右笔画分量相当，书写时右边要略强一些。

　　例：秋、辅、雕、静。（图 59）

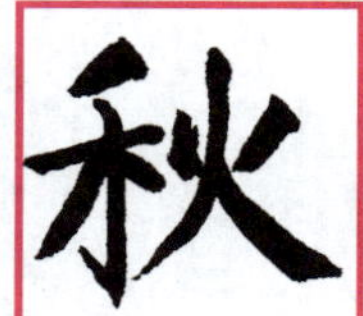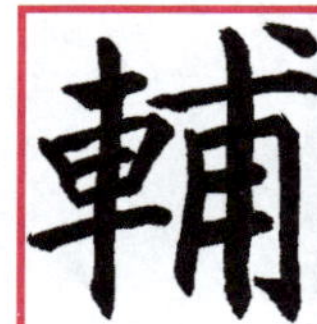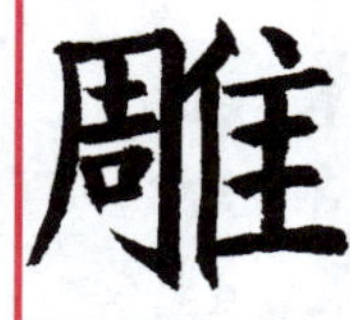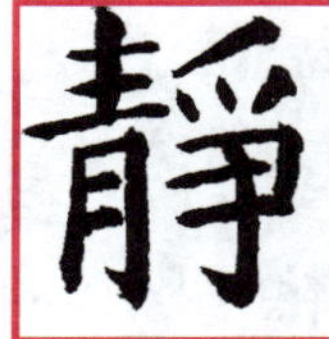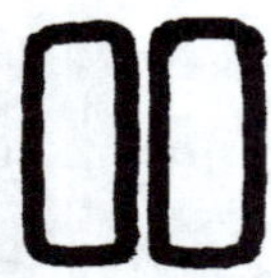

图 59　平分字形结构

4) 并排字形结构：左右笔画重复，但右边的笔画要写得长些、强些。

　　例：林、羽、竹、兢。（图 60）

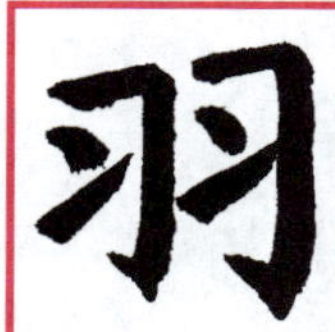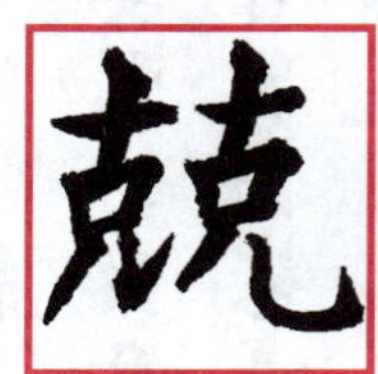

图 60　并排字形结构

2) This character has a heavier left side component and lighter right side component. In this type of structure, there are more strokes on the left side of the character, and relatively few strokes on the right side of the character. To present such structure properly, one should write strokes in the right side with increased strength. For example: 刻、钊、乳、亂. (Figure 58)

3) This type of structure has a balanced division of weight between components on the right and left sides. In writing a character in this type of structure, one needs to give the right side slightly more strength. For example: 秋、輔、雕、静. (Figure 59)

4) The right side component and the left side component in the character are a pair of the same characters (a repeated structure). In a character in this type of structure, one needs to write the right side a bit larger (stronger). For example: 林、羽、竹、兢. (Figure 60)

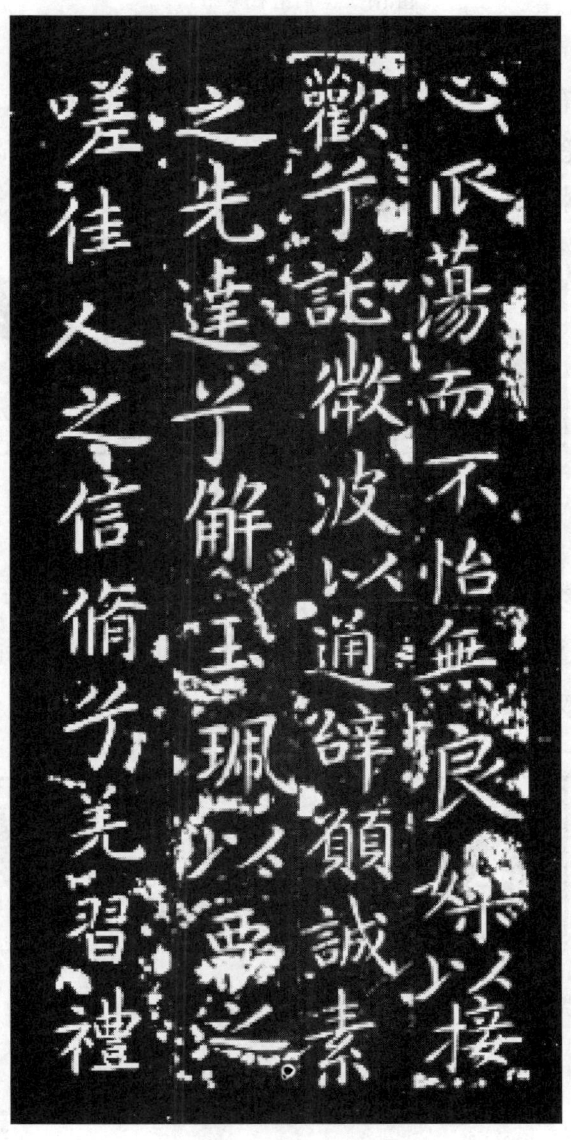

*《洛神賦》

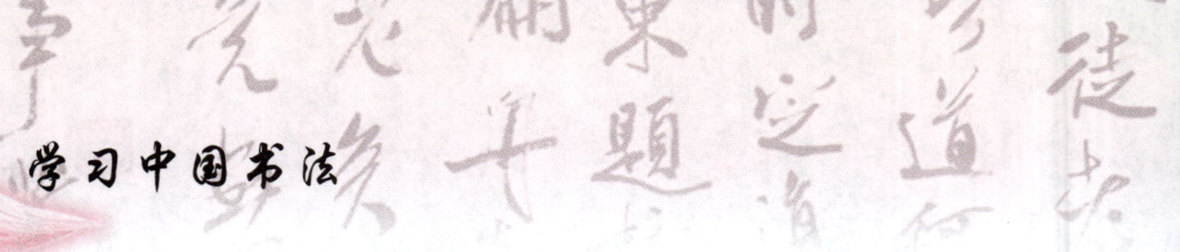

5) 左高右低字形结构：以左为正，以右为副，右让左，但右边的笔画有支
撑整体的作用。

　　例：即、却、都、部。（图 61）

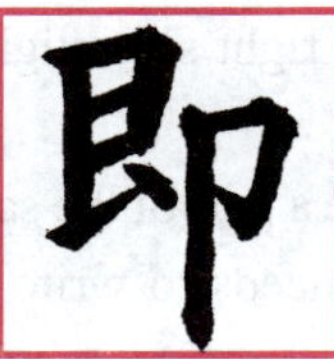 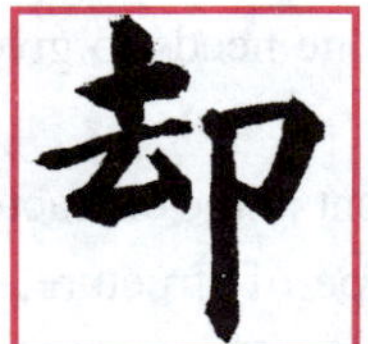 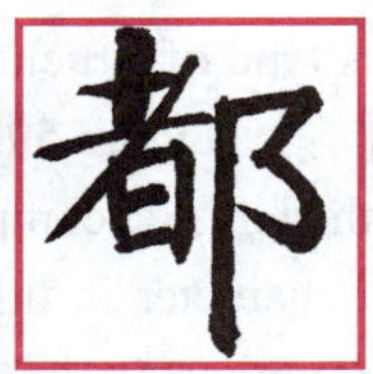 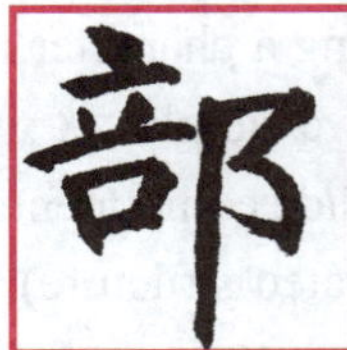 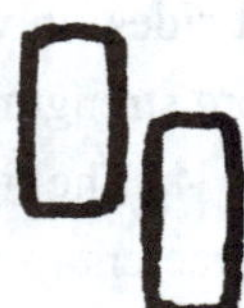

图 61　左高右低字形结构

6) 左低右高字形结构：以右为正，以左为副，左让右，但左边的笔画有辅
助右边笔画的作用。

　　例：填、球、端、峻。（图 62）

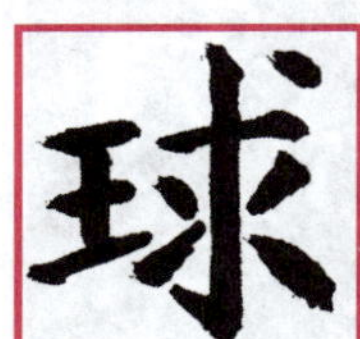 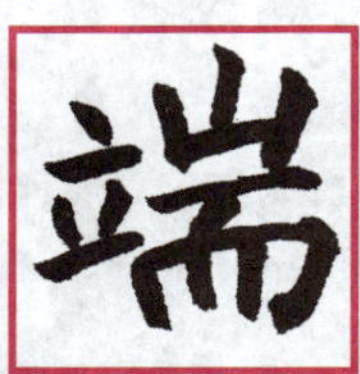 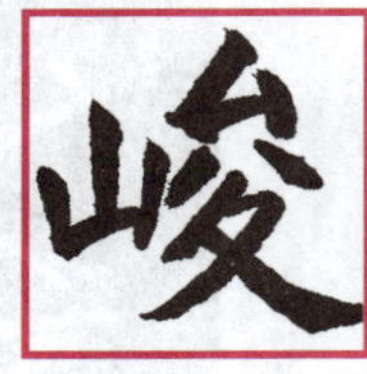 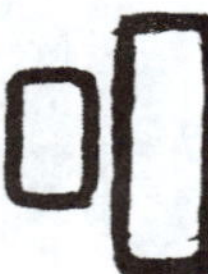

图 62　左低右高字形结构

7) 下平字形结构：左右两边下部宜平，这种字形与左高右低字形有相似
之处，书写时右边的点画居中起笔，而收笔时与左边的底部持平。

　　例：初、叙、叔、勒。（图 63）

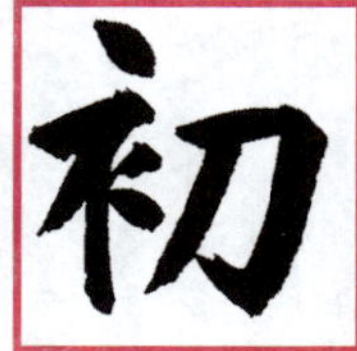 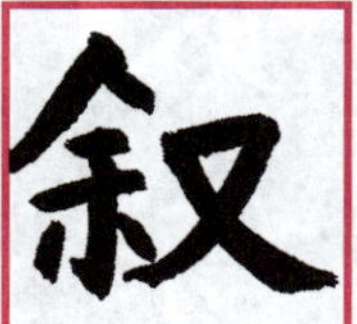 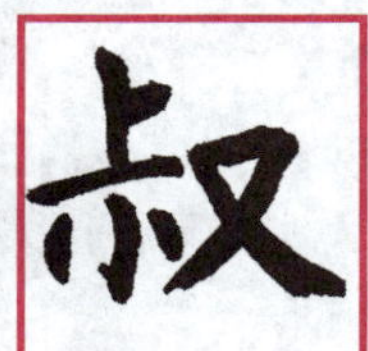 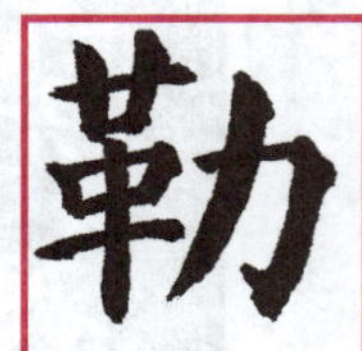 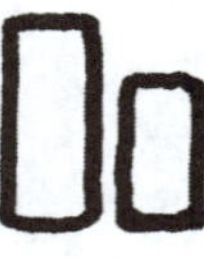

图 63　下平字形结构

5) This type of structure has a higher level left side component than right side component. The left side of the character is considered to be the primary component in the structure; and the right side is to be considered a supportive component. The right side yields to the left side but the right side strokes are necessary for the support of the structure as a whole. For example: 即、却、都、部. (Figure 61)

6) This character has a higher right side component and a lower left side component. The right side of the character is considered to be primary component; and the left side is considered to be supportive component. The left side yields to the right side but left side strokes have the responsibility to support the right side strokes. For example: 填、球、端、峻. (Figure 62)

7) This type of character has a structure with leveled lower components: The lower component on the left side and the lower component on the right side are on a same level. This structure is similar to the "higher left side and lower right side" structure. In writing a character in this structure, begin with the writing of the dot stroke in the middle of the right side, and then when writing the closing stroke, make it to be leveled with the bottom of left side component. For example: 初、叙、叔、勒. (Figure 63)

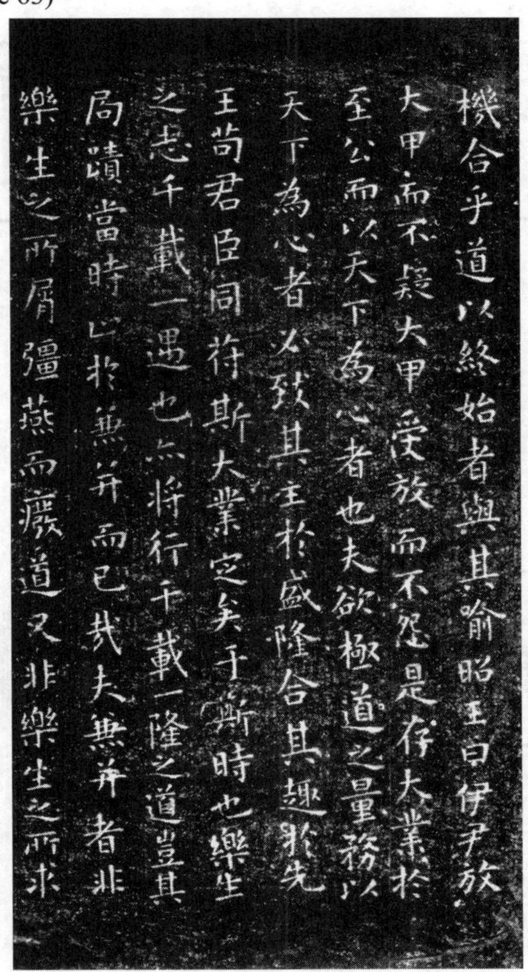

*《乐毅论》

8) 居中字形结构:左边或右边的笔画部位居中,不靠上,也不靠下。

　　例:吐、如、和、加。(图64)

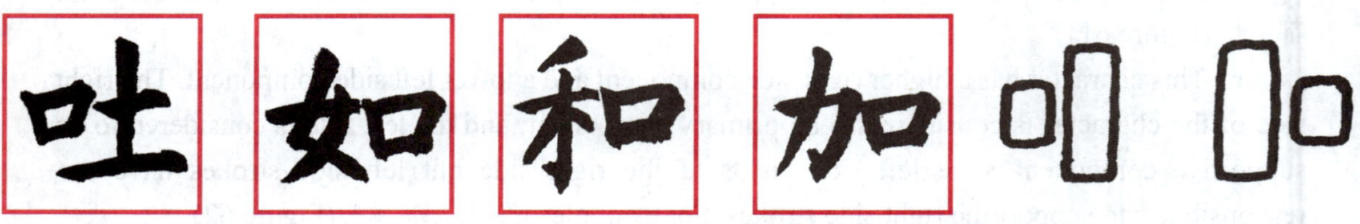

图64　居中字形结构

左右结构要注意以下组合比例。(图65)

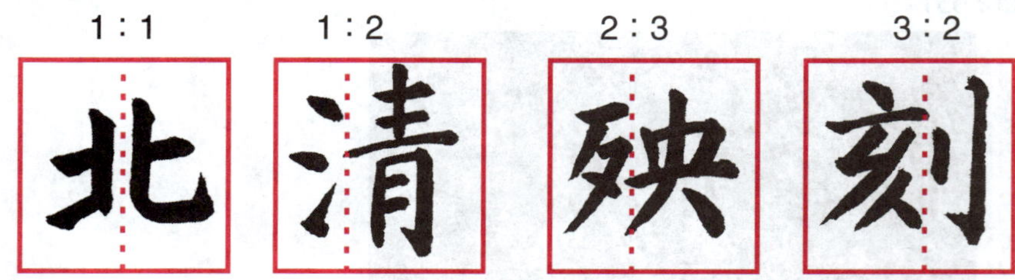

图65　左右结构比例

(2) 左中右结构:

　　1) 三分字形结构:左中右分量均等。

　　例:树、街、脚、嫩。(图66)

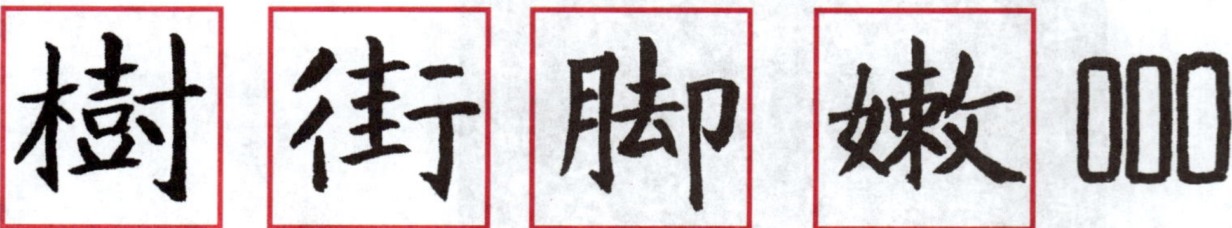

图66　三分字形结构

8) This type of character has a central structure. Strokes on the left side component or the right side component are to be centrally placed; and they are not to be placed near the top, nor near the bottom. For example: 吐、如、和、加. (Figure 64)

In writing a character with left component and right side component, one needs to pay special attention to the proportion of each side as shown in the example: 北、清、殃、刻. (Figure 65)

(2) A left, right and center structure

1) A character has three equally weighted components. For example: 树、街、脚、嫩. (Figure 66)

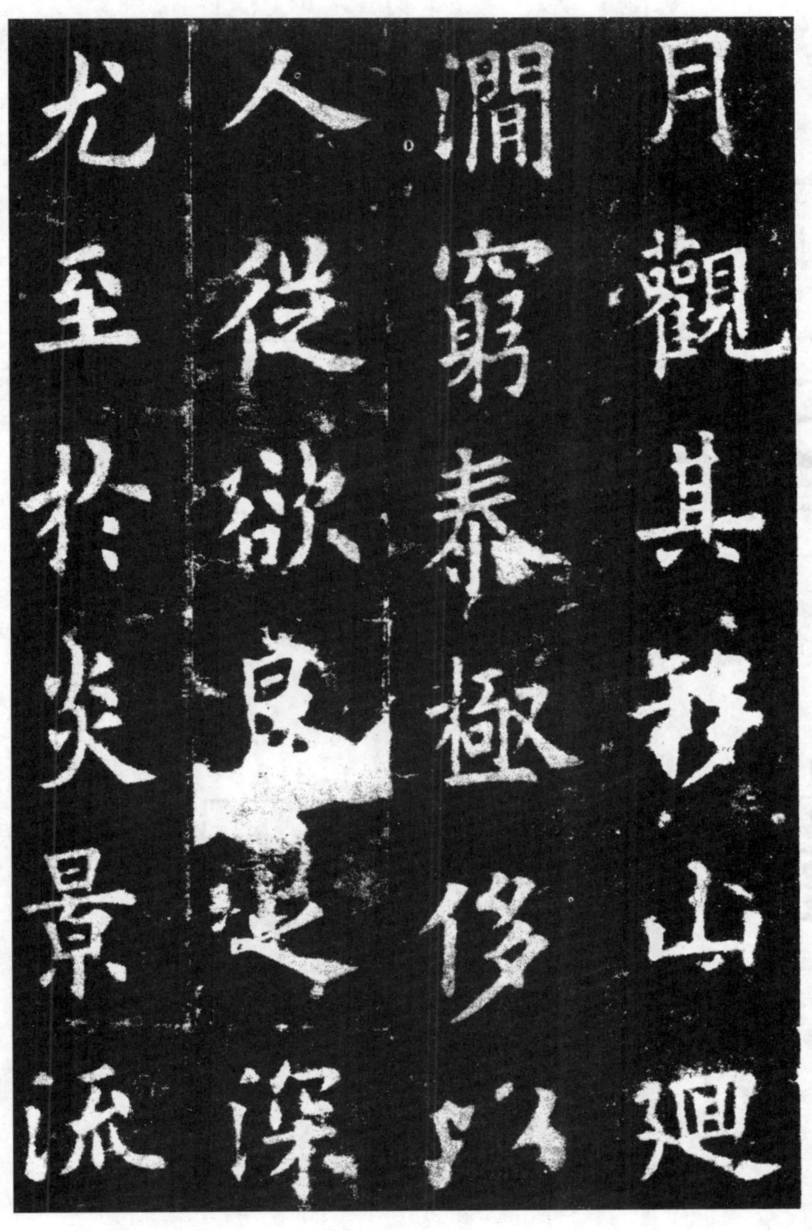

*《九成宫醴泉铭》

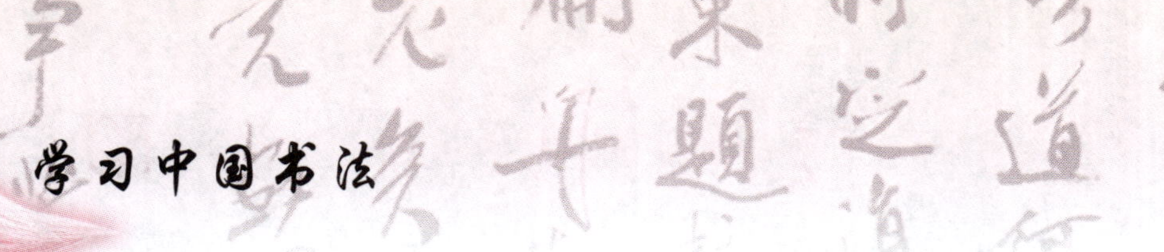

2）左简中右繁字形结构：左侧所占分量较轻，中右均等。

　　例：做、湖、凝、懈。（图 67）

图 67　左简中右繁字形结构

3）中窄左右宽字形结构：中间所占分量较小，要写得窄些，左右均等。

　　例：衍、班、袱、辨。（图 68）

图 68　中窄左右宽字形结构

左中右结构的组合比例。（图 69）

1:1:1　　2:1:2　　1:2:2

图 69　左中右结构组合比例

2) A character has three components: a simple left side; a more complex right side and a center component. For example: 做、湖、凝、懈. (Figure 67)

3) A narrow center component; but wider right and left sides structure. Because the center has a lighter weight, it is written narrower. However, the right side and the left side are written with equal weight. For example: 沩、班、袱、辨. (Figure 68)

Another types of character with three components: left, right and center but have different weights. For example: 树、沩、做. (Figure 69)

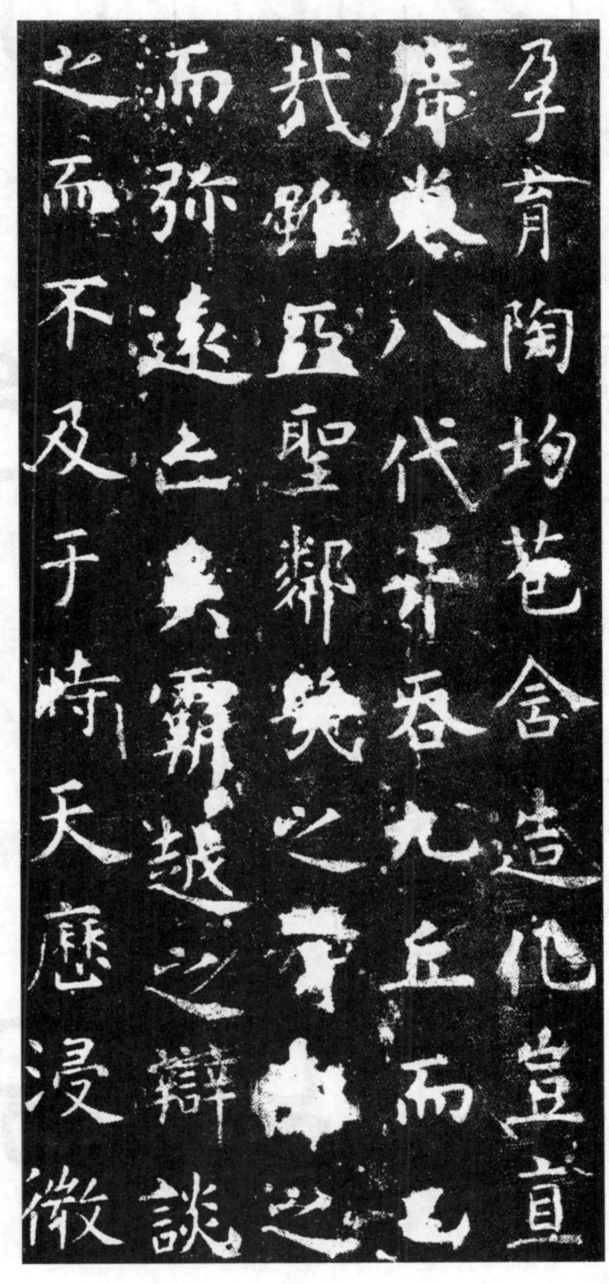

*《孔子庙堂碑》

（3）上下结构：

    1）重叠字形结构：上下点画重复，但书写时宜上小下大。

      例：昌、炎、多、哥。（图 70）

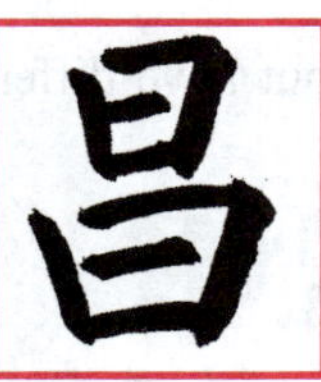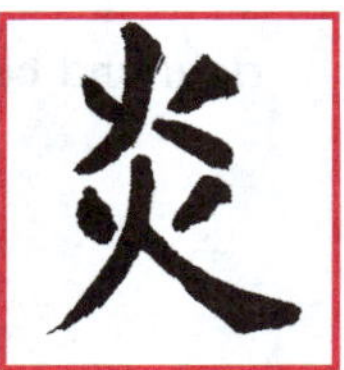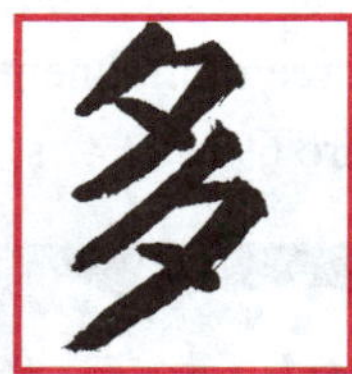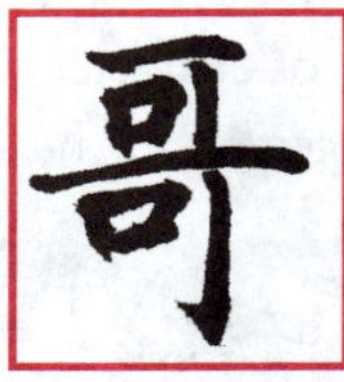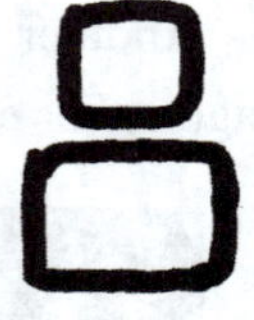

图 70　重叠字形结构

    2）上简下繁字形结构：上边笔画少，但不要写得松散；下边笔画多，要写得稍紧而匀称。

      例：最、嵌、露、羁。（图 71）

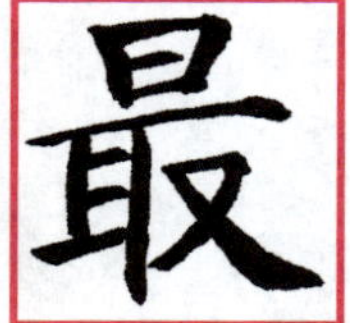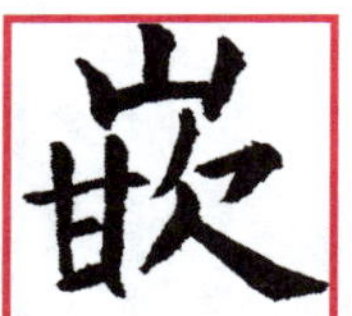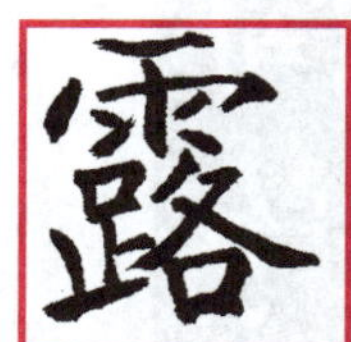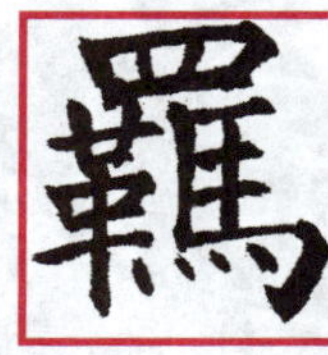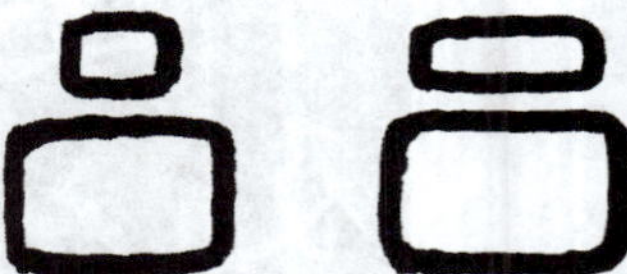

图 71　上简下繁字形结构

    3）上繁下简字形结构：上边的笔画多，要写得十分紧凑；下边的笔画少，要写得重些、粗壮些，以免头重脚轻。

      例：奥、愈、壁、整。（图 72）

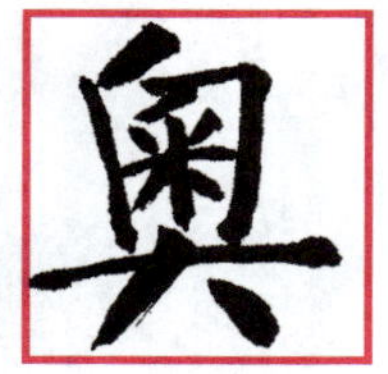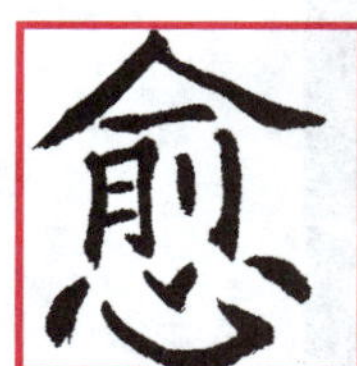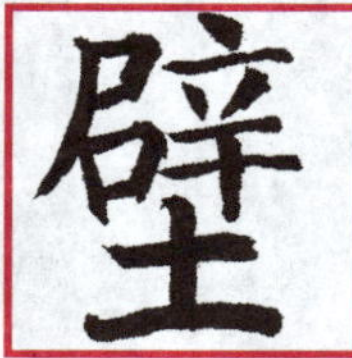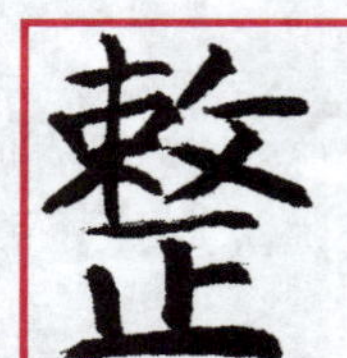

图 72　上繁下简字形结构

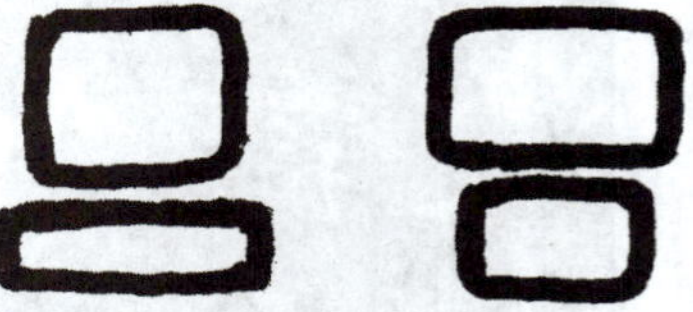

(3)　A top and bottom structure:

1) A redundant top and bottom structure: In this group of structure, there are two identical components with one placed on top of another. When writing characters in this structure, size of the top component is to be made smaller than the component on the bottom. For example: 昌、炎、多、哥. (Figure 70)

2) In this type of top and bottom structure, the top component has a simpler structure than the lower component.　For simpler stroke arrangement in the upper component,　they are not to be written in a casual and loose manner; but for the lower component where it has more strokes, they are written in a tighter and balanced arrangement. For example: 最、嵌、露、羁. (Figure 71)

3) Strokes on the top component are more complex and strokes in the lower component are simpler. Since there are more strokes on the top, they need to be written tightly together; the lower part has fewer strokes, so they are to be heavily written. For example: 奥、愈、壁、整. (Figure 72)

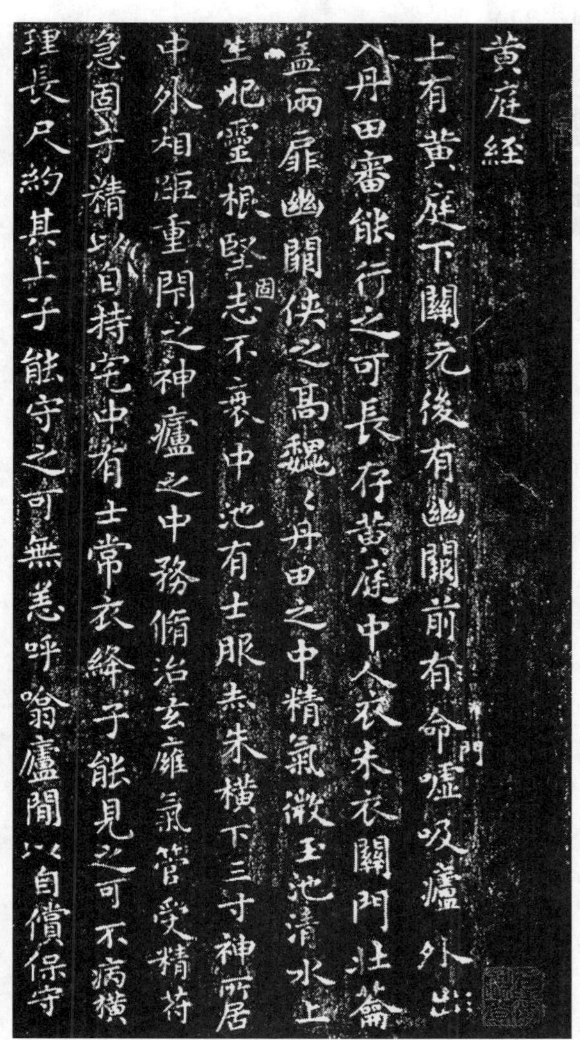

*《黄庭经》

4) 上下相等字形结构：上下两部分，不论笔画相对多或相对少，要写得分量均等。

例：思、需、留、禁。（图73）

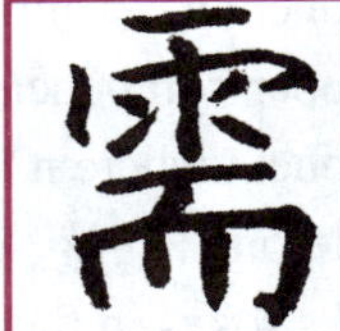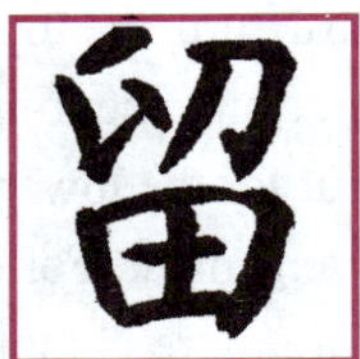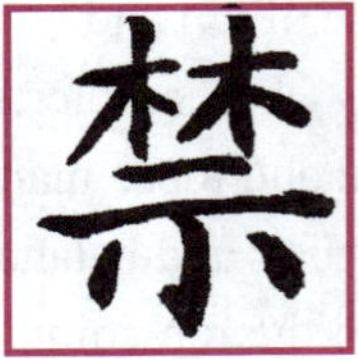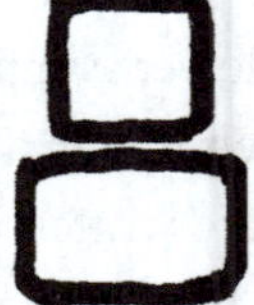

图73　上下相等字形结构

上下结构要注意以下组合比例。（图74）

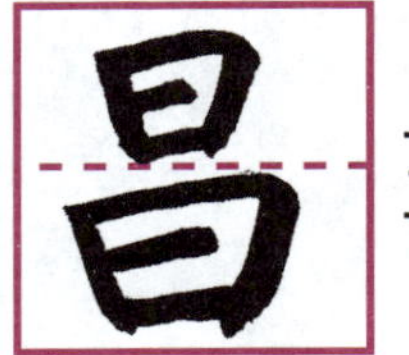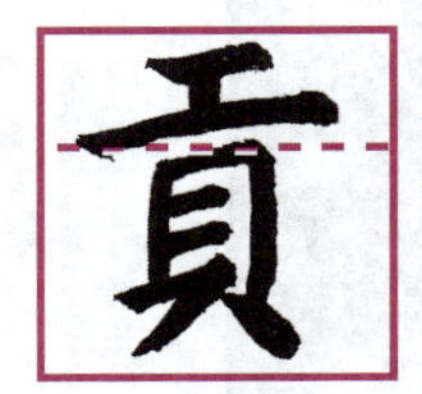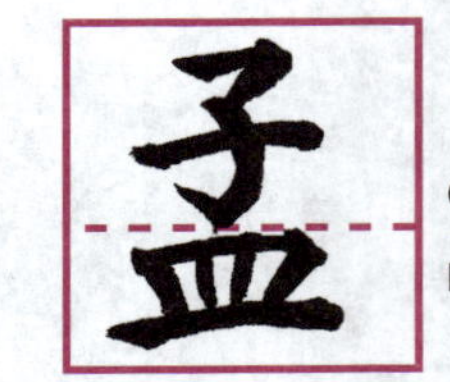

图74　上下结构组合比例

（4）上中下结构：

上中下匀称：按照上、中、下笔画的多少，妥帖、平稳地安排整体结构。

例：素、曼、翼、嚣。（图75）

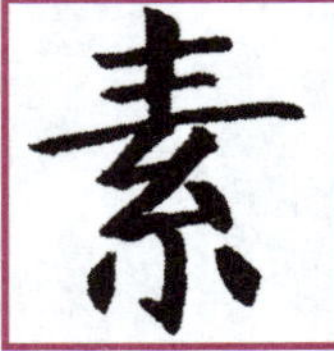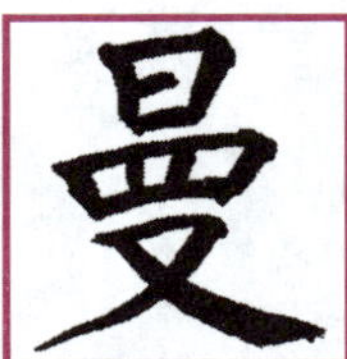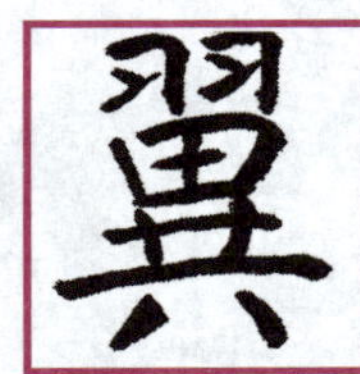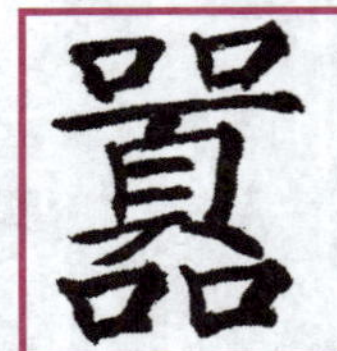

图75　上中下匀称

4) A balanced top and bottom structure. Regardless of whether there are a greater or a lesser number of strokes in the top or bottom component; each should be given equal weight in writing. For example: 思、需、留、禁. (Figure 73)

In a top and bottom structure, one should pay special attention to proportion. For example: 昌、贡、孟. (Figure 74)

(4) Top, bottom, and Middle structure:

When there is a balance of structure in the top, bottom and middle components of a character: the smoothness of stroke arrangements must be ensured. For example: 素、曼、翼、嚣. (Figure 75)

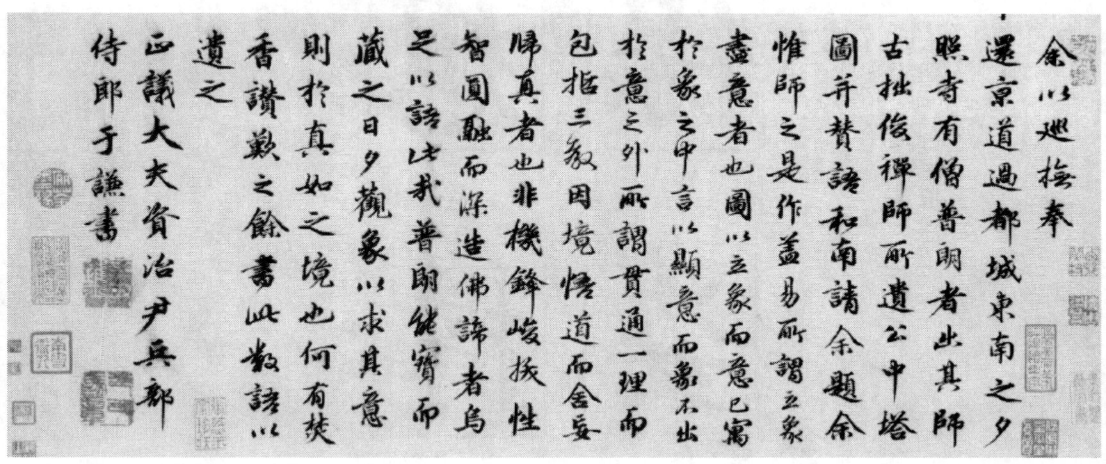

*《题公中塔图并赞》

上中下结构的组合比例。(图 76)

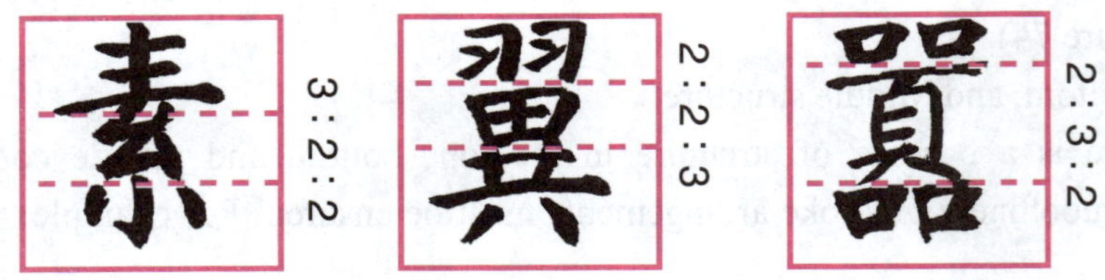

图 76　上中下结构组合比例

另外,结构较复杂的字要注意上下左右组合的比例。(图 77)

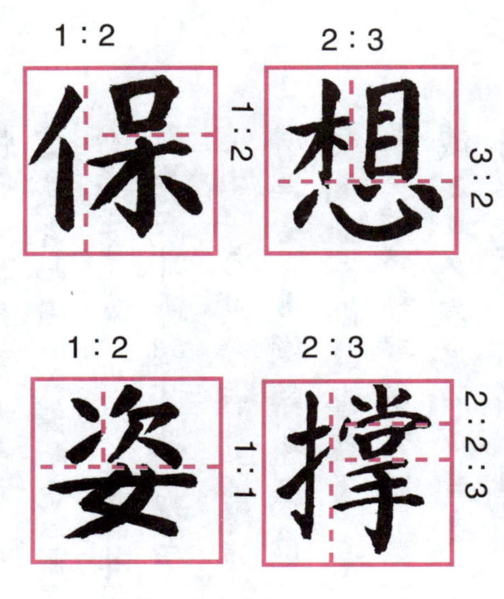

图 77　较复杂的字组合比例

A different proportion for the top, bottom and middle structure. For example: 素、翼、器.
(Figure 76)

When structure in a character is more complex，more attention should be given to the
proportion among top, bottom, left, and right component. For example: 保、想、姿、撑. (Figure
77)

*《书圣教序》

如果比例不当,写出的字是很难看的。(图 78)

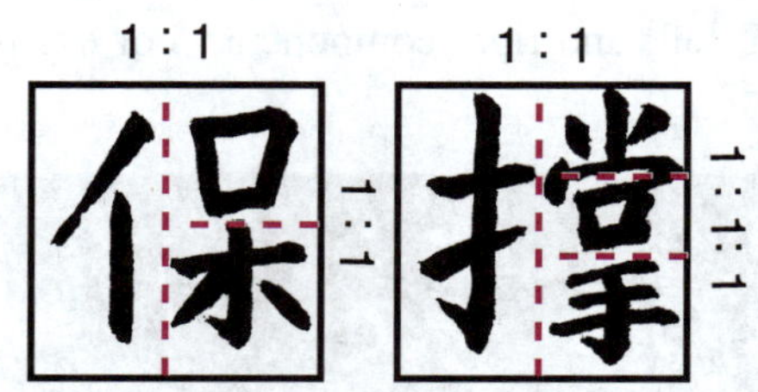

图 78　比例不当的字

(5) 半包围结构:

　　1) 上包下字形结构:书写时,被包围部分要居中而靠上,不可有下坠的
　　　感觉。

　　　例:同、周、鳳、開。(图 79)

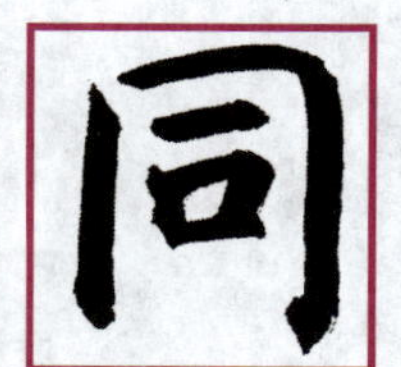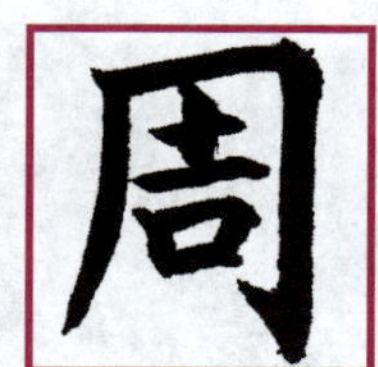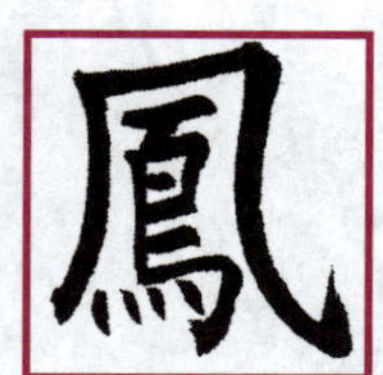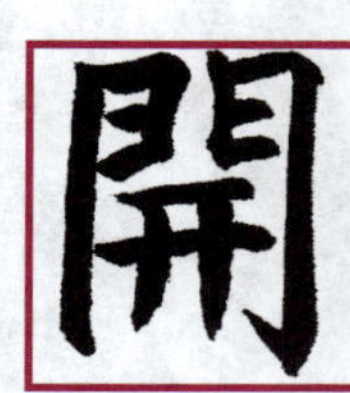

图 79　上包下字形结构

If incorrect proportion is applied to each component, the overall character will be ugly looking. For example: 保、撑. (Figure 78)

(5) When the structure is in a semi-enclosure.

1) The top part of the structure is enclosing the bottom part: In writing a character with this type of structure, the enclosed lower part should be placed in the middle and made a lean towards the top. Avoid giving the impression it is falling down. For example: 同、周、鳳、開. (Figure 79)

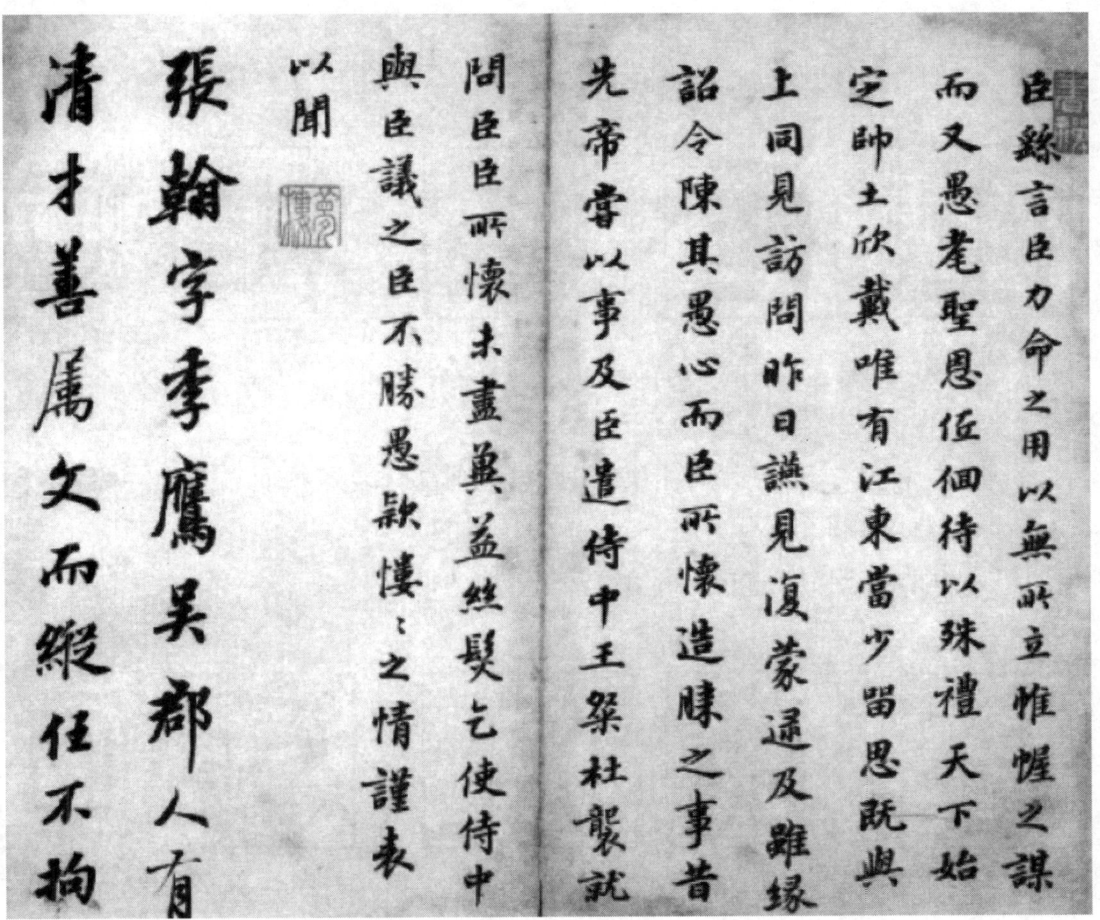

*行楷《书监帖册》

2）下包上字形结构：书写时，被包围部分要居中而靠下，不可有上悬的姿态。

例：凶、函、幽、豳（bīn）。（图 80）

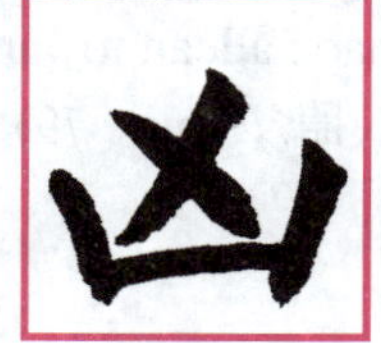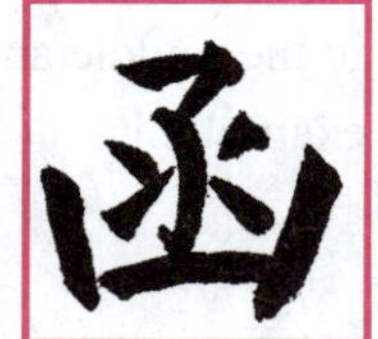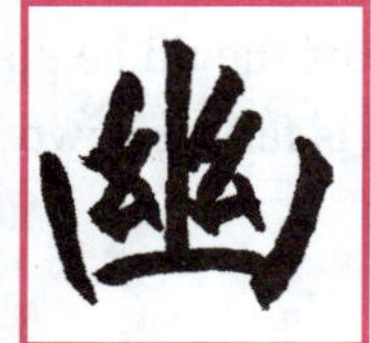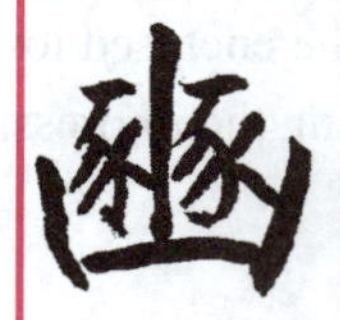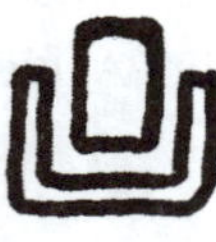

图 80　下包上字形结构

3）左包右字形结构：书写时，被包围部分要居中而靠左，还要注意整体平稳。

例：臣、匡、區、匪。（图 81）

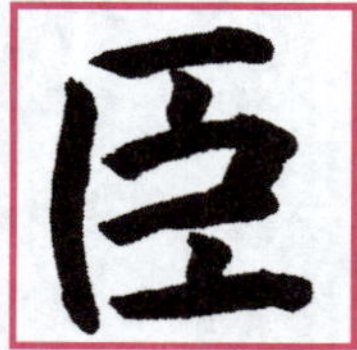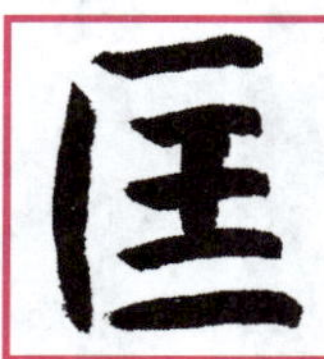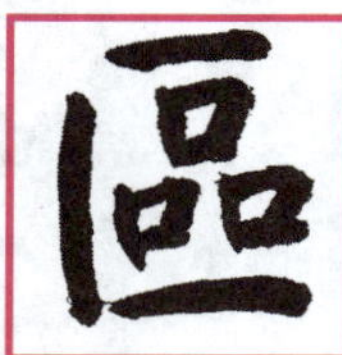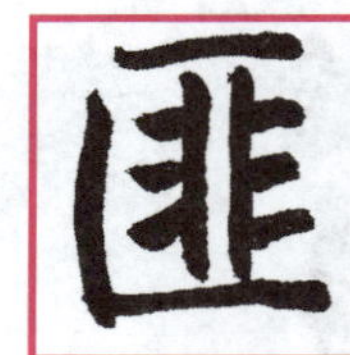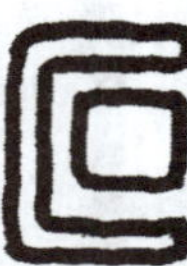

图 80　右包右字形结构

4）左上包右下字形结构：书写时，被包围部分要居中而靠左上，并且注意整体协调。

例：居、扇、度、病。（图 82）

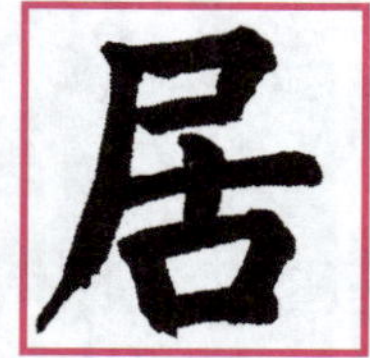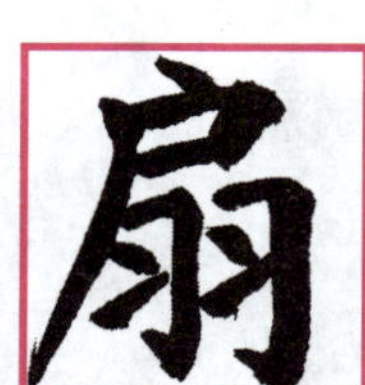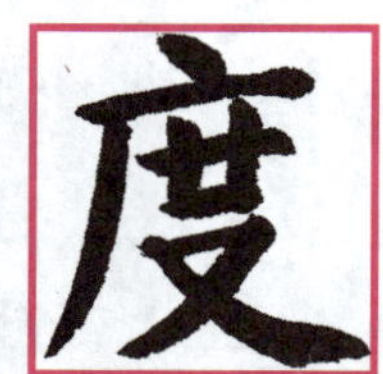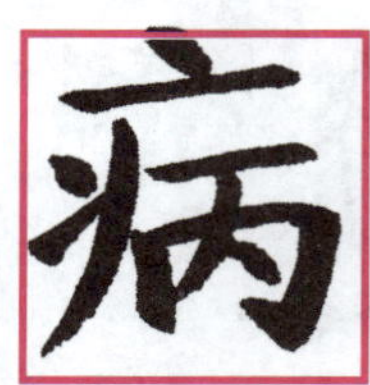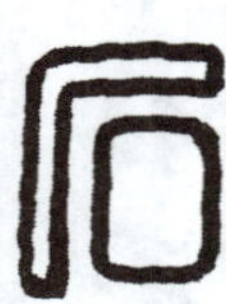

图 82　左上包右下字形结构

2) The lower (bottom) side of the character is enclosing the top side: In writing a character in this structure group, the enclosed component should be placed in the middle and closer to the bottom, otherwise, the structure will give the appearance of the character a sense of "hanging up in the air'. For example: 凶、函、幽、齒. (Figure 80)

3) The left side of the character is enclosing the right side: When writing a character in this structure group,　the enclosed components should be placed in the middle but approaching to left, and making sure a balance is still maintained for the entire character. For example: 臣、匡、區、匪. (Figure 81)

4) The left side of the top component is enclosing the lower right bottom side component: In writing a character in this structure group, the enclosed component should be placed closer to the middle but approaching to the upper left. In addition, pay special attention to the sense of harmony in the whole character. For example: 居、扇、度、病. (Figure 82)

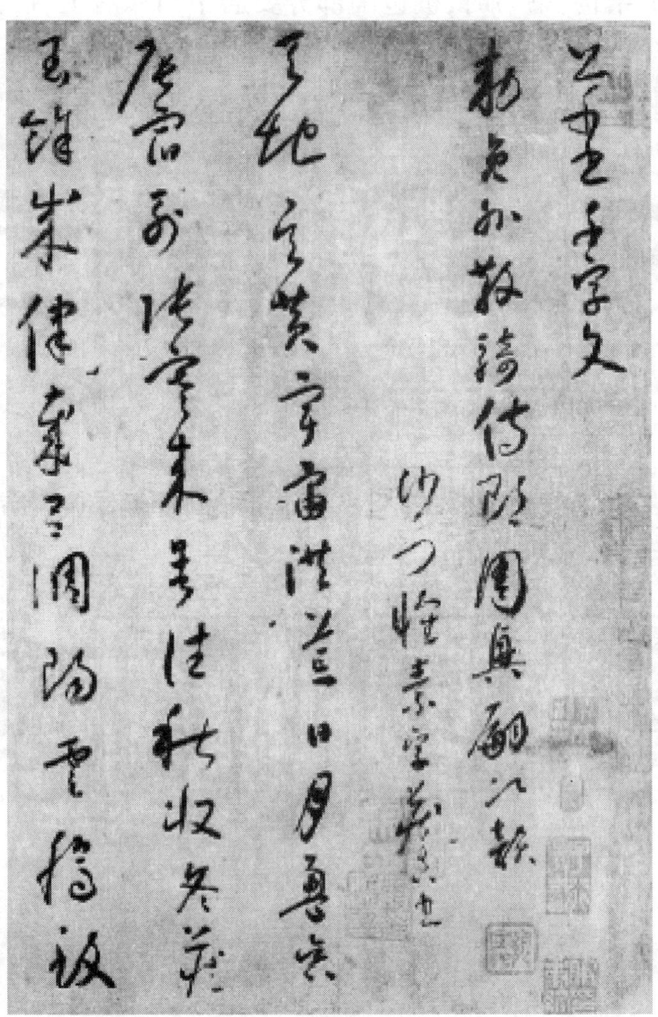

*《草书千字文》

5）左下包右上字形结构：书写时，被包围部分要居中而靠左下，并注意整体协调。

例：送、越、旭、毯。（图83）

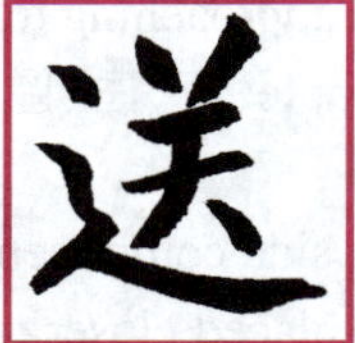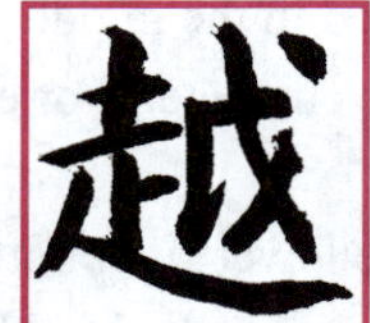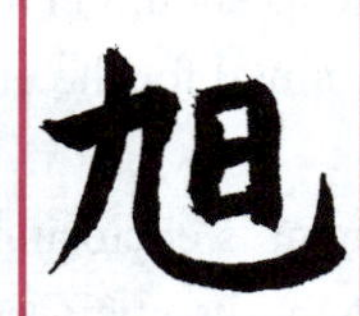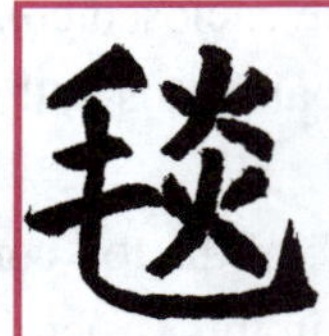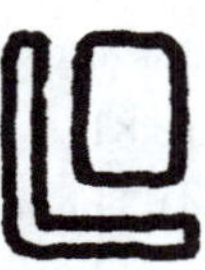

图83　左下包右上字形结构

6）右上包左下字形结构：书写时，被包围部分要居中而靠右上，但要避免拘谨。

例：句、匀、司、匍。（图84）

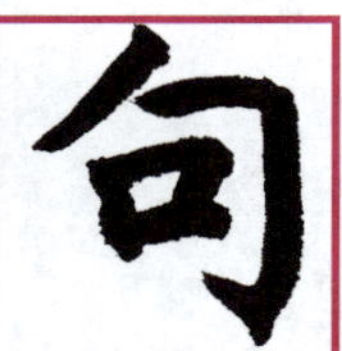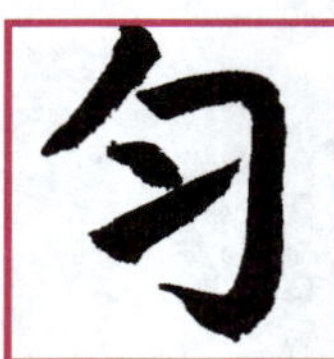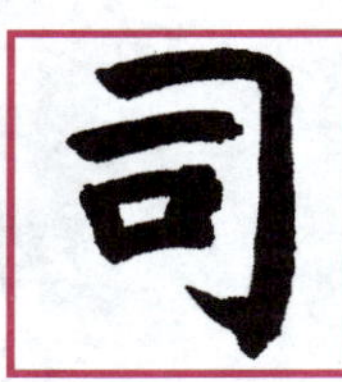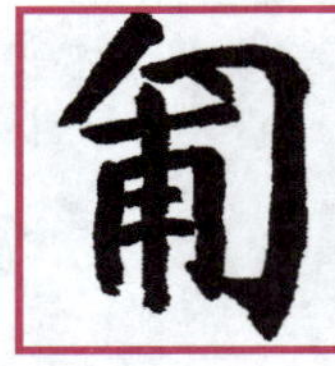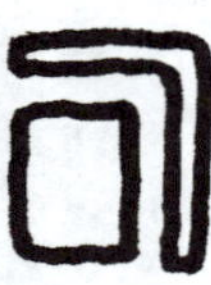

图84　右上包左下字形结构

（6）全包围结构：

内外严谨：书写时，被包围部分要居中，不要靠上、靠下、偏左、偏右。

例：因、固、國、圓。（图85）

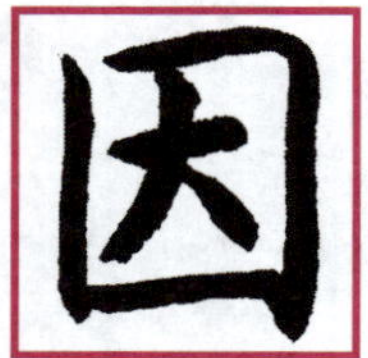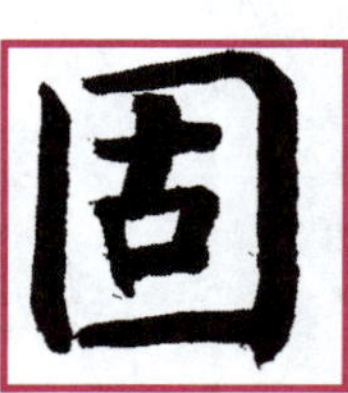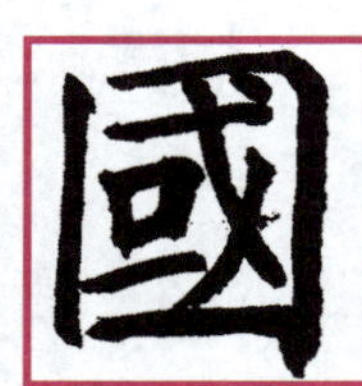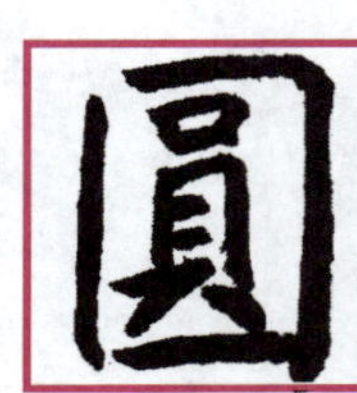

图85　全包围结构

5) The lower left side component is enclosing the top side of right component. In writing a character in this structure group, the enclosed component should be placed in the middle and made to approach the lower left side. In addition, pay special attention to the sense of harmony in the whole character. For example: 送、越、旭、毯. (Figure 83)

6) The top right side component is enclosing the lower left component. In writing a character in this structure group, the enclosed part should be placed in the middle and made to approach to right side above. Furthermore, one should avoid any sense of restraint in stroke expression. For example: 句、匀、司、匐. (Figure 84)

(6)　A completely enclosed structure.

This structure appears to be giving a solid impression from its inside and outside components. In writing a character in this character group, the enclosed part should be placed in the middle, not allowed to lean upwards or downwards, nor allowed to deviate from center to left or right. For example: 因、固、国、圆. (Figure 85)

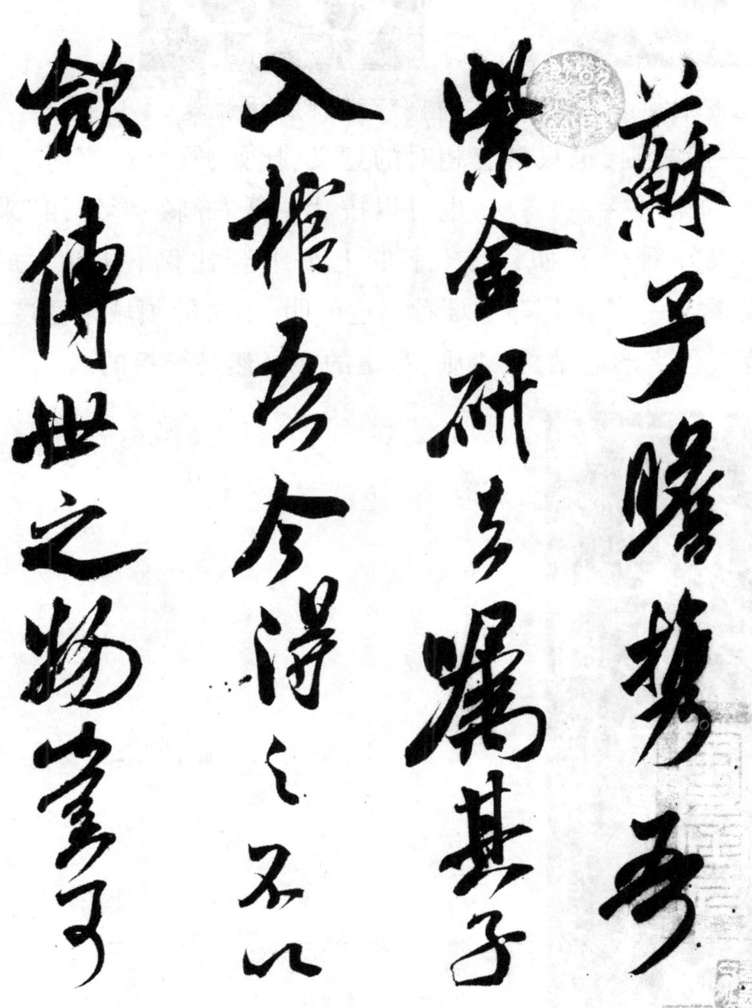

*《紫金砚帖》

　　以上讲的是结构的一般规则。按照这样的规则去做，写出的字都会比较平正、美观。然而，作为艺术品的书法来说，光讲一般规则还是不够的。结构的变化非常丰富，每一个书家都有自己独特的创造，学习时一定要细细观察、体会，掌握不同的结构形式，写出符合要求的字形来。例如，同样写一个"器"字，唐朝的书法家虞世南在《孔子庙堂碑》中写的"器"（图 86），中间的"大"宽而疏朗，下面的"口"字小而稳重；唐朝的另一位书法家柳公权在《玄秘塔碑》中写的"器"（图 87），中间的"大"字扁而挤压，下面的"口"字大而舒展。两个字的上中下结构比例均不相同。

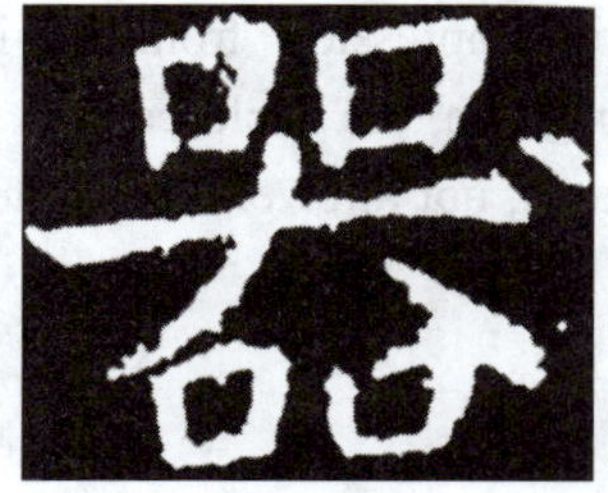
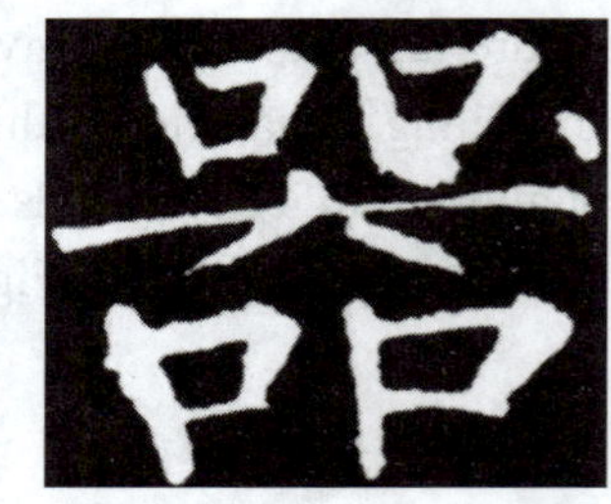

图 86　唐·虞世南《孔子庙堂碑》　　　　　图 87　唐·柳公权《玄秘塔碑》

　　另外，即使是结构的一般规则，也只具有相对的意义，比如，写"侍"字时，可以按"左轻右重字形结构"来写——"侍"，也可以按"左低右高字形结构"来写——"侍"，两种写法都很好看。又如，"贡"字的上下组合比例，可以写成 1:2——"贡"，也可以写成 2:3——"贡"，都不难看。这说明，书法的领域很宽广，不能用单一的模式来规范多种字形的结构，否则，写出的字必然是呆板的。

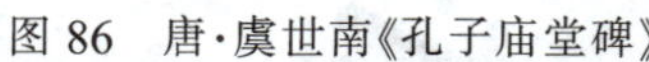

＊《欧阳通道因法师碑》

112

The structure rules presented in this chapter are for a general set of structure principles for the writing of Kai script. Following these rules, one can produce a balanced and beautiful piece of calligraphy. But, for the art of calligraphy, insistence upon rules is necessary but not sufficient. There are many variations in structure rules created by past generation Calligraphy Masters in Kai style script as well as in other scripts. We must carefully observe these rules and grasp the sense of various structures in order to benefit our own writings. In the following example of writing the same character 器, the Tang Dynasty Calligraphy Master Liu Gongquan wrote it in his *Xuan Mi Ta Bei*,　the middle component 大 was narrow and crushed;　the two 口口 was wide and open. (Figure 86)　The other Tang Dynasty Calligraphy Master Yu Shinan wrote the Chinese character 器 in his *Kong Zi Miao Tang Bei*, the middle component 大 in the character was wide and open; the components below are small and solid. (Figure 87). The proportions of the character: top, bottom and middle structure, are all different.

In other situations, although a character uses the same component in its structure, but it does not necessarily have to apply the same structure rule in writing this character. For example, in writing the character "侍", one can apply the "light left and heavy right" structure rule, or one can apply the "lower left and higher right" structure rule, appearance is good from applying with either rule. Another example, in an above and below combination of the character "贡", one can use a 1:2 proportion or a 2:3 proportion, to give the character a good appearance.

These two examples demonstrate a wide margin of structure rules in calligraphy: one should not limit applying a rigid rule in different situations;　otherwise,　one's writing will have a stiff appearance.

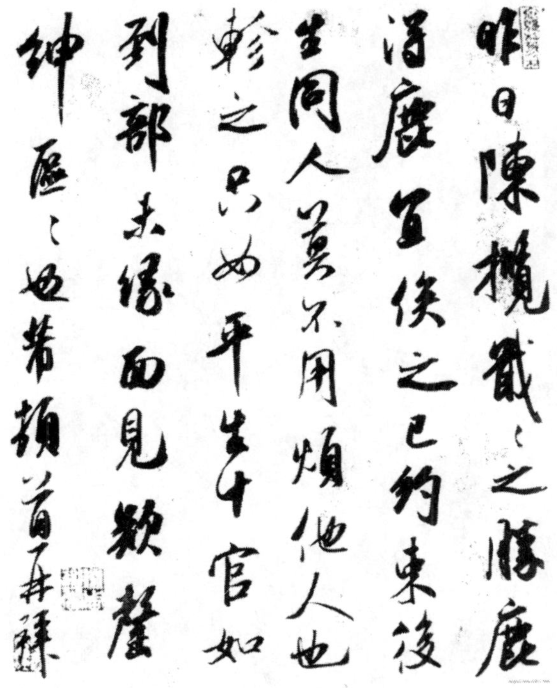

*《陈揽帖》

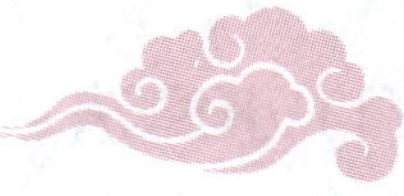

第 九 章

Chapter 9

章 法

Zhangfa (layout)

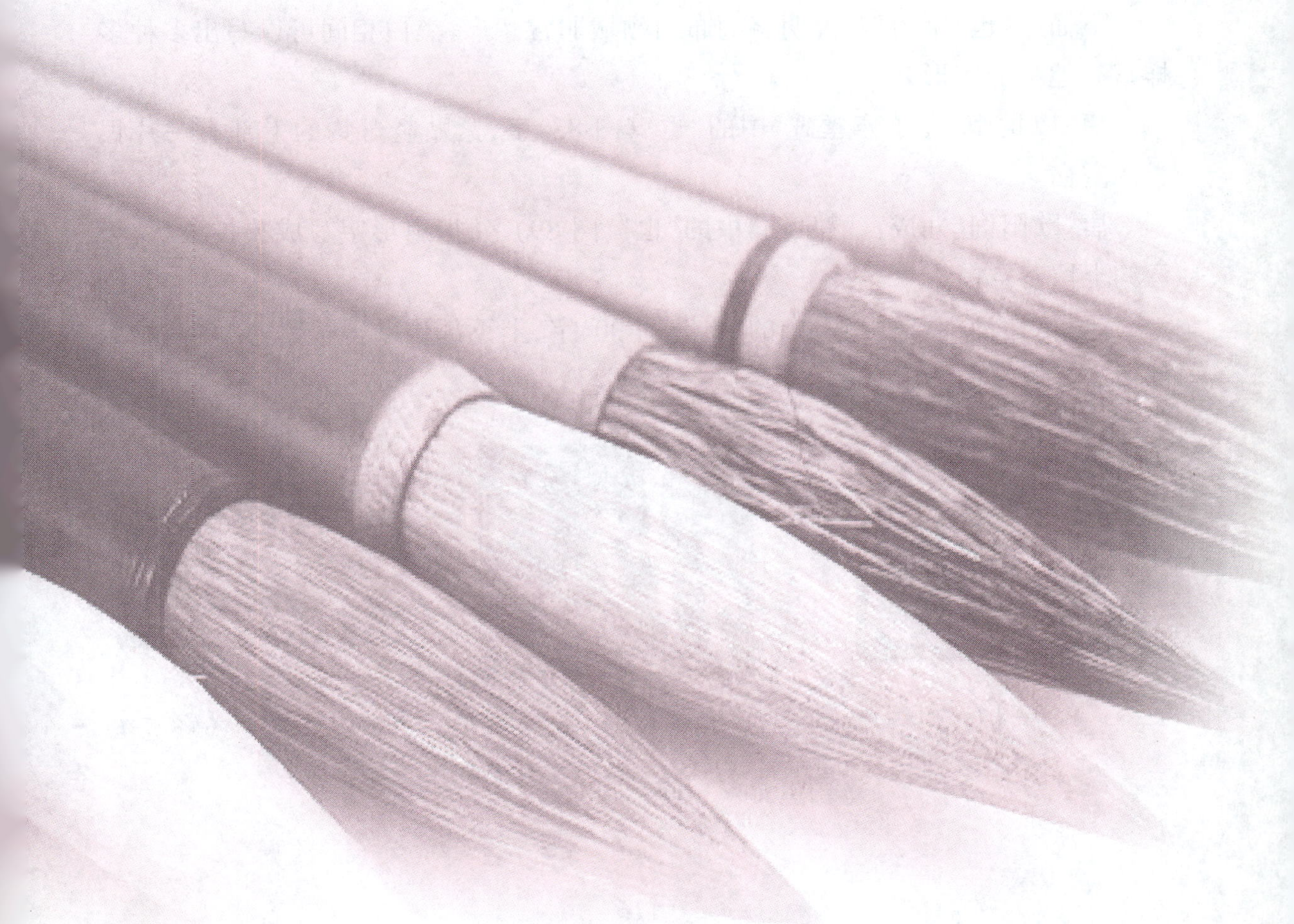

　　章法就是布局,是书法的艺术处理。

　　字有字的布局,称小章法;篇有篇的布局,称大章法。

(1) 小章法——字的布局

　　字的布局与字的结构是有关联的。从总体上说,注意字的结构与字的布局都是为了把字写得美观,但结构偏重于考虑笔画的安排、笔画的组合,布局偏重于考虑字形的完美、字形的趣味。

　　中国的书画理论在讲到章法时强调点画、线条和篇章的布白。

　　什么是布白?写字画画时,一般对黑笔画的处理容易引起重视,而对于笔画间空白处的安排容易忽略。中国的绘画理论认为作画时对空白处的经营应当像对黑笔画一样认真,讲的就是布白。书法对布白的要求也是同样的,写字时也要考虑黑笔画与空白处的疏密关系。

　　下面以"也"字为例,说明字的布白领域非常宽广,黑白相间可以写出多种多样富有趣味的字形来。

　　唐·虞世南《孔子庙堂碑》中的"也"(图 88)字,紧贴竖弯钩的上部有一片很长的空白。

　　唐·欧阳询《九成宫醴泉铭》中的"也"(图 89)字,把扁形字写成狭长形状,竖弯钩上留着空白。

　　唐·褚遂良《孟法师碑》中的"也"(图 90)字,上下部位贴得很紧,只在钩的上部留下一段空白。

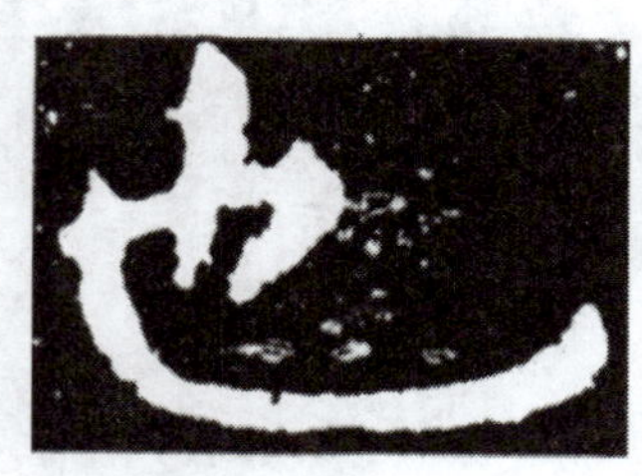

图 88　唐·虞世南《孔子庙堂碑》

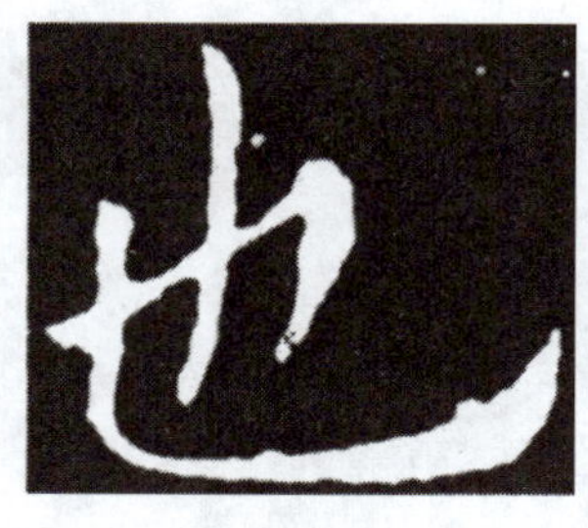

图 89　唐·欧阳询《九成宫醴泉铭》

图 90　唐·褚遂良《孟法师碑》

"Zhangfa" best translated as "Layout," is the aesthetic consideration in Chinese calligraphy. The artistic layout of a character is "Xiao Zhangfa" or (unit Zhangfa), and the artistic layout of the whole page of calligraphy is "Da Zhangfa" or the (composition Zhangfa).

(1) Xiao Zhangfa (the formation of an individual character)

The layout of a character, the "Xiao Zhangfa" and the structure of a character (previously discussed in Chapter 8 are two closely related subjects—both are issues concerning the beauty of calligraphy in its presentation. However, the structure of a character emphasizes the stroke arrangement in the character while the layout of a character emphasizes the beauty and taste in its presentation.

In the theory of Chinese calligraphy (and painting), Zhangfa places the importance of artistic expression on the relationship between dots, strokes in characters (the black stroke lines) and their surrounding background (the white space).

What is the white space or surrounding background? It is understandable that since a calligrapher uses brush to make strokes in dots and lines, the writer pays first attention to stroke control in their appearances (the appearance of black) on the paper and overlook surrounding space and background arrangement. In calligraphy, the use of white spaces is to be as serious as in the handling of black strokes in characters. The concept of layout is equally applicable in Chinese panting as well as in the Chinese calligraphy.

In the following examples of writing a 也 "ye" in each square, each "ye" exhibits a different white space. This demonstrates the distribution of white space in a character is broad, and contrast is abundant in the mixing black and white space. These varieties of black and white contrast offer an interesting range of manifestations. (See Figures 88 to 90)

In Figure 88, Yu Shinan of the Tang dynasty wrote in *A Plaque In the Confucius Temple*, the character "Ye". Above the vertical angle stroke in "Ye" has a long white blank space.

In Figure 89, Master Ouyang Xun of the Tang dynasty wrote in *A Plaque In the Jiu Ceng Temple*, the character "Ye" in a more flat shape. He left with more blank space above the vertical turn.

In Figure 90, Chu Suiliang of the Tang dynasty wrote in *Priest Meng's Plaque*, the top side and the bottom side of the "Ye" were closely attached, except for the top side of the hook is left with a blank space.

唐·颜真卿《忠义堂帖》中的"也"(图91)字,笔画敦厚,在竖弯钩的上部有一段既宽且长的空白。

汉《杨淮表记》中的"也"(图92)字,竖弯钩上有大片空白。

汉《西岳华山庙碑》中的"也"(图93)字,上半部呈扁形,下半部留大片空白。

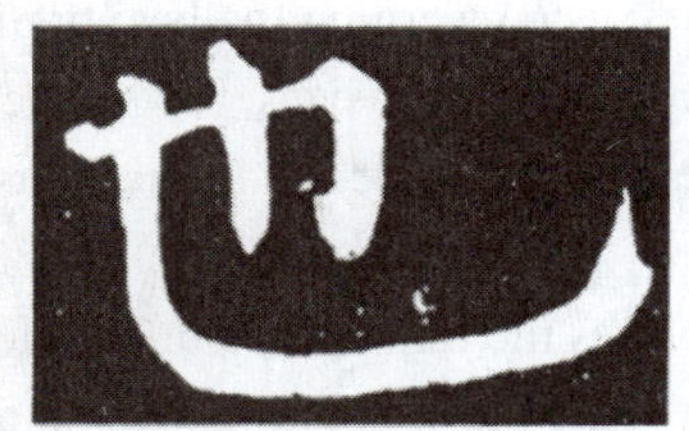

图91　唐·颜真卿《忠义堂帖》

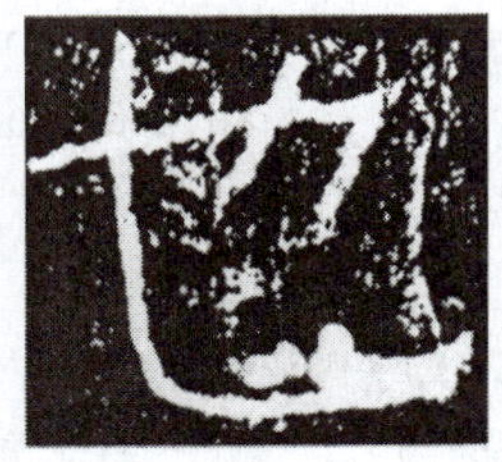

图92　汉《杨淮表记》

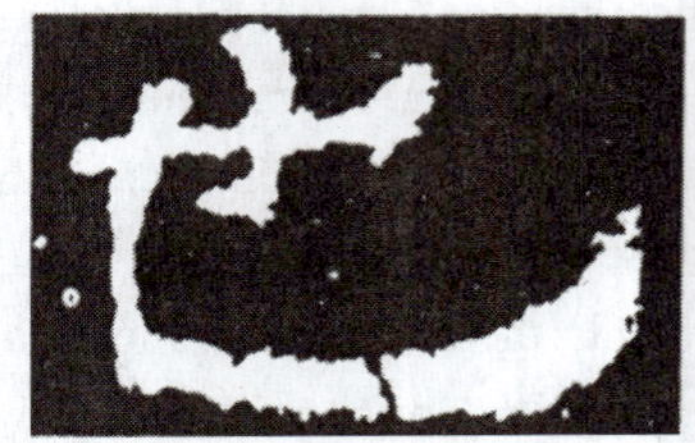

图93　汉《西岳华山庙碑》

行草书中"也"字的黑白处理更加丰富多采。

汉·张芝《终年帖》中的"也"(图94)字,左边横竖画起笔处相粘,给右边留下大片空白。字形如飞鸟出林。

唐·怀素《圣母帖》中的"也"(图95)字,笔画有断裂处,把字形自然分割成两个部分,既散乱,又相连。

宋·苏舜元《停云馆法帖》中的"也"(图96)字,横画斜伸,右部空白呈方形,字体犹如一条修长的钓杆。

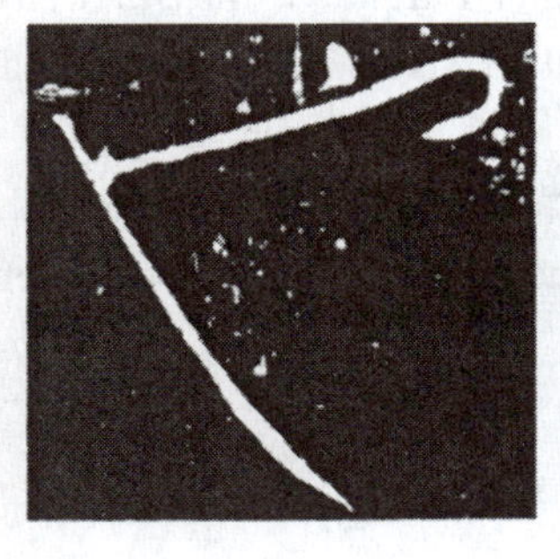

图94　汉·张芝《终年帖》

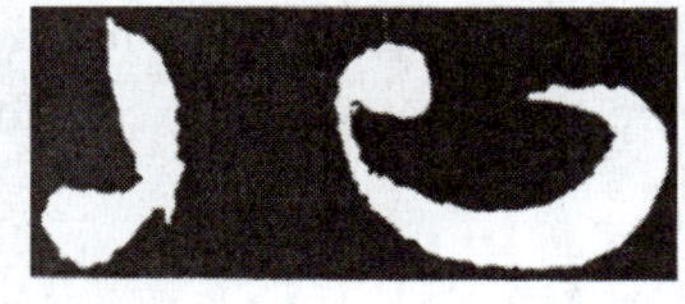

图95　唐·怀素《圣母帖》

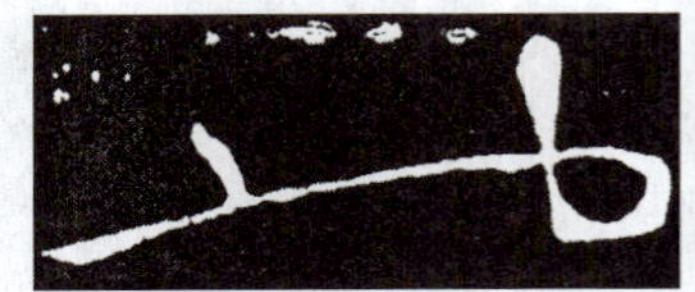

图96　宋·苏舜元《停云馆法帖》

In Figure 91, Yan Zhenqing of the Tang dynasty wrote the character "Ye" in *A Plaque In the Loyalty Temple*, his strokes were shown be honestly solid! Except there is a block of long and wide empty blank space left behind.

In Figure 92 is "Ye" of the Han dynasty in *Yang Wei Biao Ji*. At the top of the vertical hook there is a large blank space.

In Figure 93 is "Ye" of the Han dynasty in *A Plaque in the Hua Mountain Temple*. At the upper side of the character "Ye" there is a large blank space.

In Figure 94, Zhang Zhi of the Tang dynasty wrote "Ye" in *Zhong Nian Tie*, he wrote the left side of the character "Ye", the starting points of the horizontal and vertical strokes are connected, thus eaving a large (white) blank area; the shape of the character looks as if a flock of birds were flying out of a forest.

In Figure 95, Huai Su of the Tang dynasty wrote in *An Ode for Mother God*, it appears strokes in "Ye" are divided into two separate components.

In Figure 96, Su Shunyuan of the Song dynasty in *Ting Yun Guan Fa Tie* wrote "Ye" with a horizontal strokes rises up in an angle. The white space on right side is a square; the whole character looks like a long fishing pole.

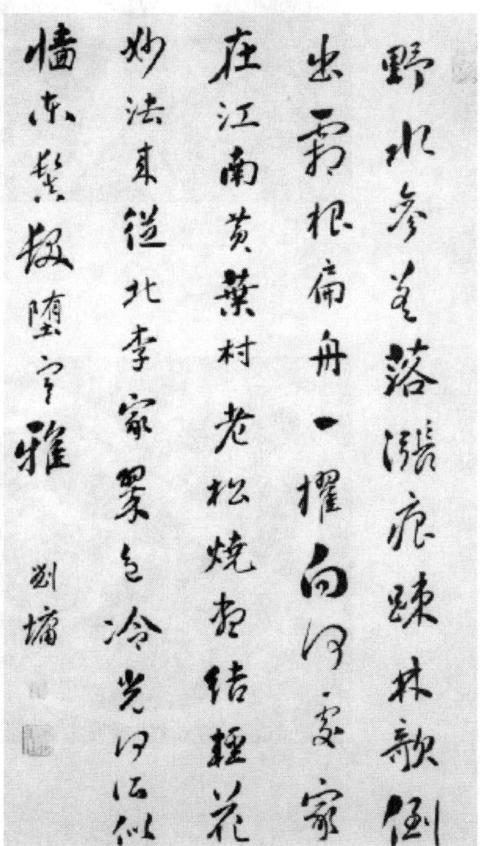

*行书《七绝二首诗轴》

119

晋武帝《平阁帖》中的"也"（图97）字，笔画连接处呈现出方形、圆形两个空白。

明·解缙《停云馆法帖》中的"也"（图98）字，笔画运转，形成大环套小环的环形空白。

明·文徵明《与野亭书帖》中的"也"（图99）字，笔画运转应形成的空白处采取相反的处理办法，密而不疏。

宋·苏轼《醉翁亭记》中的"也"（图100）字，运笔沉着痛快，最后一笔直落右下方，竖画两边留下大片空白。

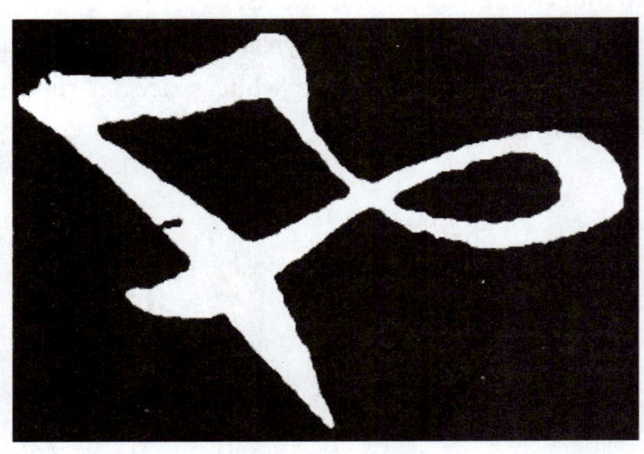

图97　晋武帝《平阁帖》

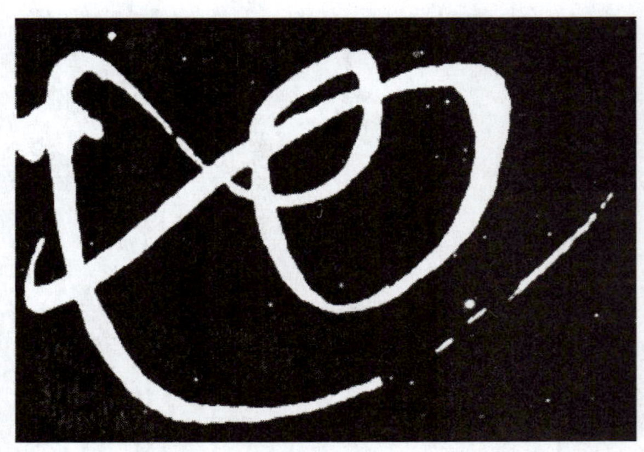

图98　明·解缙《停云馆法帖》

In Figure 97, Jin Wu Emperor wrote a "Ye" in *Ping Ge Tie* At the juncture of strokes, there are a square shaped blank space and a round shaped blank space.

In Figure 98, Jie Jin of the Ming dynasty wrote "Ye" in *Ting Yuan Fa Tie*. His blank space is drawn in a process opposite to the normal Process—tight but not loose.

In Figure 99, Wen Zhengming of the Ming dynasty wrote "Ye" in *Yu Ye Ting Shu Tie*.

In Figure 100, Su Shi of the Song dynasty wrote *A Note In the Drunk Man's Pavillion*, with a steady and solid stroke movement! Finally, the stroke drops down to the right lower side, and leaves with a large amount of blank space on both side of the vertical stroke.

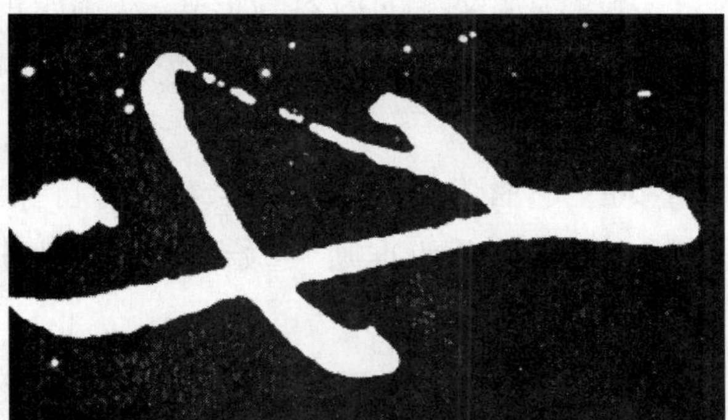

图 99　明·文徵明《与野亭书帖》

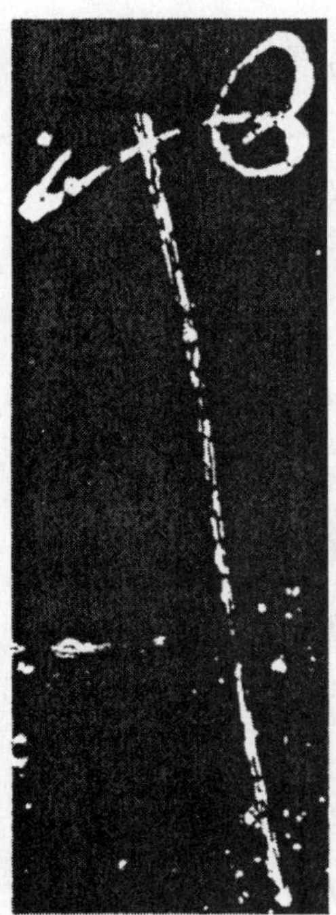

图 100　宋·苏轼《醉翁亭记》

（2）大章法——篇的布局

　　字的布局美只是局部的美，篇的布局美才是全局性的美。篇的布局中最重要的是自始至终气势如一，上下连贯。要做到这一点，除了扎实的基本功以外，与作者的总体设计、书写技巧、艺术趣味、临场发挥以及作者平和的心境、开朗的情绪都有关系，如果心情紧张、心态拘谨是写不好字的。

　　篇的布局应注意哪些问题？

　　1）写字之前，要考虑全局：

　　写字之前，要做好全篇字的总体设计：从文字的内容到形式，从确定的书体到字的多少、大小，以及分行和终始，何处题款、盖章等等，都要做到心中有数。

　　2）第一个字要统领全篇：

　　写好一篇字的第一个字是很重要的，它常常成为整篇字要看齐的目标。这就好比一队士兵的排头兵一样，后面的士兵要以他为准则。起始字的线型决定后面字形的发展、变化。

　　3）行气贯通：

　　一切好的书法作品，都少不了气脉。有了气脉，一字字、一行行就能圆润流转。各种书体都是这样，行书、草书尤其突出，可以说行、草书的神韵全在于气脉。

　　有时看一幅字，形式上歪歪扭扭，字的大小不一，但细细玩味一番，我们会发现，前后连接如贯珠，有时笔断气连，有时形断意连。一篇字，个别地看，不见得是好字，连起来看，却是非常精彩的字，这就是以行气取胜。

(2) Da Zhangfa (the layout of a composition)

The composition of a beautiful character is but one step in an overall piece of beautiful writing. The unit beauty is important but with the beauty of each and every beautiful character arranged within the artful layout of the overall writing, they then produce a beautiful piece of writing. The arrangement of layout from the beginning to the end; and from the top to the bottom is the "Da Zhangfa" or (the composition layout). It requires the calligrapher to develop an understanding of "qi" in the pursuit of solid basic training in the Da Zhangfa. The "qi" in the calligraphy includes the basic training of calligraphy method which includes the technical aspect of calligraphy skill, the layout planning, the historical styles of calligraphy masters, and knowledge in the layout of a beautiful piece of calligraphy. In addition to know the technical method in calligraphy, a person with an uptight mind could not possibly write a free flow and beautiful piece of calligraphy.

What are the essential elements in layout arrangement?

1) A careful planning of the overall presentation. Before writing the first stroke on a page, one needs to think through the overall process: from the content to the style of the calligraphy script in mind, from the decided script to the number of characters to be included; what is the size of each character; where to divide lines; where the beginning and the ending spots lie; where to place the signature and which seal to use. All of these are parts of the overall planning.

2) The first character lays down the commanding posture. The beginning of the first stroke decides the structure of the character; the first character on the page commands the direction of the whole piece. As if it were a platoon of soldiers, the lead soldier uses his position to guide the rest of the members of the formation.

3) A thorough and free moving of "qi". In every famous calligraphic creations, they all contain the "qi". Qi is the necessary element in smooth free flow of characters, qi is required in every script, and it is exceptionally pronounced in the running mode and the cursive mode of writing. One might consider the spirits of running mode and cursive mode are entirely in the free flow of qi.

In some calligraphy pieces, one sees inconsistent shapes and sizes of characters, yet in a more careful examination, one finds the existence of continuous free flow of buried "pearls". Sometimes the strokes are disconnected and sometimes strokes shows disrupted lines. From the first appearance of these individual characters each does not seem to follow the conventional rules of good quality calligraphy, but if one observes their overall character together, they represent a beautiful piece of calligraphy. This is known as the "flow of qi".

　　唐·颜真卿的《自书告身》(图101)，写的是楷书，但明显地看到字形有大，有小，有长，有短，有正，有斜，并无一定之规。字与字之间有时舒展，有时密集，然而行气连贯，趣味无穷，四行字曲行而下，有如凤尾的形状。(图102)

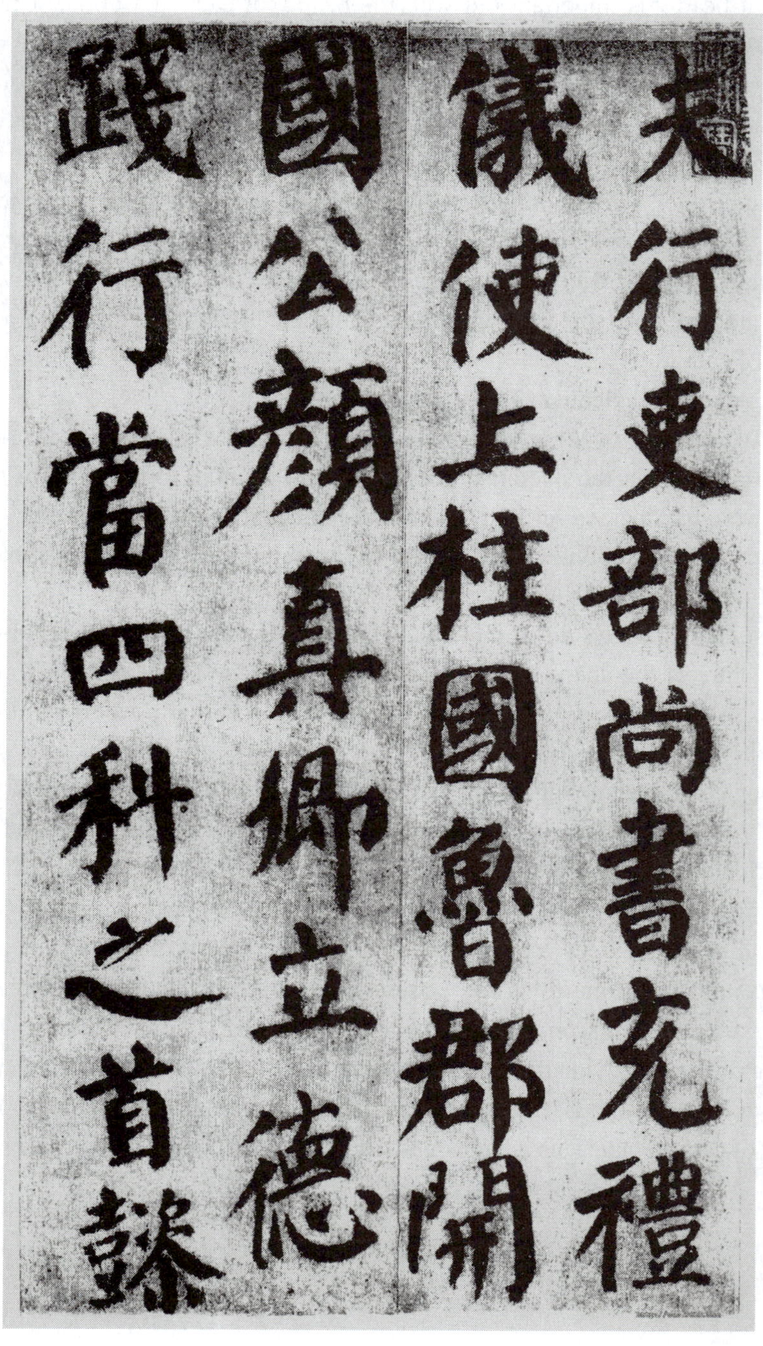

图 101　唐·颜真卿《自书告身》

124

Figure 101 *Zi Shu Gao Shen* is a piece of Kai Shu written by Yan Zhenqing of the Tang dynasty. Although it is a piece of Kai Shu, written in standard script, but characters have large and smaller sizes, longer and shorter shapes, and in straight standing or tilt positions. Furthermore, the first two characters of each line are written in open and free mode. In Figure 102, the last character in the first, second, and fourth lines are tightly compressed, with free flow of "qi" to provide an interesting appearance. The curve and downward slide of characters in every line, as if they were shaped like the tail of a phoenix.

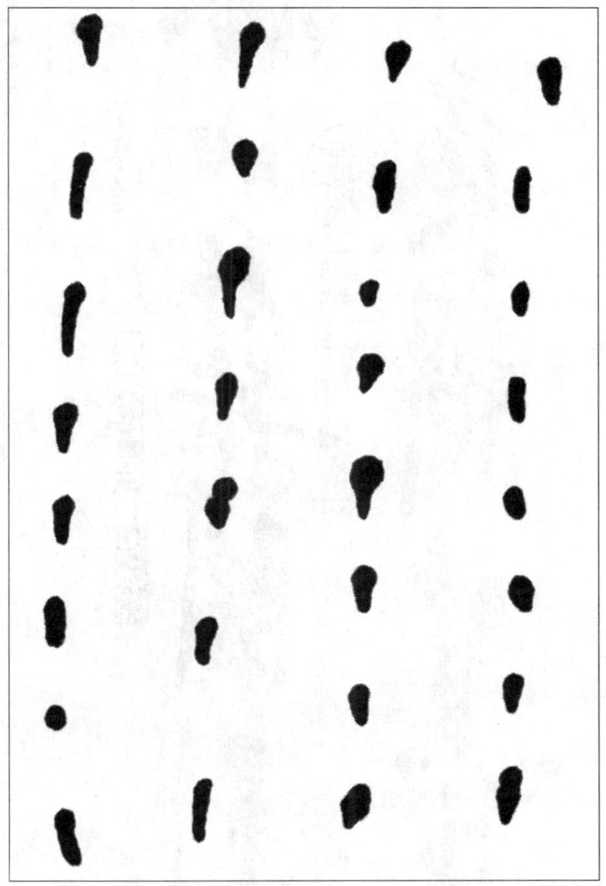

图 102　《自书告身》章法

　　宋·黄庭坚的《松风阁诗》(图103)，行书，字形是朝着同一个方向倾斜的，两行字气势相连，形成两条斜行的平行线。(图104)

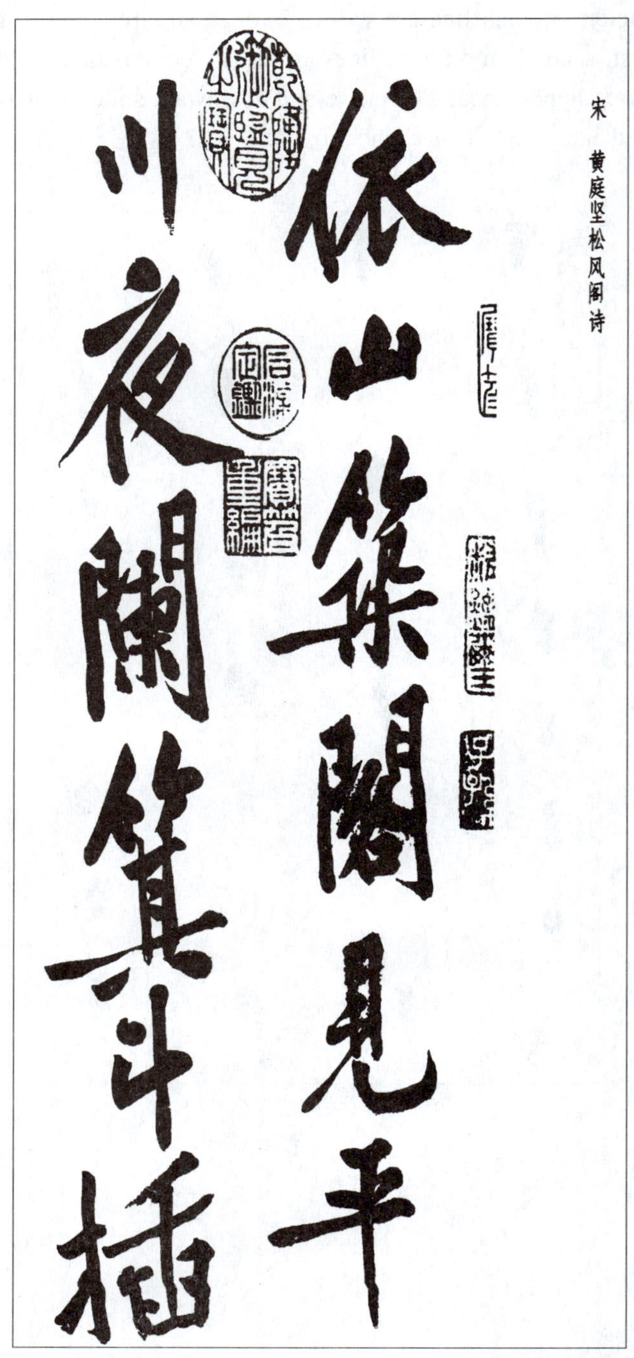

图 103　宋·黄庭坚《松风阁诗》

Figure 103 *Song Feng Ge Shi* is a form of Running Script written by Huang Tingjian of the Song dynasty. His characters are written tilting toward a common direction. In Figure 104, two lines of characters are maintaining a common and connected "qi", —they formed two parallel and angular lines.

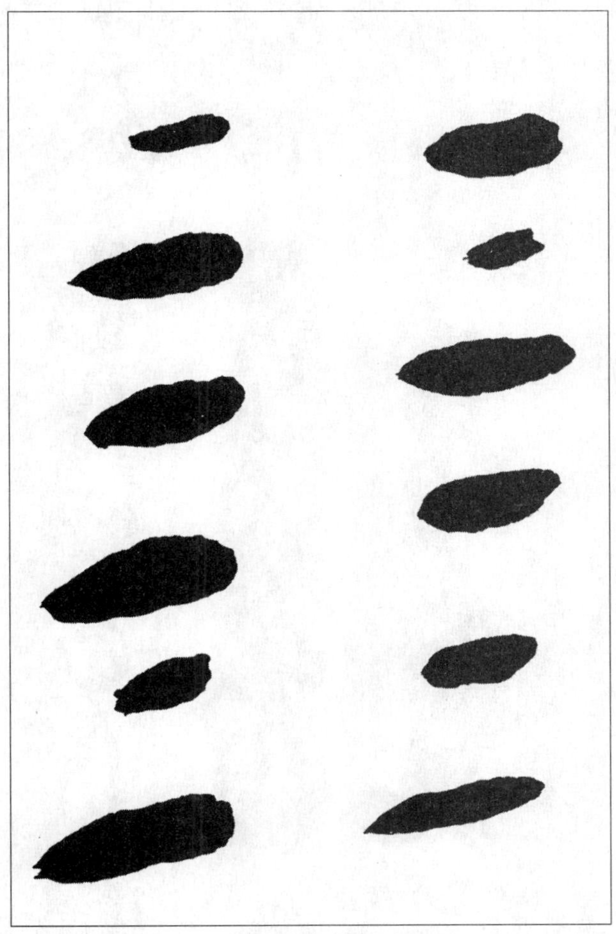

图 104　《松风阁诗》章法

127

　　晋·王献之的《中秋帖》（图 105），草书，因体势相连，一笔而成，世称一笔书，偶有不连处，亦气脉不断，有如风行水上，每个字的衔接都非常自然流畅。（图 106）

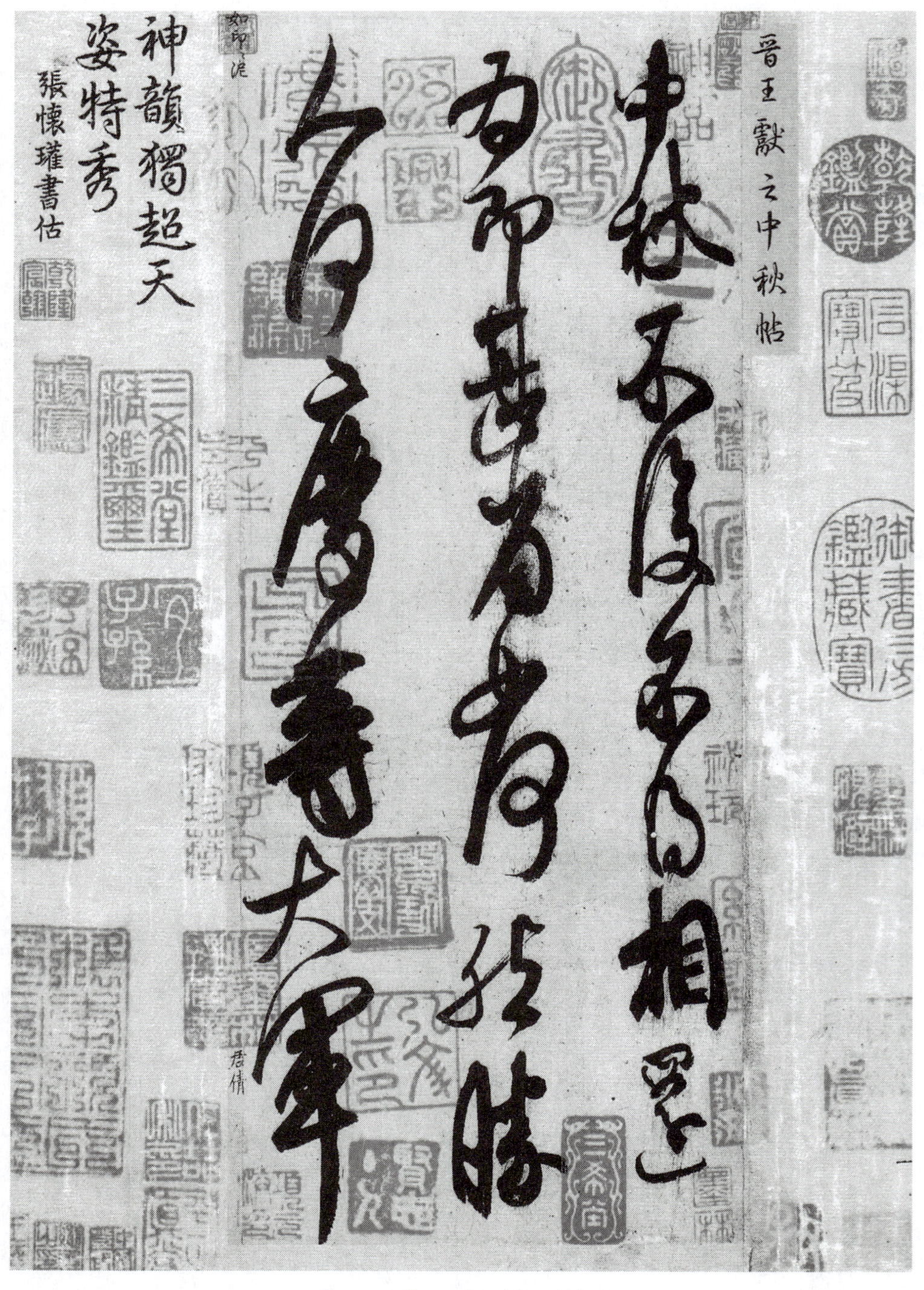

图 105　晋·王献之《中秋帖》

Figure 105 *Zong Qiu Tie* is Cursive writing written by Wang Xiezhi of the Jin dynasty. Because it is in Cursive script, characters are continuously connected as if completed in one continuous stroke—people named this style a one-stroked-writing. Although there are missing connections in places but they did not interrupt the flow of "qi". This demonstrates the flow of "qi" is always subtle and natural.

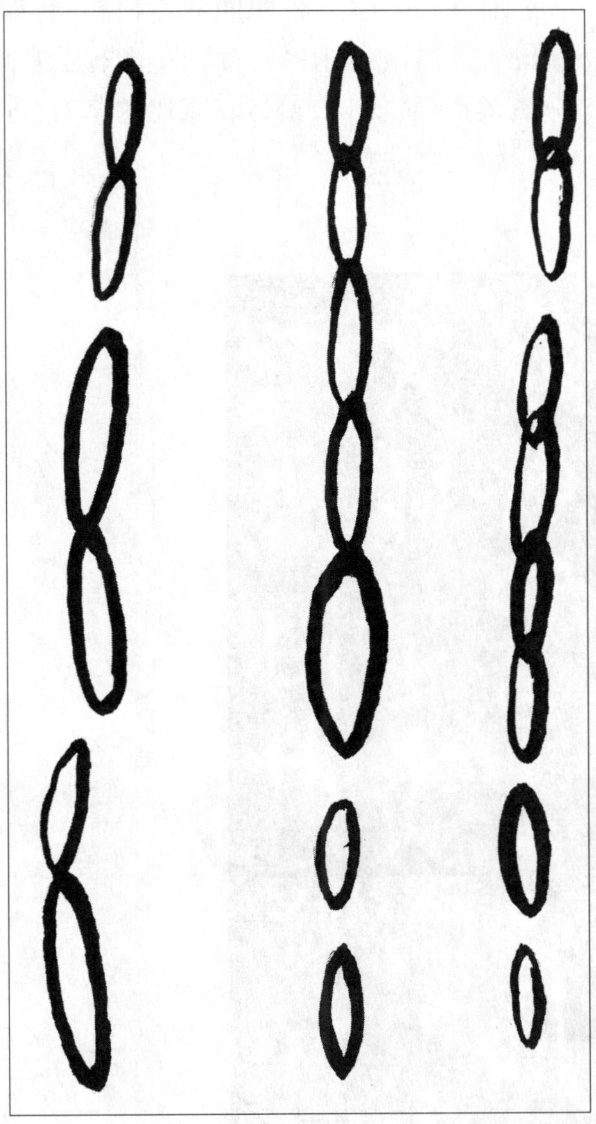

图 106　《中秋帖》章法

4）字距、行距匀称、协调：

字距、行距间空白的多少，取决于书体的要求和书家的审美趣味，体现着作品的艺术风貌。一般地说，篆书的行距宽、字距窄，如：西周《毛公鼎》（图 107）；隶书的字距宽，行距相对地窄，如汉《鲜于璜碑》（图 108）、汉《孔宙碑》（图 109）；楷书，包括魏碑和唐碑，字形方正，字距、行距间的空白相当，如：北魏《郑文公碑》（图 110）、唐·虞世南《孔子庙堂碑》（图 111）；行书、草书连绵，行距比字距相对地宽，如宋·米芾的行书《苕溪诗卷》（图 112）、唐·张旭的草书《古诗四帖》（图 113）。

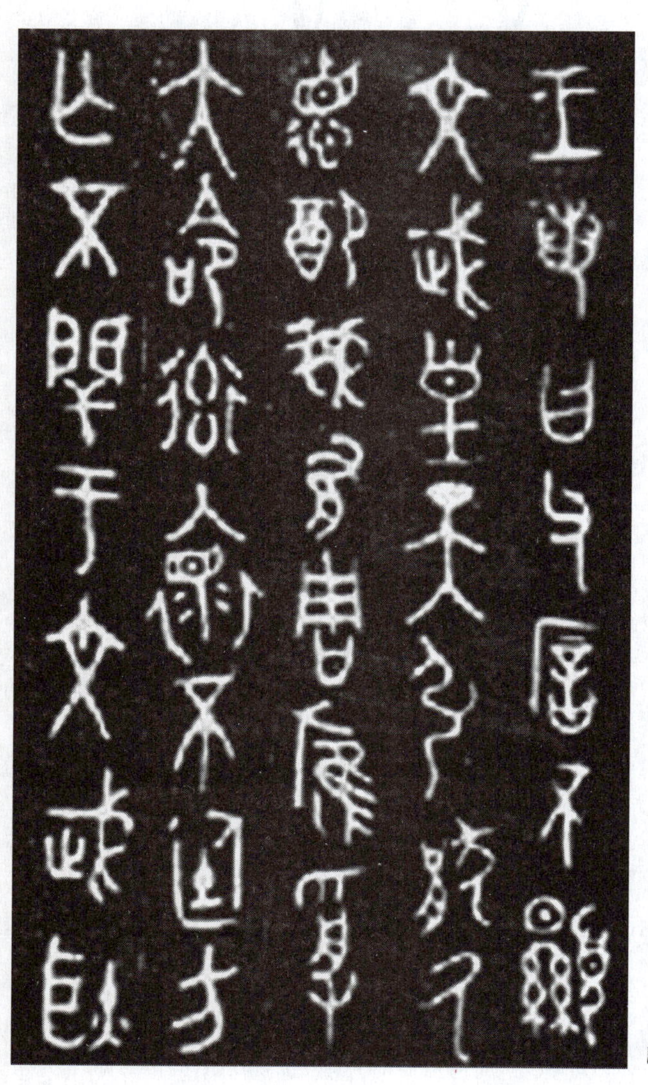

图 107　西周《毛公鼎》

4) An equal and balanced space among characters and lines

The dividing spaces among characters and the dividing spaces among lines are determined by the mode of characters and the artistic taste of the calligraphy artist. In general, Zhuan mode of script requires a wider line space, but a narrower space among characters; For example in Western Zhou *Mao Gong Ding* (Figure 107). The Li mode of script requires wider space among characters but a narrower space among lines; For example in Han dynasty *Xianyu Huang Bei* (Figure 108) and Han dynasty *Kong Miao Bei* (Figure 109). Regular Kai mode scripts, including Wei Bei and Tang Bei are square-shaped which requires the same amount of space among characters and lines. For examples Northern Wei dynaty *Zheng Wen Gong Bei* (Figure 110); and Tang dynasty Yu Shinan *Kong Nan Miao Tang Bei* (Figure 111). In running mode and in cursory mode scripts, characters are often connected with other characters, thus spaces among lines are wider, relative to the spaces among characters. See examples in Song dynasty, Mi Fu, *Tiao Xi Shi Juan* (Running script) (Figure 112) and Tang dynasty, Zhang Xu *Gu Shi Si Tie* Cursive script, (Figure 113).

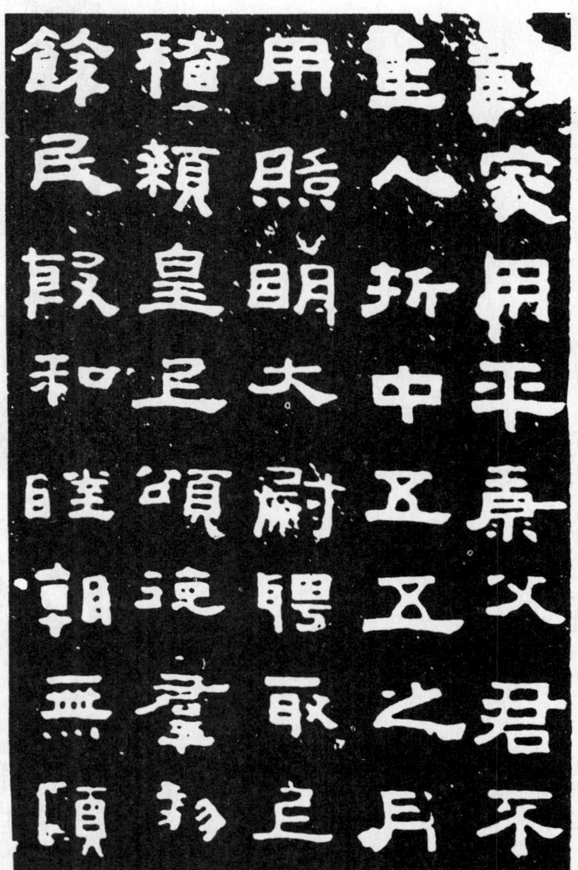

图 108　汉《鲜于璜碑》

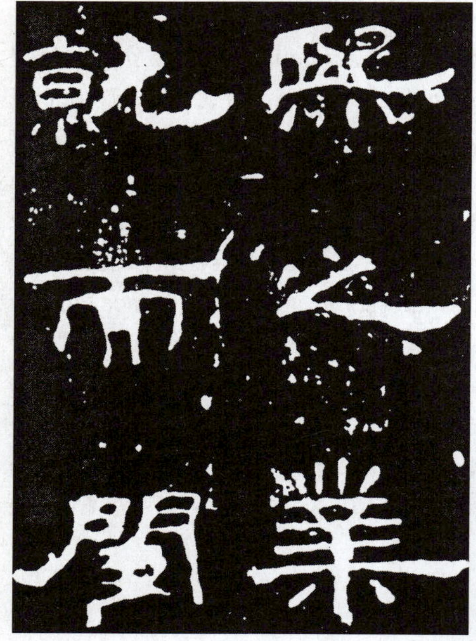

图 109　汉《孔宙碑》

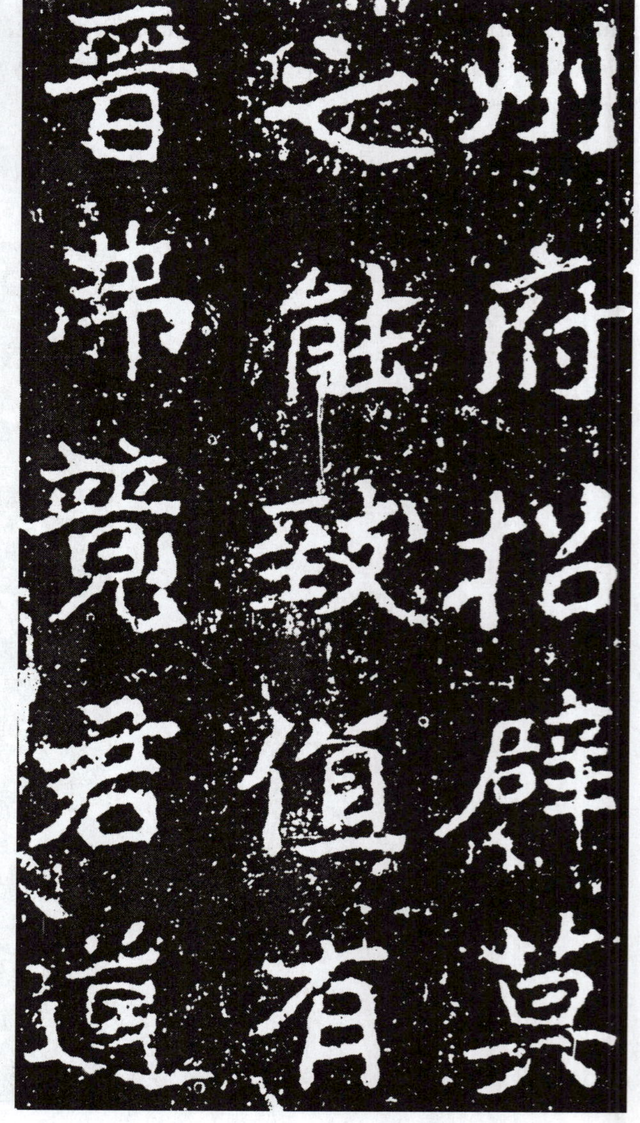

图 110　北魏《郑文公碑》

132

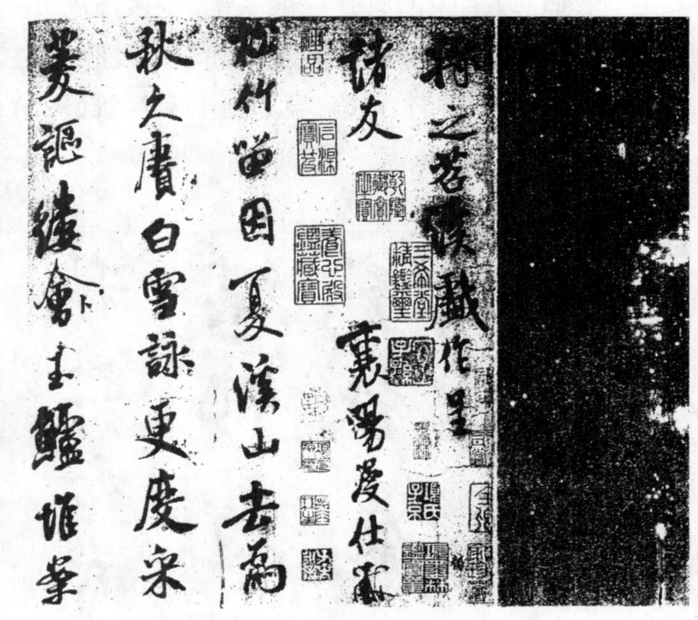

图111　唐·虞世南《孔子庙堂碑》

图112　宋·米芾 行书《苕溪诗卷》

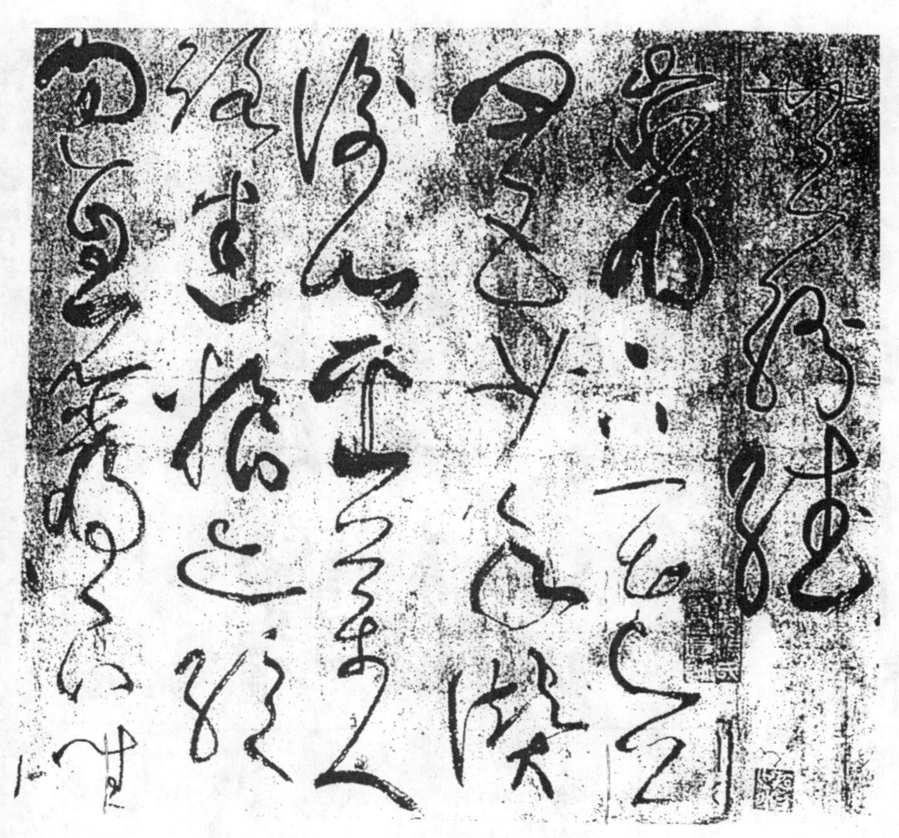

图113　唐·张旭 草书
《古诗四帖》

　　然而，以上说的只是一般状况，很多情况并不如此。五代·杨凝式的《韭花帖》（图114）在处理字距、行距方面就非常大胆。这幅字，字距、行距疏密相间，疏处比密处多，行距前窄后宽，显示出书家淡雅、随意、疏朗的风格，字与字参差错落，确有飘风斜雨的味道。（图115）

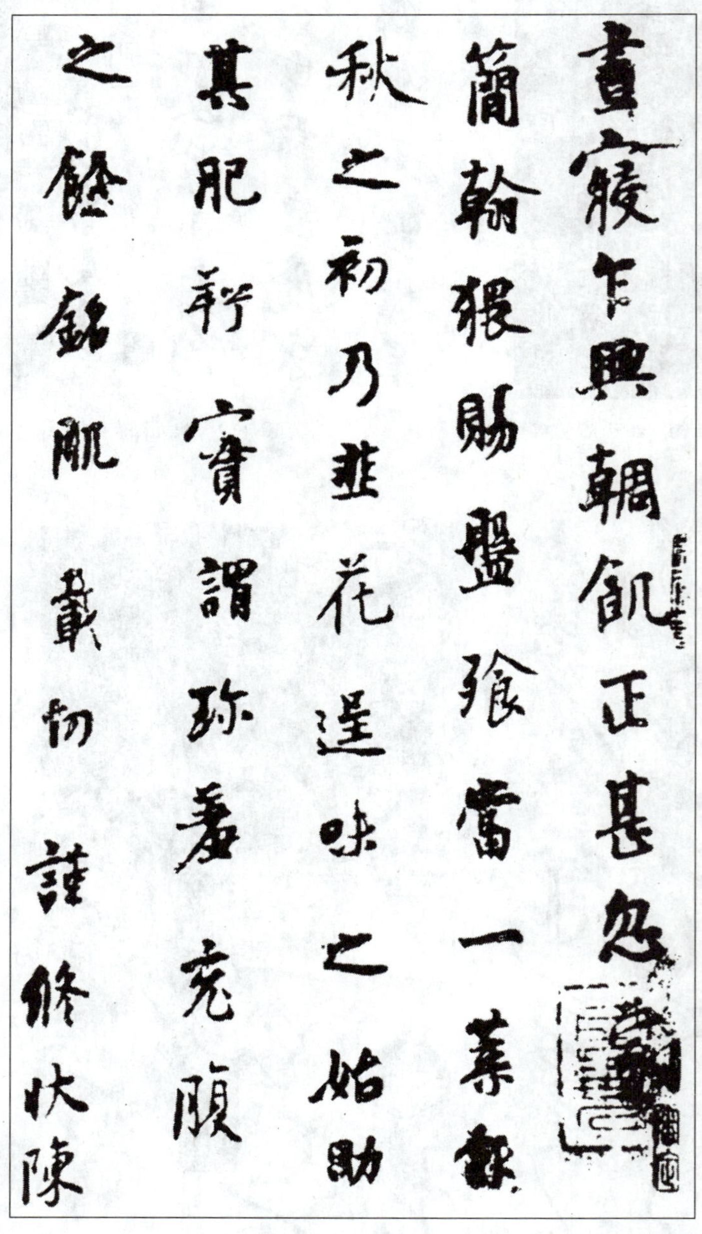

图114　五代·杨凝式《韭花帖》

The material described in above represents dividing space for normal and common situation; and exceptions are abundant. In Figure 114, during the "Five Dynasties" (907—960 AD), Master Yang Ningshi was unconventionally and brave in handling the line spaces and character spaces in *Jiu Hua Tie*.

In Figure 115, spaces among characters, and spaces among lines have mixed looseness and thickness. Although there are more looseness than tightness, a narrower line space in the beginning and a wider line space in the rear seem to express the Calligrapher' scholarly, earthly, and open mind attitudes. These intermingled characters have left with the observer an image of drizzling rain falling along in breezes.

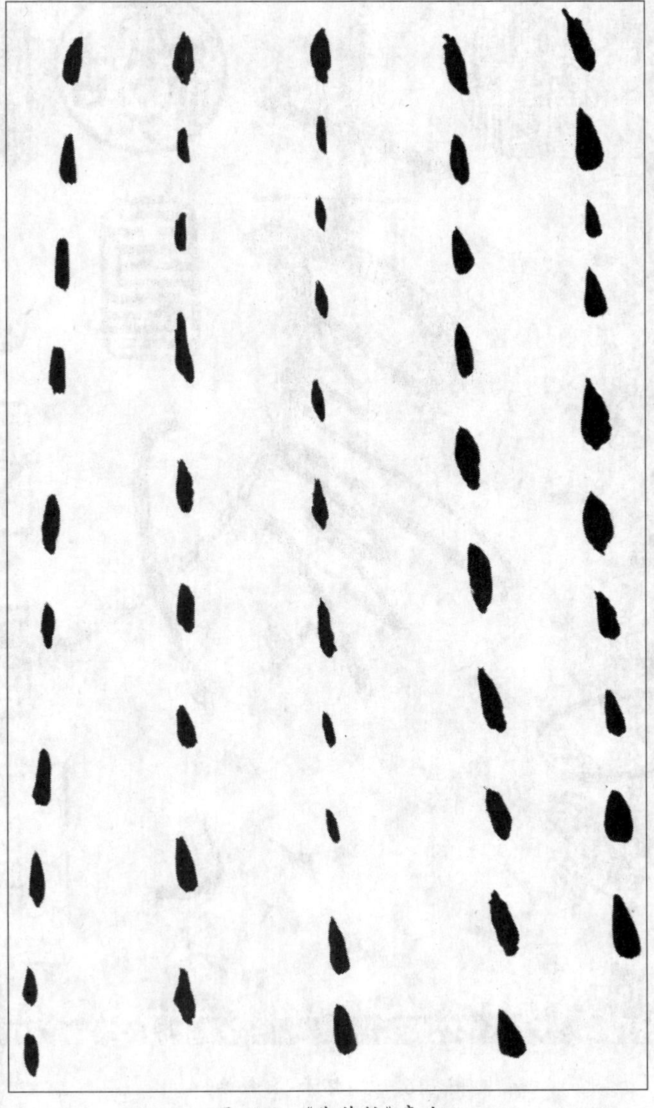

图 115　《韭花帖》章法

5）突出主字、主笔：

一幅字中有主字，一个字中有主笔。有时主字、主笔非常突出，引人瞩目，好像众星捧月，使全幅字色彩斑斓。这在行、草书中格外明显。

唐·怀素《自叙帖》(图 116)中"戴公又云驰毫骤"数字，一个"戴"字占了三分之二的篇幅，就是突出的例子。

宋·苏轼《黄州寒食帖》(图 117)中一个"帋(纸)"字的竖画(主笔)使满纸生辉。

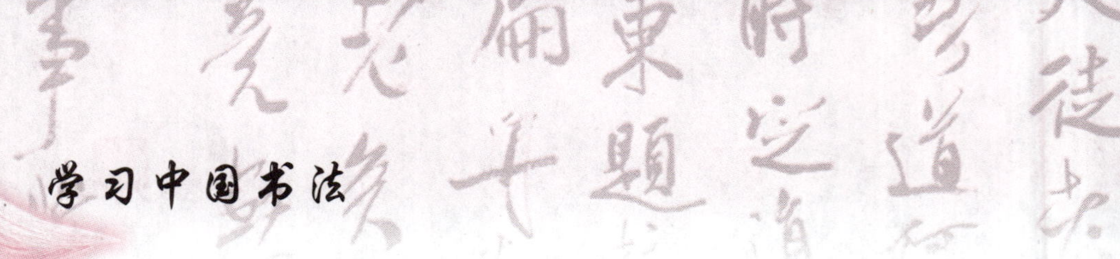

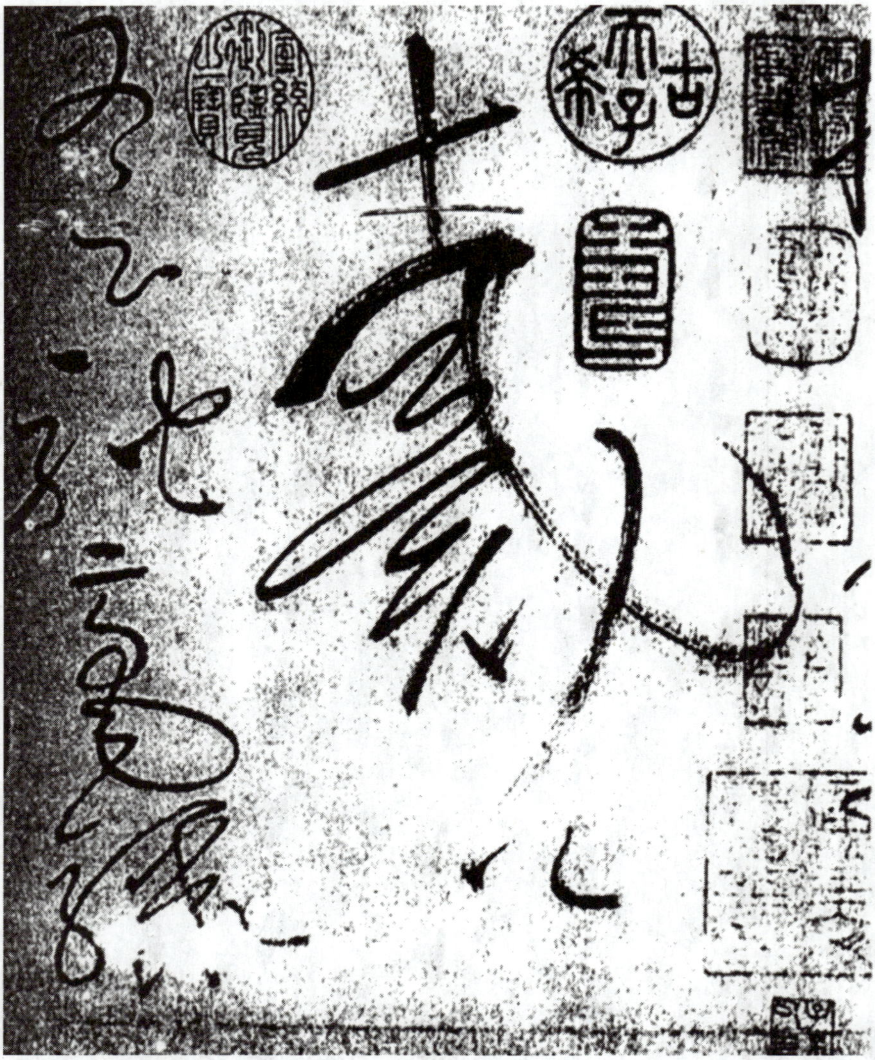

图 116　唐·怀素《自叙帖》

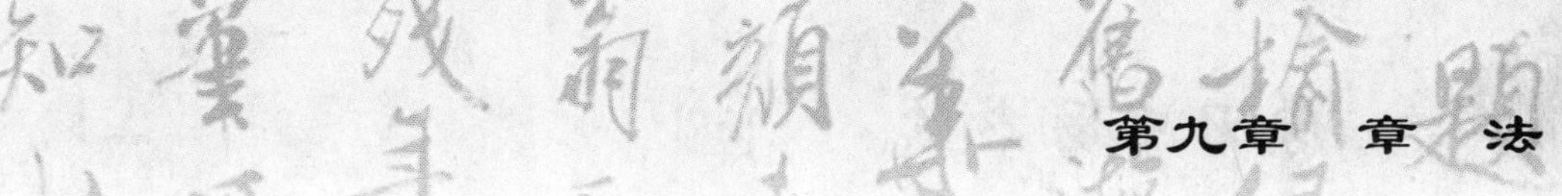

5) A stand out major character and major stroke.

There are major characters standing out in a piece of calligraphy, and there are major strokes standing out in a character.　Sometimes,　these major characters and major strokes are extremely striking to observers. They appear as images of shinning stars holding up the moon; or expressing the obvious contrast of brightness and darkness in the sky. The outstanding major characters and major strokes are even more striking in running or cursory scripts. The following are but a few examples:

In Figure 116,　the Tang dynasty Master Calligrapher Huai Su in *Zi Xu Tie* wrote the first character "dai" to occupy 2/3 of total available space. This is an example of exception.

In Figure 117, Su Shi of the Song dynasty wrote an unusual style for the character "zhi" in his *Huang Zhou Han Shi Tie*. This gives an exceptional distinction to the whole piece of calligraphy.

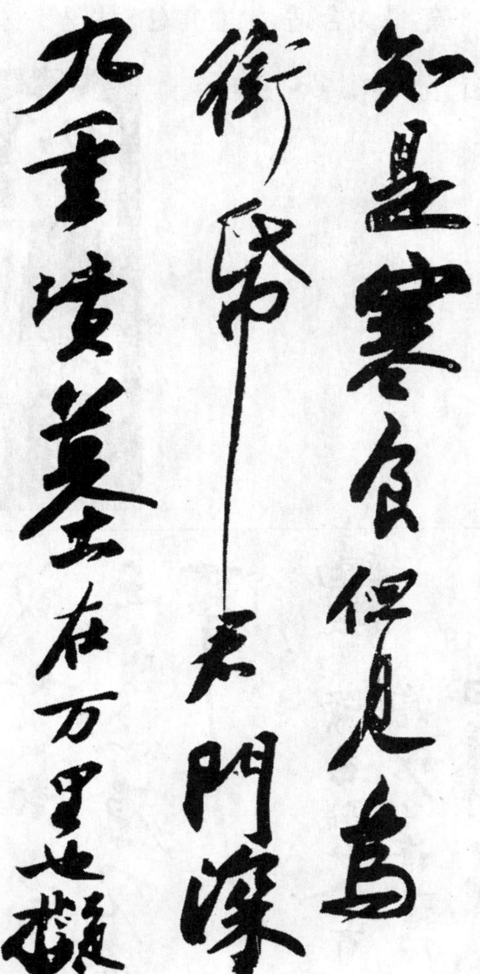

图 117　宋·苏轼《黄州寒食帖》

唐·颜真卿《裴将军诗》(图 118)中"麟臺"二字安排奇特,一斜一正,而"麟"字的最后一笔特别长,斜贯到底,占据了"臺"字的右半部。"麟"是极精彩的主字,而其中又有突出的主笔。

6) 最后一行、一字决定全局:

愈是写到最后,愈要谨慎从事。

如果最后一行、一字写得很拘谨,不舒展,或轻率马虎,可能导致全篇遗憾告终。

宋·王诜《行草书自书诗卷》(图 119),姿态甚美,气脉连绵,最后的"耳"字写得酣畅淋漓。

又如:行书"百年树人"(图 120)四字,"人"的最后一笔,A、C 都不好,惟有 B 的一笔最为合适,它立得住,站得稳,使全幅字变得有力量、有生气。

图 118　唐·颜真卿《裴将军诗》

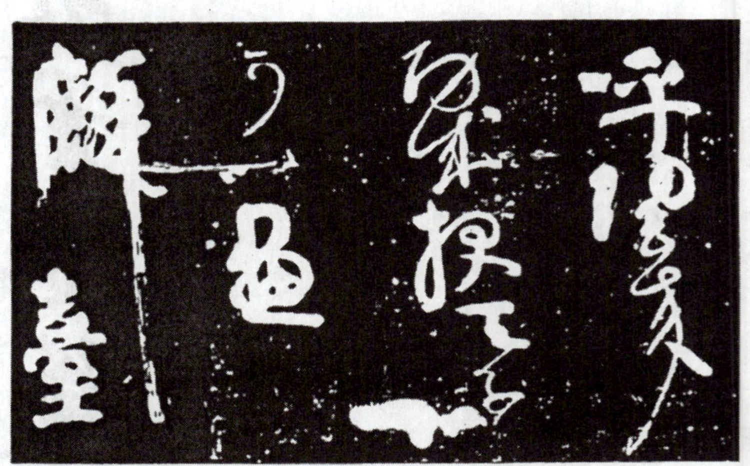

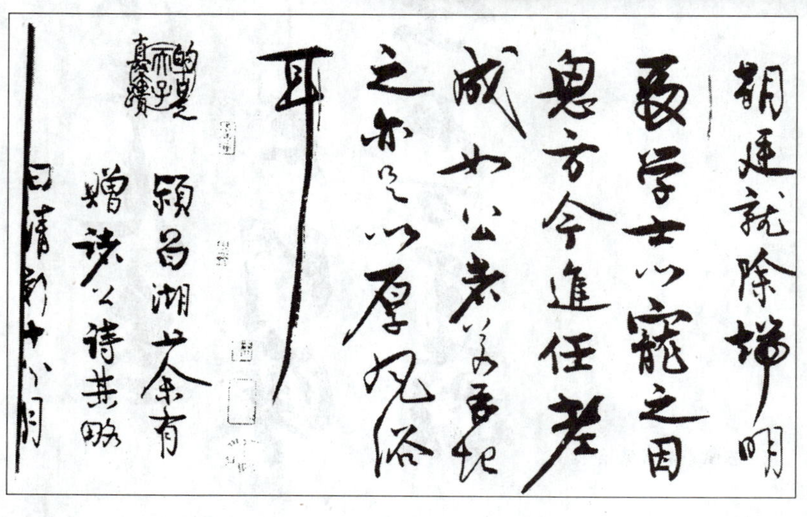

图 119　宋·王诜《行草书自书诗卷》

In Figure 118, Yan Zhenqing of Tang dynasty wrote in his *Pei Jiang Jun Shi* two characters "Ling Tai" in an unusual arrangement—one leans to one side and the other standing straight up, and the last stroke in the character "麟" is exceptionally long. The character "lin" slopes all the way down, and takes away half of space for the character "臺". The character "麟" is a major character standing out in the piece; and in it has outstanding strokes.

6) The final line and the last character in a total piece of calligraphy determined the overall quality.

Towards the end of writing a piece, it is most important to write with caution. If the final line and the last character in a piece is hastily written; and the writer's mind has already wondered away; that change might result in a total loss of the presentation.

In Figure 119, Calligraphy Master Wang Shen in his *Xing Cao Shu Zi Shu Shi Juan* has a beautiful presentation. He creates the writing with a free flow of "qi", in which the free flow seems to resemble waves of water. Finally, the character "耳" begins its writing in a running mode and continued into a wild cursive mode, a thoroughly free expression!

In Figure 120, Xing Shu wrote *Bai Nian Shu Ren*. The last stroke of the fourth character "人" has labeled A, B, and C. Except the "B" stroke is eloquent; it can stand up in solitude which makes the whole composition lively and powerful.

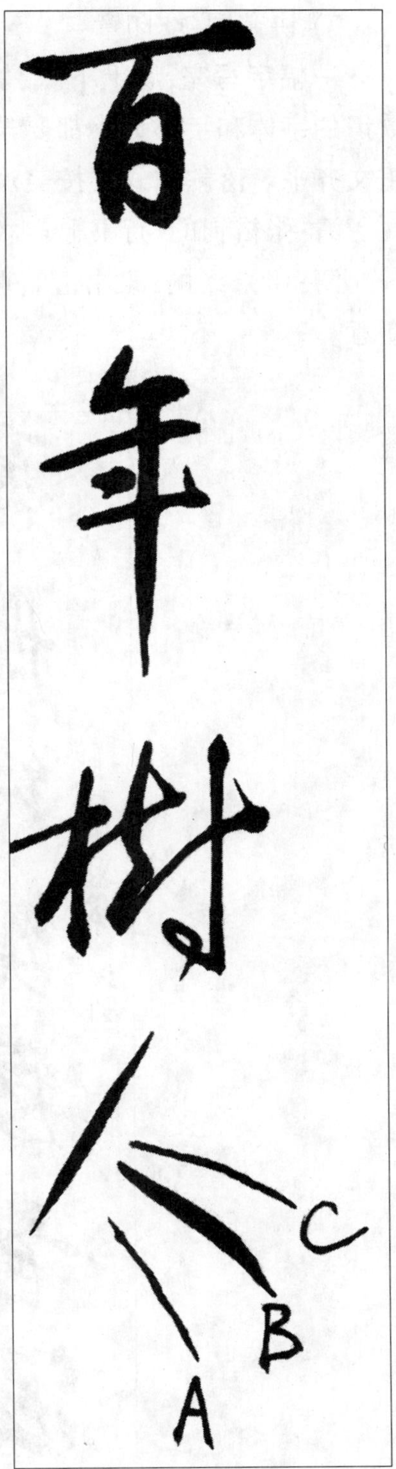

图 120　"百年树人"

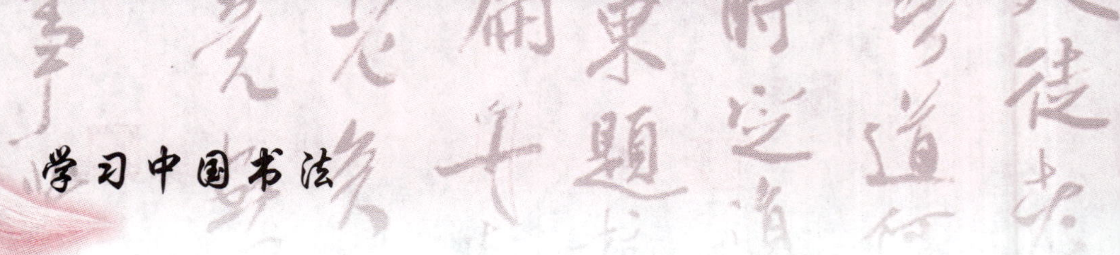

7）讲究题款、印章：

一幅字写完，题上下款，加盖印章，就成了一幅完整的字，上下款题在两边。款识的字体和字形大小都要与正文协调，字形要比正文略小，上下两端都不能与正文齐平。落款方式要按美观的要求配合正文作灵活的处理。

清·张裕钊的《行书七言联》（图 121），上下款识均端庄清峻。

清·伊秉绶的《隶书五言联》（图 122），上下款识与一般的落款方式不同，有新意。

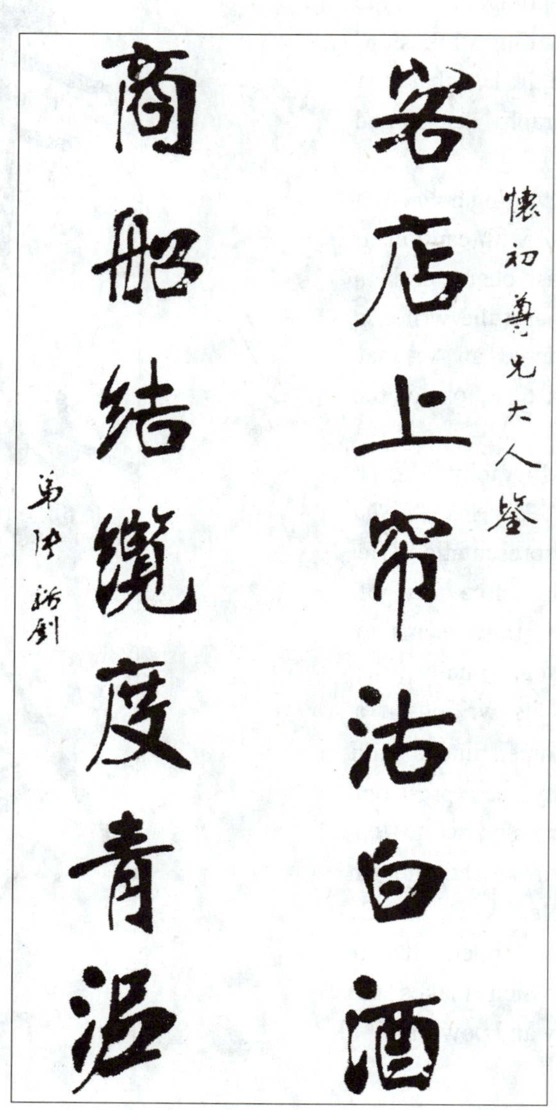

图 121　清·张裕钊《行书七言联》

7) A sophisticated signature signed by the calligrapher and his proper placement of seal(s).

When the writing is completed, the signature of the calligrapher and his seal(s) are properly placed, then the creation of a piece of calligraphy is completed.

The calligrapher's seals are normally placed on the (right) top side and (left) lower side of the calligraphy piece. The styles and sizes of signature placed on the piece should be slightly smaller yet not inconsistent. The size of the heading and signature should harmoniously be aligned with the major content. The signature should follow the aesthetic requirement; and to be certain they are flexible and coordinated to supplement major content.

Here is the signature of Qing Master Zhang Yuzhao *Xing Shu Qi Yan Lian* (Figure 121), it has square and disciplined strokes, and also round and smooth strokes. The signature on the upside and the lower side are clear-cut.

Qing Master Yin Bingshou, *Li Shu Wu Yan Lian* (Figure 122), his signature on the upper left and lower right uses a new idea but unconventional styles than other calligraphers.

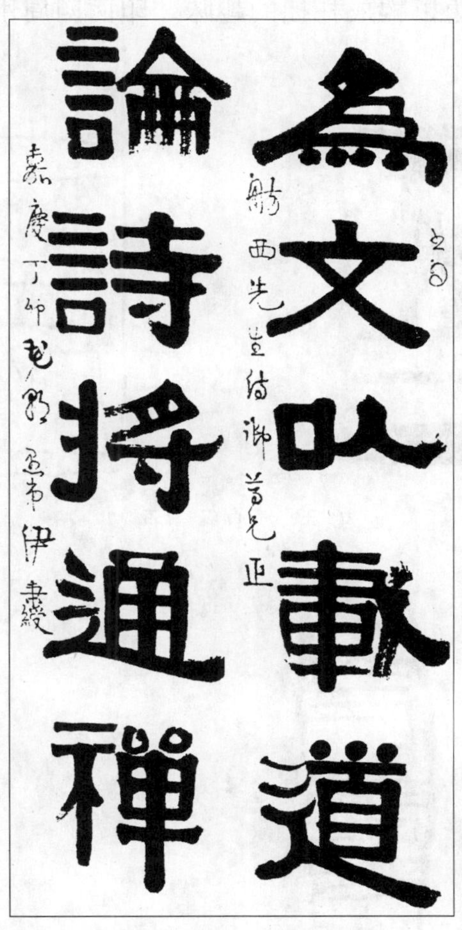

图 122　清·伊秉绶《隶书五言联》

　　印章有三种：一为名章；二为压脚章，盖在名章之下；三为引首章，多加于右上角。后二者为闲章。加盖印章可以增加全幅字的艺术美和趣味性。

　　印章中笔画凸出的称朱文，笔画凹进的称白文。印章一般都刻篆字，仿秦汉印，表现古朴的金石气。从篆书的布局中最能看出印面的章法来。

　　现代书画、篆刻大师齐白石的名章"白石"（图 123），朱文，线条大刀阔斧，"白"字笔画多在下部，"石"字笔画多在上部，印面被分割成大小不同的三角形和方块，多斩削的线条，给人以空旷、大方、对比、协调的感觉。

　　齐白石的印章"人长寿"（图 124），朱文，线条细长挺拔，三字右竖均与印面粘连，字形由小到大，笔画由少到多，每个字既有密集的线条，又有宽阔的空间，呈现小、中、大的节奏。此章可作引首章。

　　现代书画、篆刻大师吴昌硕的压脚章"园丁书画"（图 125），用刀锋锐，笔画粗壮，印面底部添加厚边以构成朴拙的趣味。印面四周用重笔(刀)敲边，更增加了印章古拙的气韵。

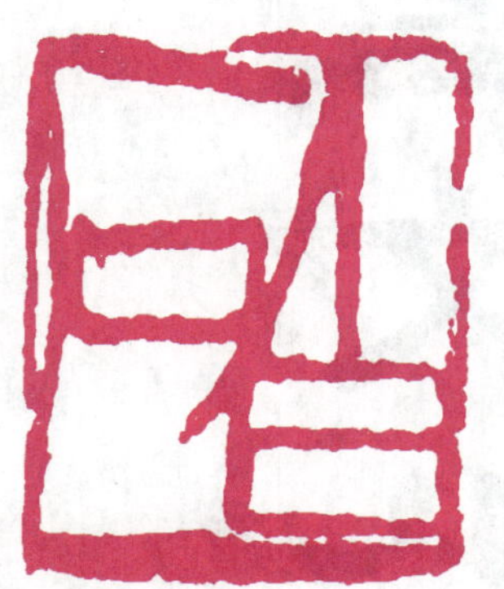
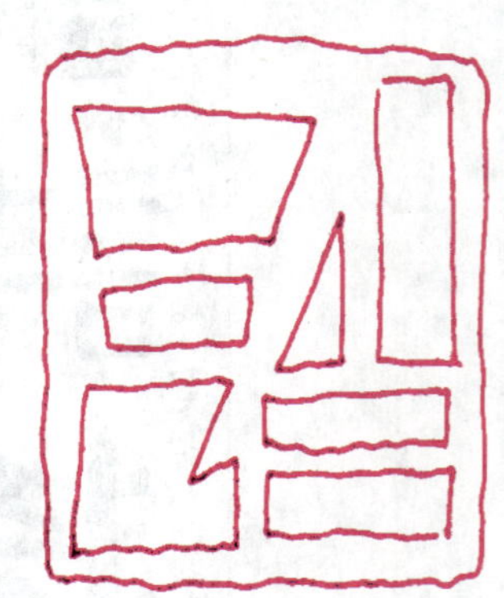

图 123　齐白石"白石"

图 124　齐白石"人长寿"

There are three kinds of seals: one seal has the name of the calligrapher; one is the step stone seal, placed below the name seal; and the third is a forward seal, usually placed on the right top corner. The last two seals are leisure seal. They are placed on the paper to enhance the overall aesthetic of the calligraphy.

The carvings bulged out from the seal are "zhu wen", and the carvings caved into the seal are "bai wen". Most seals are carved with Zhuan script to imitate the seals carved in Qin-Han dynasties. These scripts have a classical and solid sense. From the arrangement of Zhuan script, one can clearly see the layout on the seal surface.

Among modern day artists, in Figure 123, Master Qi Baishi uses bold strokes in his name seal. The character "白" has more strokes in the lower side, and the character "石" has more strokes in the top side. Furthermore, the character "白" has an extra vertical stroke in the middle. The surface of the seal is carved into different sizes square and triangle. There are sharp lines to give observers a sense of broad, generous, opposite, and homonymous.

In Figure 124, Qi Baishi's seal *ren chang shou*, has narrow and long strokes. When one looks at it casually, it gives appearance of many horizontal lines dividing the seal surface, when one makes careful examination, one will find in them just a few horizontal and parallel strokes. Three vertical strokes of the three characters attach closely with the seal surface, but each uses a different method. Each of the three characters has a different size, (from a smaller size to a big size), and each has different strokes. A loosely laid division line, and a tightly laid division gave a different sense (the large, the medium and the small). This seal is often used as the lead seal.

In Figure 125, the step stone seal *Yuan Ding Shu Hua* of modern day Calligraphy and Zhuan script carving master Wu Changshuo, his seal has sharp knife cuts and bold strokes, and a thick edge on the bottom side of the seal creates an interesting impression of bold and humble feeling. Furthermore, the beating scar seen around the seal also increases this humble feeling.

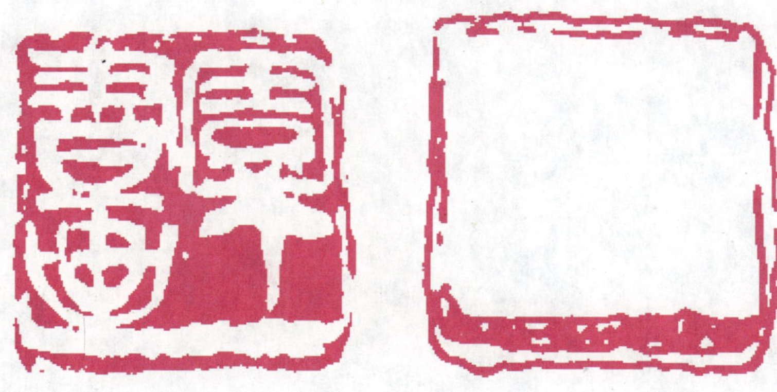

图 125　吴昌硕"园丁书画"

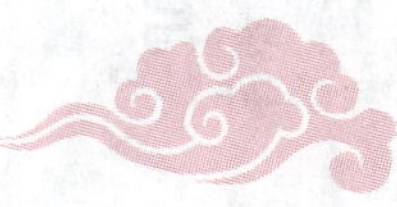

第 十 章

Chapter 10

习 字 的 方 法

Methods for practice and exercise

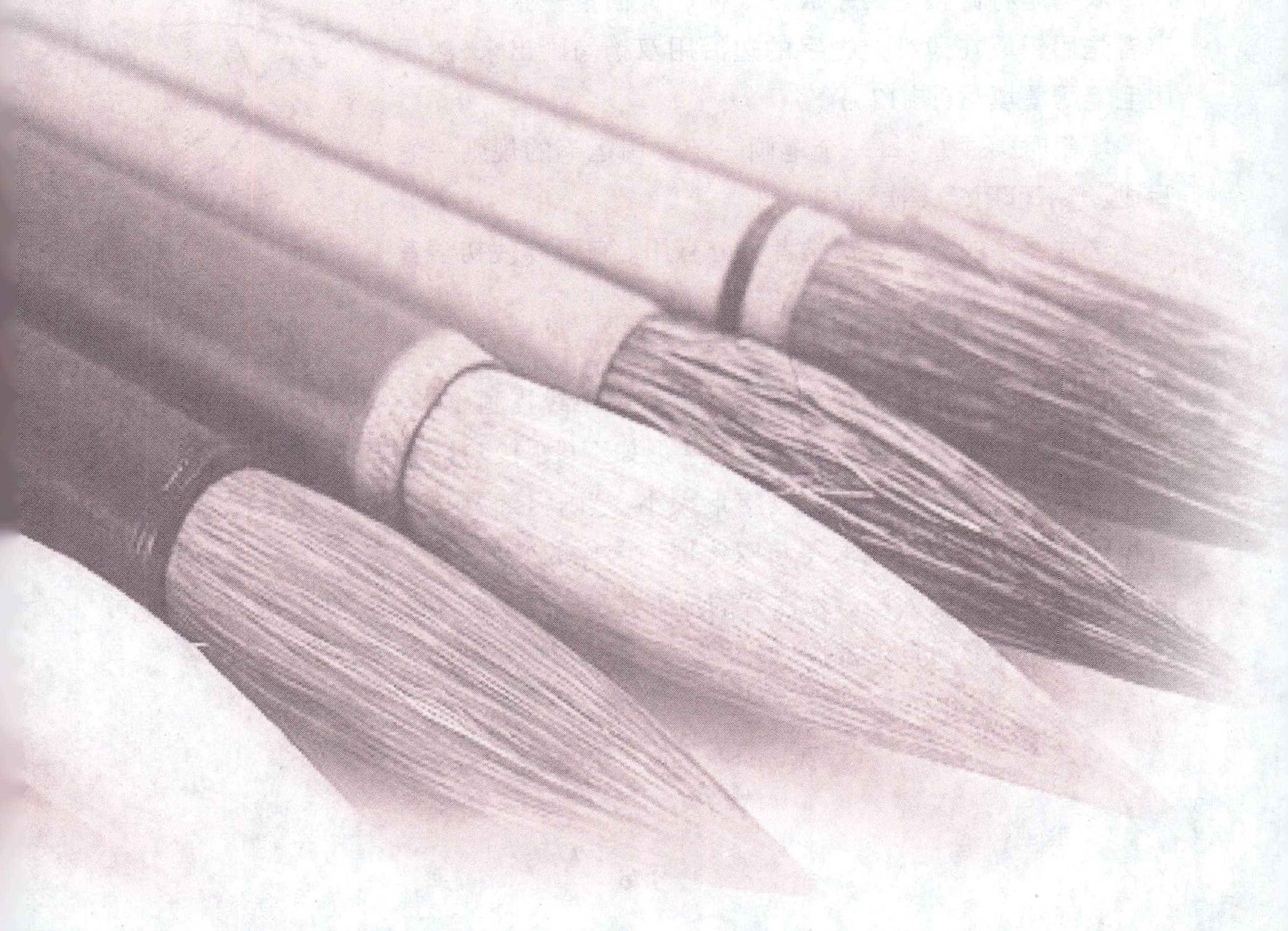

摹写与临写，统称临摹。下面分别叙述这两种习字的方法。

（1）摹写

摹写是初级的习字法，却是花时间少而见效快的一种办法。中国人幼年习写汉字多用此法。具体地说，有以下四种方式：

1）描摹字形：

这是最初级的习字方法，要求用毛笔把红色的范字描成黑的。描成的黑字，笔画要和红色的范字保持一致。这种方法俗称描红模字。

2）仿影：

仿影就是在描红模字的基础上进行的，它将范字放在下面，上面覆一张薄纸，从上面可以看到下面范字的影子，按照范字的影子用毛笔写出字形。

3）双钩填墨：

双钩是将碑帖上的字放在下面，上面覆一张薄纸，习字者先用铅笔在薄纸上把字的边沿用双钩勾画出来，然后用毛笔蘸墨填写（图 126）。

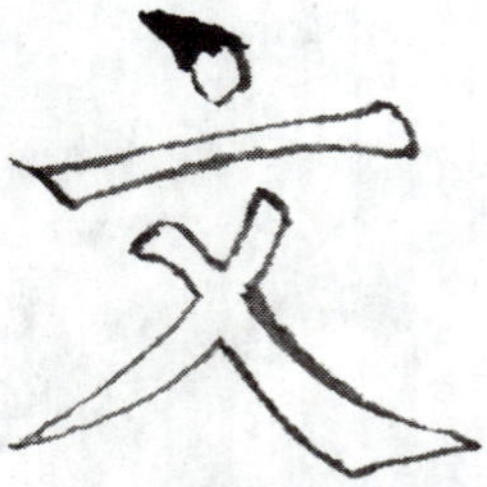

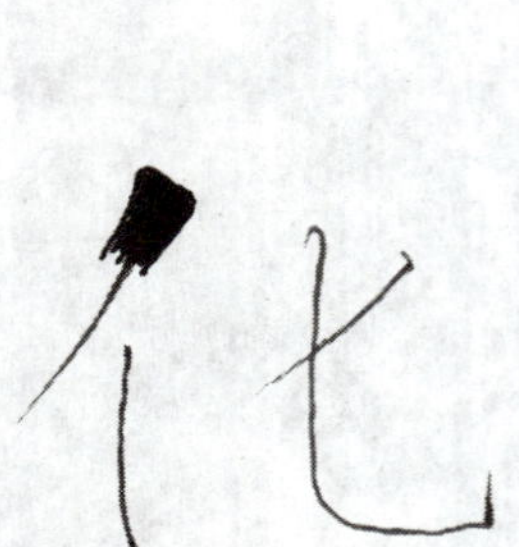

图 126

填墨时须注意：每一个笔画一定要用运笔的规则一笔写成，绝不可用笔多次涂抹。

这种习字的方法对初学者十分有用。它可以使初学者找到笔画的位置，掌握结构的安排。

4）单线摹写：

单线摹写是用铅笔把范字每一笔画的中线描画出来，然后用毛笔写成黑字。单线描画的字形如下（图 127）：

图 127

用毛笔摹写时，写出的字，字形大小、笔画粗细要与范字相同。这种练习可以取得与双钩填墨同样的效果，而它的自由度又比前者大些。须注意的地方是：应严格地按照范字的字形来写，不可脱离范字的字形而自由发挥。

To Mo and to Lin are "Lin Mo", or learn to write Chinese calligraphy. These two methods of learning are described in detail below.

(1) Filling blank strokes from a pattern book

Mo Xie is a beginning method to learn Chinese calligraphy.　This method requires the least amount of learning time yet it accomplish the most.　In China,　all youngsters use this method to learn the writing of Chinese characters.　More specifically,　there several kinds of this beginning method:

1) Miao Mo Zi Xing

This is the very basic method of learning to write Chinese. It requires learner to use brush and black ink to cover the red colored sample characters on the sample plate. The finished "Miao Mo" should be in the same shape as the sample character. This method is also commonly referred to as Miao Hong Mo Zi.

2) Fang Ying

It uses the same foundation as Miao Hong Mo Zi. The learner covers over the sample character sheet with a transparent blank sheet;　then uses a brush and black ink to write over shadow characters seen on the blank sheet.

3) Shuang Gou Tian Mo

The learner places a sheet of thin paper over the sample characters. Thus, shadows of the sample characters are made to penetrate the thin paper. Then a pencil is used to trace all edges of the shadow sample below. This thin sheet of paper with pencil tracing, will be used as an alternative to a Miao Hong Sheet. (Figure 126) When the sheet of tracings is used in practice, one must still use the correct rule of Yun Bi. That is, to fill each blank stroke, tracing with a brush and ink; one should write it once and only once.

4) Dan Xian Mo Xie

Dan Xian Mo Xie is to use pencil to trace only the middle line of shadow characters below. The brush and ink are used to write following the pencil lines. (Figure 127)

When brush is used in Mo Xie, size of each character and the width of each stroke, should be approximate to those on the sample sheet. In doing so, one gains the same benefit as if a practice sheet of Shuang Gou Tian Mo is used; yet it offers greater latitude to learner. A word to remind learner using Mo Xie: one needs to follow closely the shape of the sample characters and not to do a free hand.

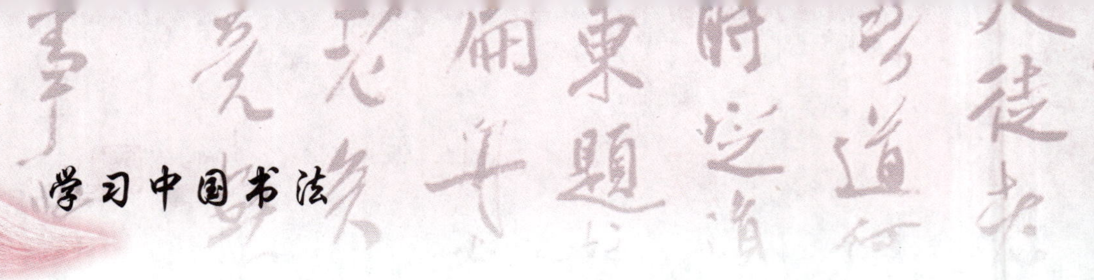

（2）临写

临字是选择好的碑帖范本，照着其中的范字一笔一画地学写。临写是摹写的提高阶段，也是书法学习者需要长期使用的方法。临写也有四种方式。

1）对临：

对临就是把碑帖放在旁边，对照着碑帖上的字认真地书写。书写时，要细致观察字的笔画和结构安排。初学者最好是看一笔，写一笔，每个字的书写速度不宜过快，每一个字可以多写几遍，尽量做到：使自己的字和范本上的字基本相似。

2）背临：

背临是离开碑帖，默着写出碑帖上的字。经过较长时间的对临以后，临写出来的字已基本上与碑帖上的范字相似，这时可以把碑帖合上，背着默写碑帖上的范字，然后对照检查，看自己的字与碑帖上的字差距在哪里。这是对临的基础上提高书写能力的另一种有效的练习方法。

3）空临：

空临是离开碑帖，默想碑帖上的字形，用手指临空写字。古人学习书法，常用这种方法。三国·魏的大书法家钟繇躺在床上，用手指画被，以致把被都划破了；唐朝的书法家虞世南用手指在自己的肚子上画写，常常达到废寝忘食的程度。空临的方法随时可以使用，非常方便，但它和背临一样，必须有扎实的书法根底才可使用。否则，名为背临、空临，实际上还是按照自己的书写习惯去写字，这样学习书法是毫无用处的。

4）意临：

意临是临帖的最高阶段。意临是在临写的过程中不追求每一个笔画的绝对酷似，而要把碑帖的精髓和风格展现出来。这是书法家在临写时的高标准和高要求，一般人是较难做到的。

我们主张：学习书法的人要把主要精力放在踏踏实实的对临上。

(2) Copying characters from a pattern book

Lin xie needs the selection of a pattern sheet with good sample character or a sample character sheet tapped off from a stone template.

1) Dui Lin

Dui Lin is to place the sample sheet near-by to the writing table. The learner can see the sample sheet well and copy the same stroke and structure of all characters carefully. The learner also follows one stroke at a time, and not to be in high speed. He or she may write repeatedly the same character many times; and to match all strokes seen in the sample sheet.

2) Bei Lin

Bei lin is to put away the sample sheet;　and to follow the example character stored in the memory. One may compare the writing with the sample sheet afterwards.

3) Kong Lin

Kong Lin is a method used to remember the character as seen on the sample sheet; and write out the memorized character in the air.　It is convenient because it does not limit the learning to a particular place, that is, to practice writing on a table.

Some Chinese calligraphers in the past often use their fingers to Kong Lin write while lying in bed. As a result, a person who is very diligent to practice would have damaged his bed spread. Or, other calligraphers would use fingers to Kong Lin write on their stomach while lying in beds. As a result of their diligent practices, they often forget to eat or sleep.

4) Yi Lin

This method is the highest order of Lin Xie. Yi Lin does not ask a learner to mimic the exact shapes written on the sample sheet but wants the learner to be able to express the same flavor and style of calligraphy as expressed by the Master on the sample sheet.　Yi Lin is a very difficult requirement for a learner.

Our recommendation:　The learner should place his or her primary energy in the Dui Lin method.

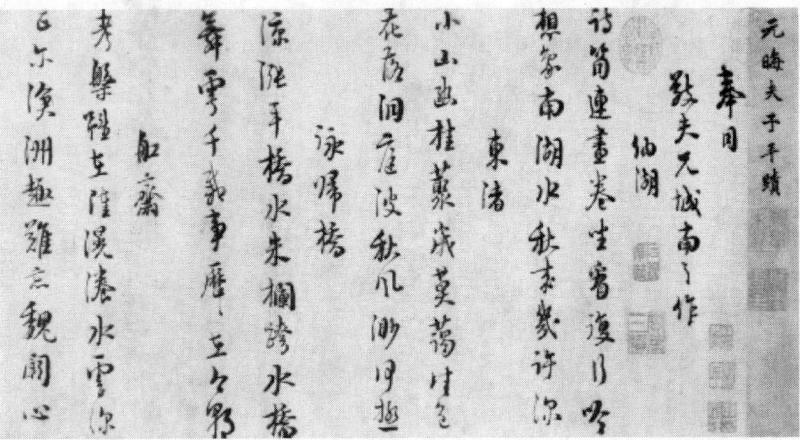

*《城南唱和诗》

为了更好地掌握范字的点画位置和字形结构,在中国,普遍采用米字格(图128)和九宫格(图129)的正形方框作为习字的辅助性工具。

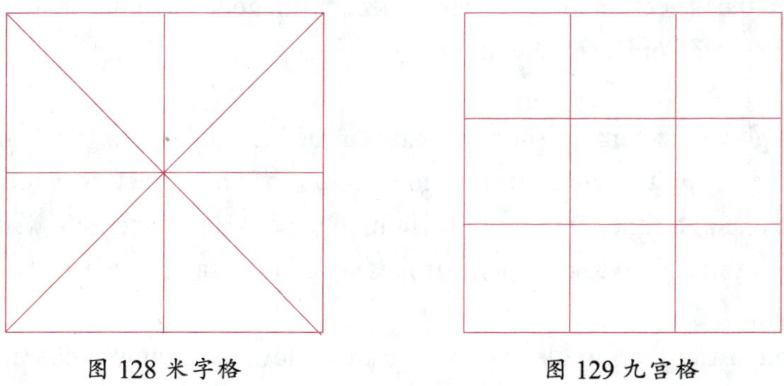

图 128 米字格　　　　　　　　　图 129 九宫格

米字格,自中心点向四面八方射出八条直线,形成米字形。以米字格作为辅助工具,临写时,既容易掌握字的中心,又容易使字形舒展得体,尤其是写撇、捺、点、折笔画多的字,更为有益。

九宫格,把正形方框分割成九个方格,形成井字形。当中的方格叫中宫。临写时,认定字的中心点以后,再四面展开,安排结构,对于写横、竖画多的字,容易掌握字形。

还有一些其它的字框可作为临写的辅助工具,但不普遍。为了把字练好,只要采取一种措施就可以了。

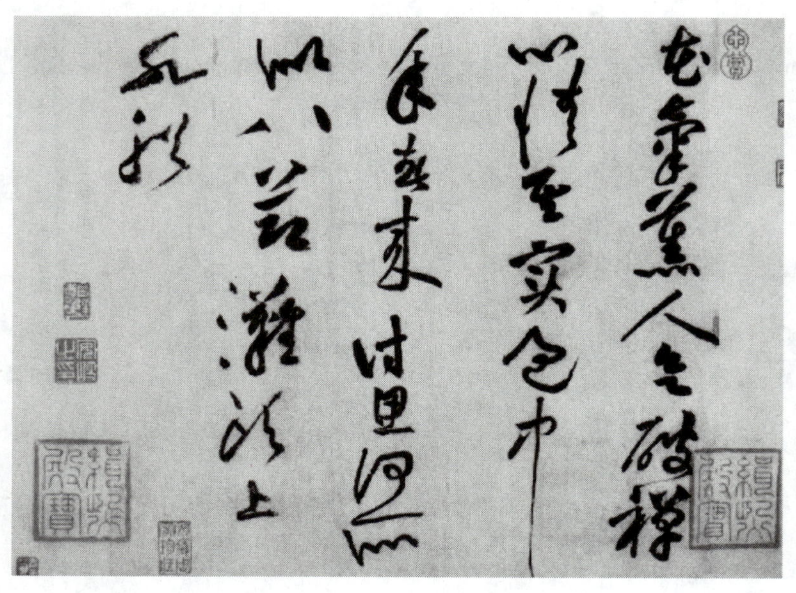

*《花气诗帖》

In order to place all the strokes of characters and their correct structure of a sample sheet in a square, Chinese beginning learners use two types of square paper to help them. One is having the character or the shape of "米"printed in red on the sheet to divide each block into separate spaces (Figure 128). Another kind is to use straight lines to divide a block into nine smaller spaces in the shape of the Chinese character "井" (Figure 129).

On the practice sheet with a character"米" printed on it, it has eight lines dividing the block. In using this type of practice sheet, one can easily determine the center of a character; and to locate the spread of various strokes in their desired directions. This type of practice sheet is very convenient to practice "Pie ", " Na", "Dian", and "Zhe" or characters with many strokes.

On the practice sheet with a character 井 printed on it, it has nine equal size smaller blocks, the center block is called a center hall. After the learner identified first the center of a character; other strokes in the character may be spread to other blocks. It is more convenient to arrange the structure of a character; and it is easier to handle characters with more horizontal and straight lines.

There are other tools on the market to assist Lin Mo but not common. For convenient sake, select any one recommendation above will suffice.

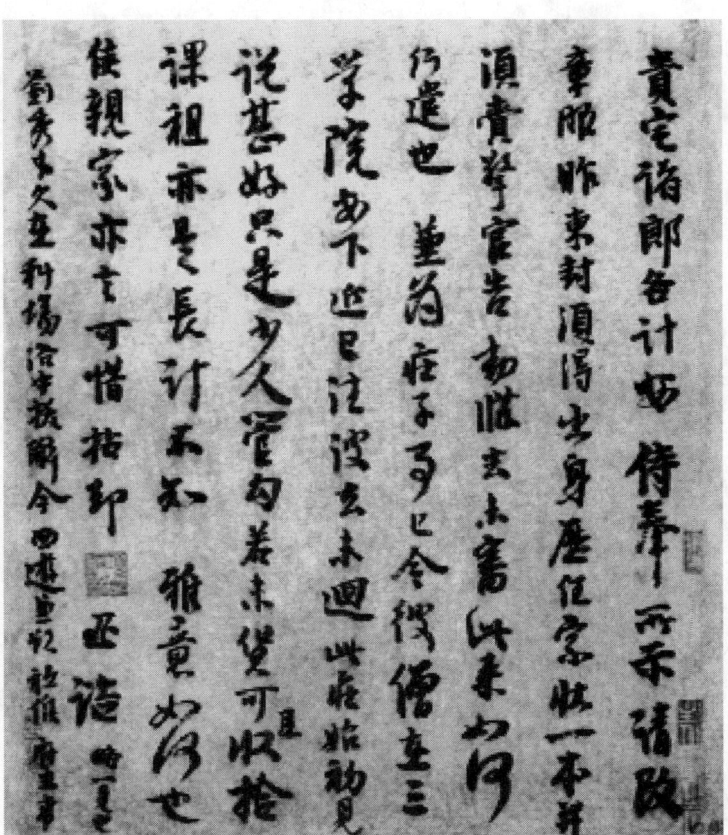

*《贵宅帖》

151

Chapter 11

楷书四大书体简介

A brief introduction of four major schools of kaishu

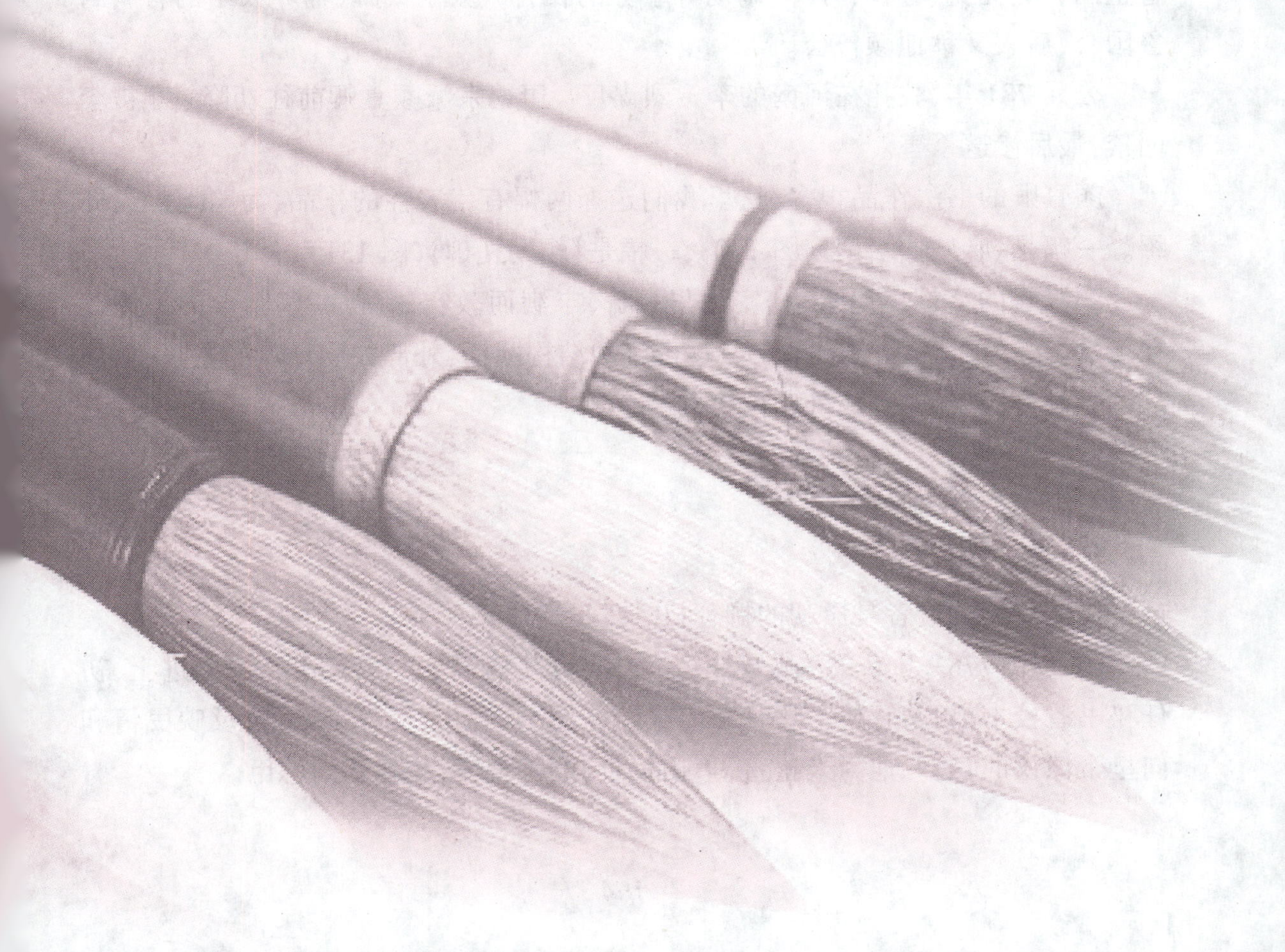

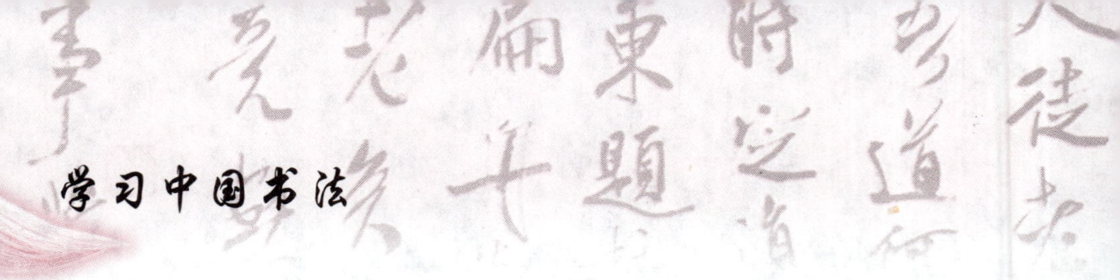

学习中国书法

当我们有了书写汉字的基础知识、掌握了书写汉字的基本技法以后,我们总想借鉴前人的经验,写出优美的汉字来。中国的书法艺术,历史悠久,从古至今,产生过许多影响后世的大书法家。这里我们仅以楷书为例,简略地介绍几位著名的书法家和有代表性的楷书字体。

(1) 颜体字

颜体字的创造者是唐朝的颜真卿。

颜真卿(709—785),字清臣,京兆万年(今陕西西安)人,二十六岁中进士,因为遭受权臣的排挤,离开长安到平原郡(今属山东)当太守(郡的行政长官),所以人称颜平原。公元 757 年,安禄山发动叛乱,颜真卿联合他的族兄、常山(今属河北)太守颜杲卿起兵讨贼,颜真卿被推为盟主。他统兵二十万与叛军激战,打了大胜仗。颜氏一家有三十多人牺牲在战场上。叛乱平息后,颜真卿升任吏部尚书(掌管全国官吏任免、考核、升降、调动等事务的长官)、太子太师(辅导太子的官),封鲁国公,后人又称他颜鲁公。

公元 781 年,驻扎在河南的李希烈谋反。唐德宗派颜真卿前往劝降。颜被李囚禁,最后惨遭杀害。

颜真卿的书法作品很多,这里我们选择两幅有代表性的作品,简略地加以介绍。一幅是《麻姑仙坛记》(图 130),一幅是《颜勤礼碑》(图 131)。

颜真卿的字端庄厚重,朴实无华,肌肉丰满而敦实,好像一座圆形的塔座落在地基上。笔画粗壮,雄浑有力。整个字的结构圆浑,外部如同环状的紧箍,而内部的笔画是舒展的,形成外密内疏的特色。

(2) 柳体字

柳体字的创造者是唐朝的柳公权。

柳公权(778—865),字诚悬,京兆华原(今陕西耀县)人,二十八岁中进士,初任秘书省校书郎(掌管校对历代法制文献与图书的官),后任右拾遗(反映民情和向皇帝谏议的官)。他为人正直,不畏权贵,敢于直言,是朝廷的忠臣。

When one has acquired the fundamental knowledge in Chinese calligraphy art, and have grasped the basic method of writing Chinese, one feel able to begin to reproduce the experience of expert Masters: to produce beautiful writings ourselves. Chinese calligraphy art has a long history; from years back in history to modern days, and there have been many great calligraphy masters, who have contributed to the calligraphy art. In the present chapter, we shall illustrate the Kaishu, thw Standard Script, by reference to four prominent Calligraphy Masters.

(1) Yanti Zi

The founder of Yanti Style Kai Script was Yan Zhenqing in the Tang dynasty.

Yan Zhenqing (AD 709—785), also named Qing Chen, was born in Shan Xi, Xi'An; and obtained his academic degree Jinshi at age 26 through competitive examination. Because he was not accepted by the power clique in the government, he left the Capital Zhang An and went to Ping Yuan Jun, Shan Dong to be an area governor. He was often addressed as Governor Yan by his people. In AD 757, the rebellion force of An Lushan began, Yan organized soldiers with his cousin, Yan Gaoqin to battle the rebellion. Yan Zhenqing was elected leader to lead the defense force and brought with him 200,000 men to fight the rebellion force. He has more than 30 members of his family perished in different battles. After the war, Yan was promoted to the position of Minister of Civil Service in the Central Government (a position in charge of appointment, promotion, examination, evaluation,and remove civil servants); teacher of the princes; and Duke of Lu. People often address him with the honorary title "Yan Lu Gong".

In AD781, another rebellion force began in He Nan. The King of Tang dynasty De Zong sent Yan to negotiate with the rebellion force which was lead by General Li Xilie. His effort failed and Yan was killed after taken prisoner.

Yan has written a prolific amount of calligraphy. The famous *Ma Gu Xian Tan Ji* (Figure 130) and *Yan Qing Li Bei* (Figure 131) are but two more representative works.

Yan's writing is dignified and generous; plain and not flashy; his strokes are honest and full, each character is like a pagoda sat solidly on its foundation. Strokes in his writing are forceful; the external area of his characters like being tightly crowned together; and internal strokes of his characters are being loosely assembled.

(2) Liuti Zi

The founder of Liuti Zi was credited by Liu Gongquan in the Tang dynasty. Liu Gongquan (AD 778—865), also uses the name Cheng Xuan. He was born in Shaanxi Yao county. He obtained his academic degree "Jingshi" through the national examination. He served in the royal court as a proof- reader in legal documents. He was promoted to "Youshi Yi" (an official to reflect people's concern in public policies to the King). He has a straight forward personality; does not afraid to speak out the truth.

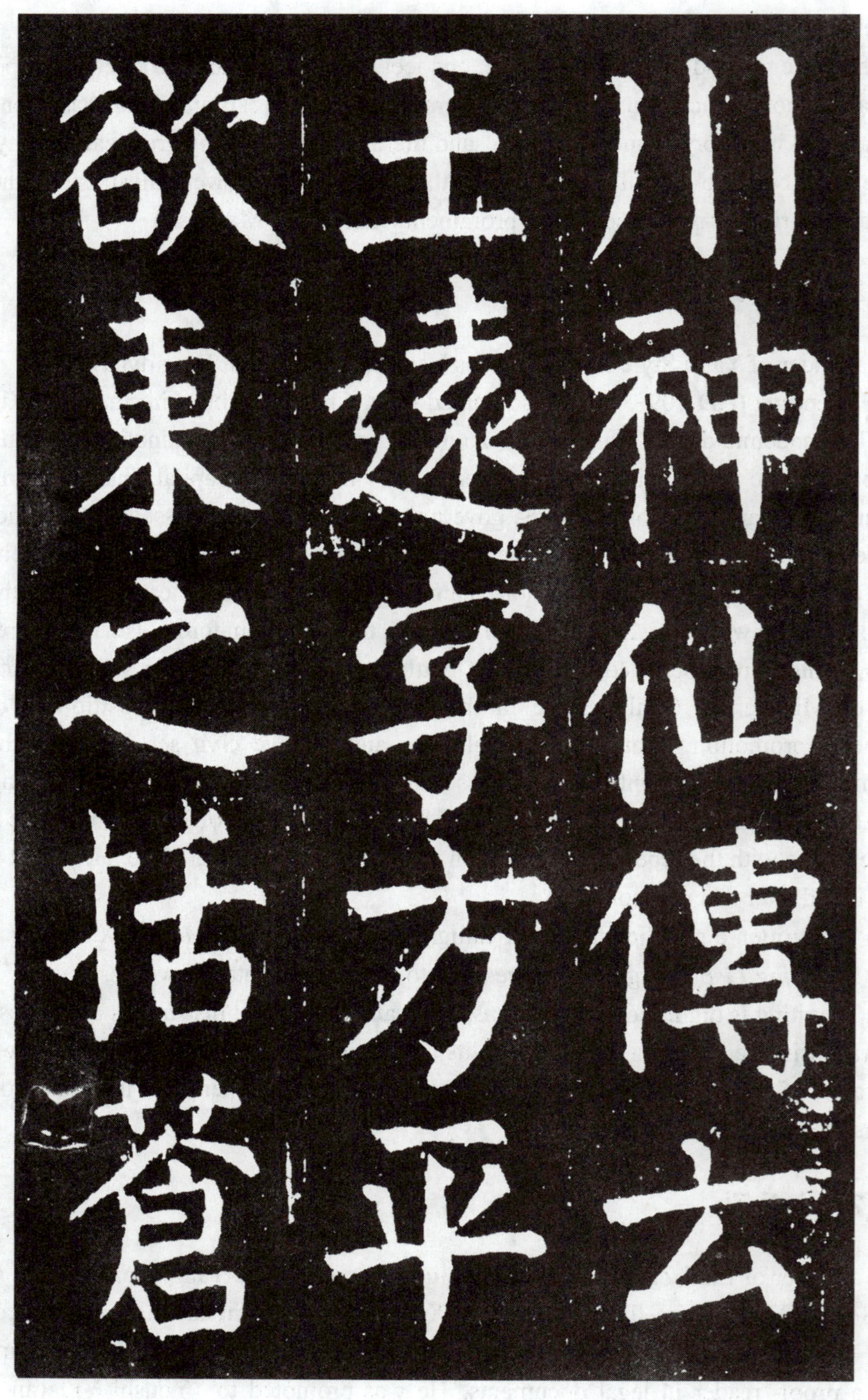

图 130　唐·颜真卿《麻姑仙坛记》

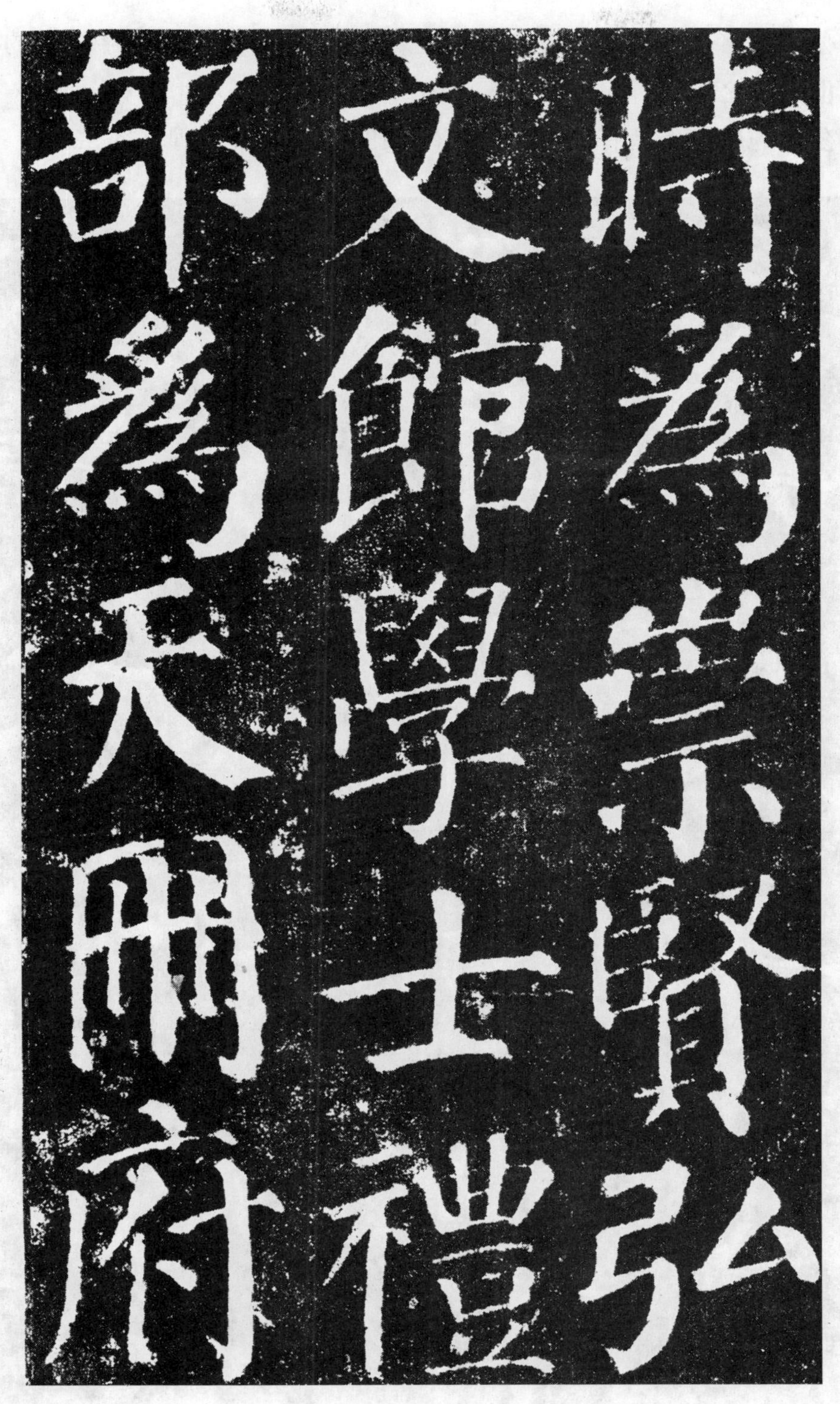

图 131　唐·颜真卿《颜勤礼碑》

　　柳公权的字在当朝就居正统的地位。很多初学者是从学柳字入手的，可见柳体对后世影响之深。

　　柳公权的代表作品有《玄秘塔碑》(图 132)和《神策军碑》(图 133)。

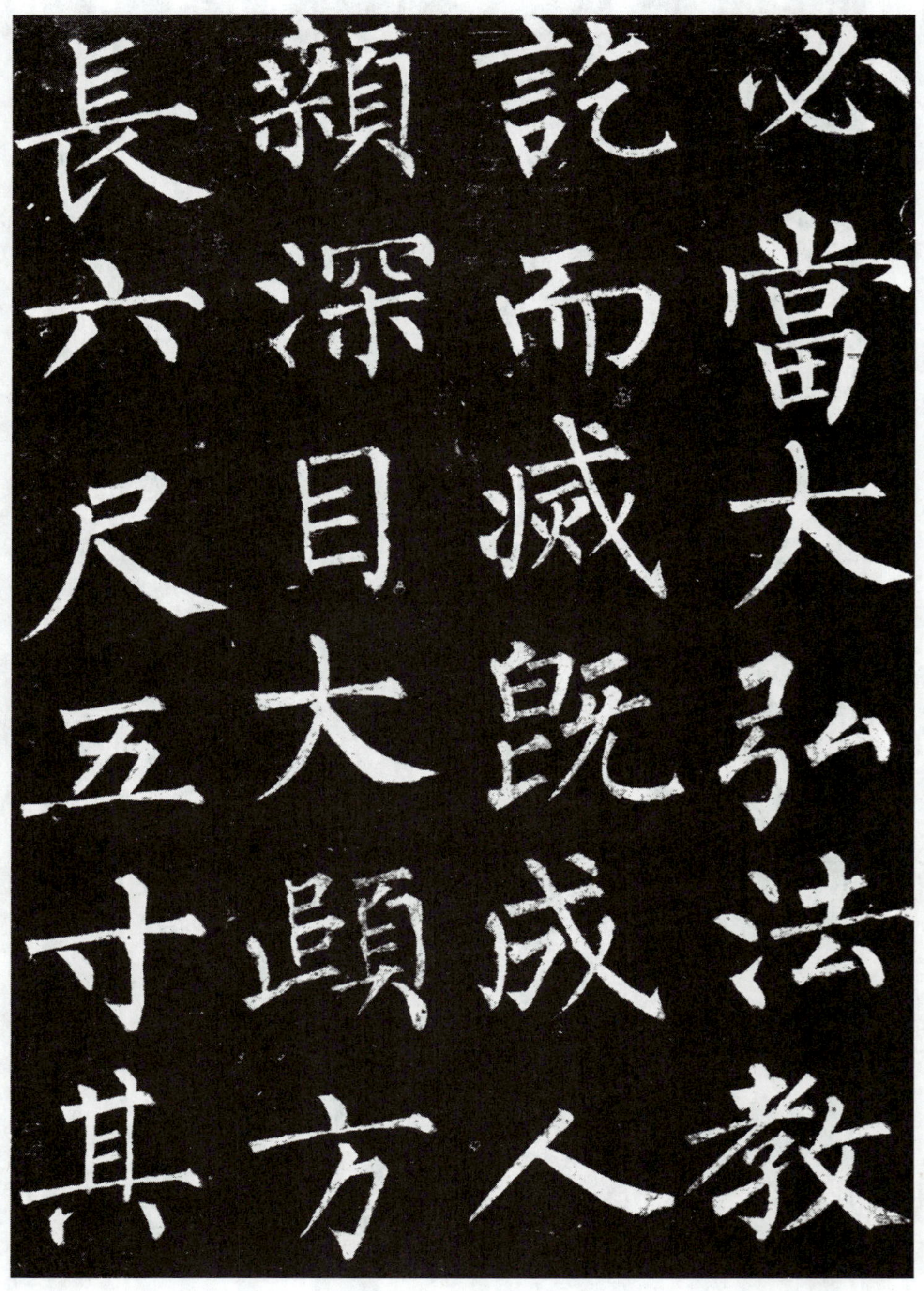

图 132　　唐·柳公权《玄秘塔碑》

　　Liu Gongquan was the authority and an influential person in Liu Style Kai Script; many beginners in calligraphy art practiced this style in the entry level of learning calligraphy art.

　　Among his famous representative writings were *Xuan Mi Ta Bei* (Figure 132) and *Shen Ce Jun Bei* (Figure 133).

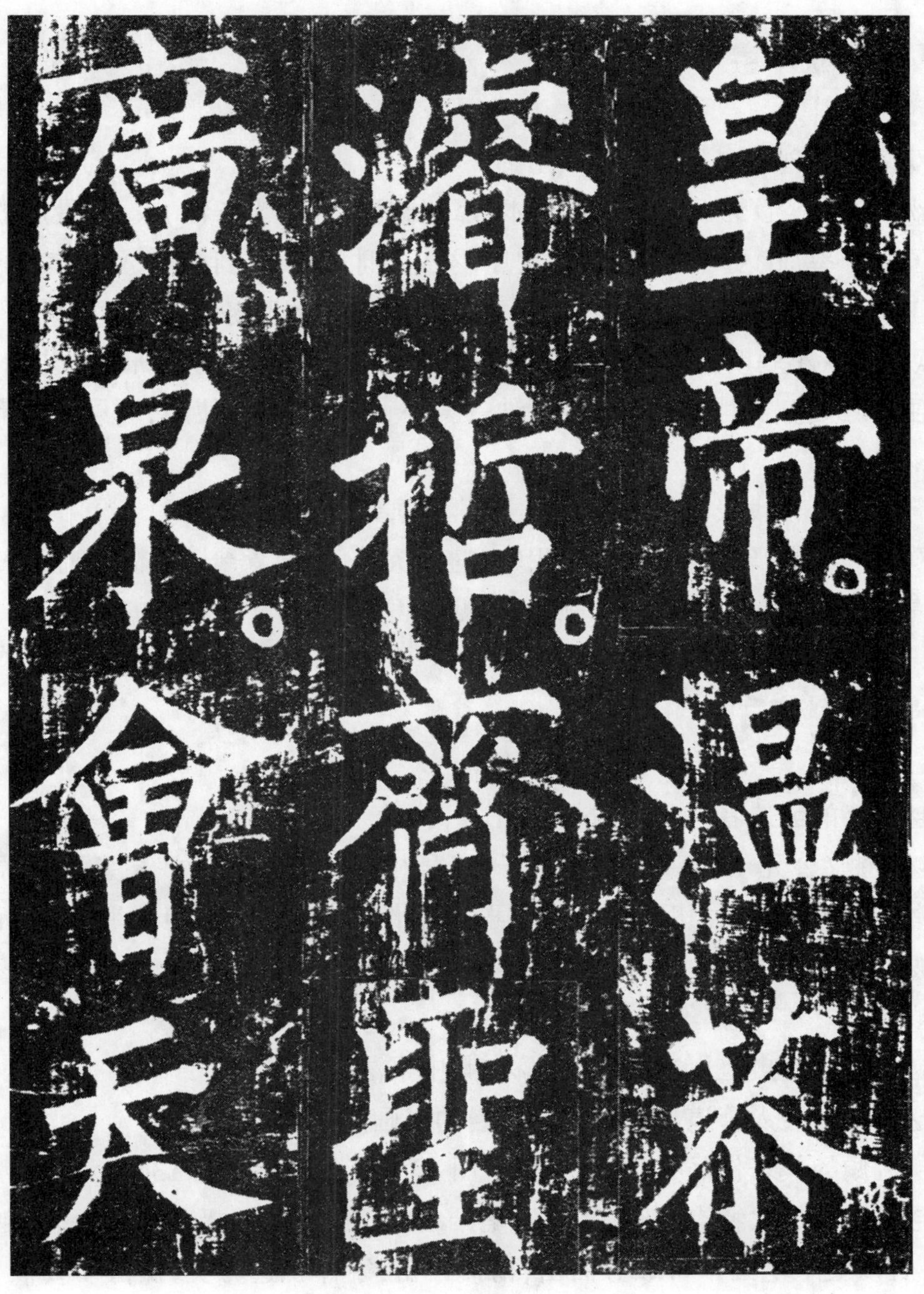

图 133　唐·柳公权《神策军碑》

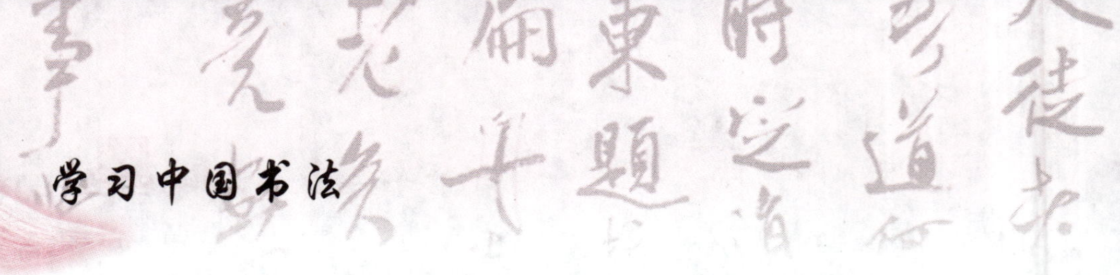

　　柳体字有一个很大的特点,就是筋骨强盛而外露。他的字,笔笔都送到末端,十分劲健。笔画向字的中心聚攒,整体结构内密外疏。《神策军碑》比《玄秘塔碑》更显得苍劲有力。

(3) 欧体字

　　欧体字的创造者是唐朝的欧阳询。

　　欧阳询(公元 557—641),字信本,潭州临湘(今湖南长沙)人,他最后的官职做到了太子率(lǜ)更令(掌管宗族次序、礼乐、刑罚等事的官职)、弘文馆学士(掌管校正图书、教授学生,并参议朝廷制度礼仪改革的职务),所以也称他欧阳率更。欧阳询从小聪明过人,读过许多经史之类的书,尤其努力钻研书法艺术,楷书更有独到之处。当时的人如果得到他一篇字,多作为范本使用,可见欧字影响之大。

　　欧阳询最有代表性的作品是《九成宫醴泉铭》(图 134)。

　　欧阳询的字,笔画一丝不苟,用笔方整、沉着,法度森严,字体瘦削而刚劲,结构严谨而疏朗。有些字体似乎倾斜,却见平正,像一座斜而不坠的塔。

(4) 赵体字

　　赵体字的创造者是元朝的赵孟頫。

　　赵孟頫(公元 1254—1322),字子昂,号松雪,湖州(今浙江吴兴)人,原为宋代皇帝宗亲。南宋灭亡后,他在家闲居,读书作画。后来经程钜夫举荐,在元朝政府供职,受到元世祖忽必烈的信任和器重,1316 年升任翰林学士,掌管编修历史和草拟文稿。

　　赵孟頫在历史上以书画兼优著称,其中书法影响更大。

　　赵孟頫的夫人管道昇也是一位著名的书画家。

　　赵孟頫的代表作品有《妙严寺记》(图 135)、《胆巴碑》(图 136)。

　　赵体字的最大特点是圆润流畅。笔画之间,互相迎让,极为协调。由于赵字行笔快,所以上下笔画常常顺势而出,衔接紧密,字体飘逸秀美,潇洒多姿。《胆巴碑》比《妙严寺记》更显老练、多彩。

The special feature of Liu Style Kai Script gives a strong and boney appearance. In his style of writing, every stroke in a character reaches its final destination with force. In his writings, strokes are clustered toward the center of the character; and his character is written tightly in the center and looser on the exterior. Characters in his *Shen Ce Jun Bei* is shown to be written more forcefully than his *Xuan Mi Ta Bei*.

(3) Outi Zi

The founder of Outi Zi was "Ouyang Xun" in the Tang dynasty. Ouyang Xun (AD 557—641), also named 信本 (Xin Ben), was born in "Tan Zhou Lin Xiang" (Today's "Hunan Changsha"), his last official capacity was "Tai Zi Lv Gen Ling Ren" (a position in charge of managing royal family tree, court music, and punishment etc.); "Hong Wen Guan Xue Shi" (In charge of proof reading official publications, teaching students, and participating in the setting of Official Ceremony, and recommending changes in court procedures), thus he was alternately being addressed Ouyang Lü Gen. He was a very brilliant person; studied many classic books; and particularly diligent to master his calligraphy art skill, with an unique contribution to Kai script writing. His contemporary often uses his writing to practice calligraphy!

The most representative work by Ouyang Xun is *Jiu Cheng Gong Li Quan Ming* (Figure 134)

In Ouyang Xun's writing, every stroke in every character is meticulously placed. His writing is organized, well composed, and all rules are observed. His characters are thin but firm, structure is rigidly followed but loose. Some of his characters look tilted but in reality, were not; they resemble a tilted pagoda but in no danger of falling over.

(4) Zhaoti Zi

The founder of Zhaoti Kaishu was "Zhao Mengfu". Zhao Mengfu (AD 1254—1322), also named "Zi Ang" and "Song Xue", born in "Zhe Jiang, Wu Xing", was a relative of the Royal family. When "Nan Song dynasty" was overturned, he stayed home to read and to paint. Later he was recommended by a friend "Cheng Jufu" to serve in the new Yuan dynasty government. He became a trusted official in the new Government of the new king "Hu Bilie". In 1316, he was promoted to be a scholar in the royal court and in charge of editing history and drafting royal orders.

Mrs. Zhao Mengfu "Guan Daosheng" was also a brilliant calligrapher and painter.

Among Zhao Mengfu's famous works are *Miao Yan Si Ji* (Figure 135) and *Dan Ba Bei* (Figure 136).

The best feature of Zhaoti Zi is its smooth flow and fluid character. Among his strokes and characters applied, each is deliberately to supplement other with harmony. Because he applies rapid brush movement, there is a logical connection between characters. His style of character writing is beautiful and carefree. His *Dan Ba Bei* is even more experienced and beautiful than *Miao Yan Si Miao Ji*.

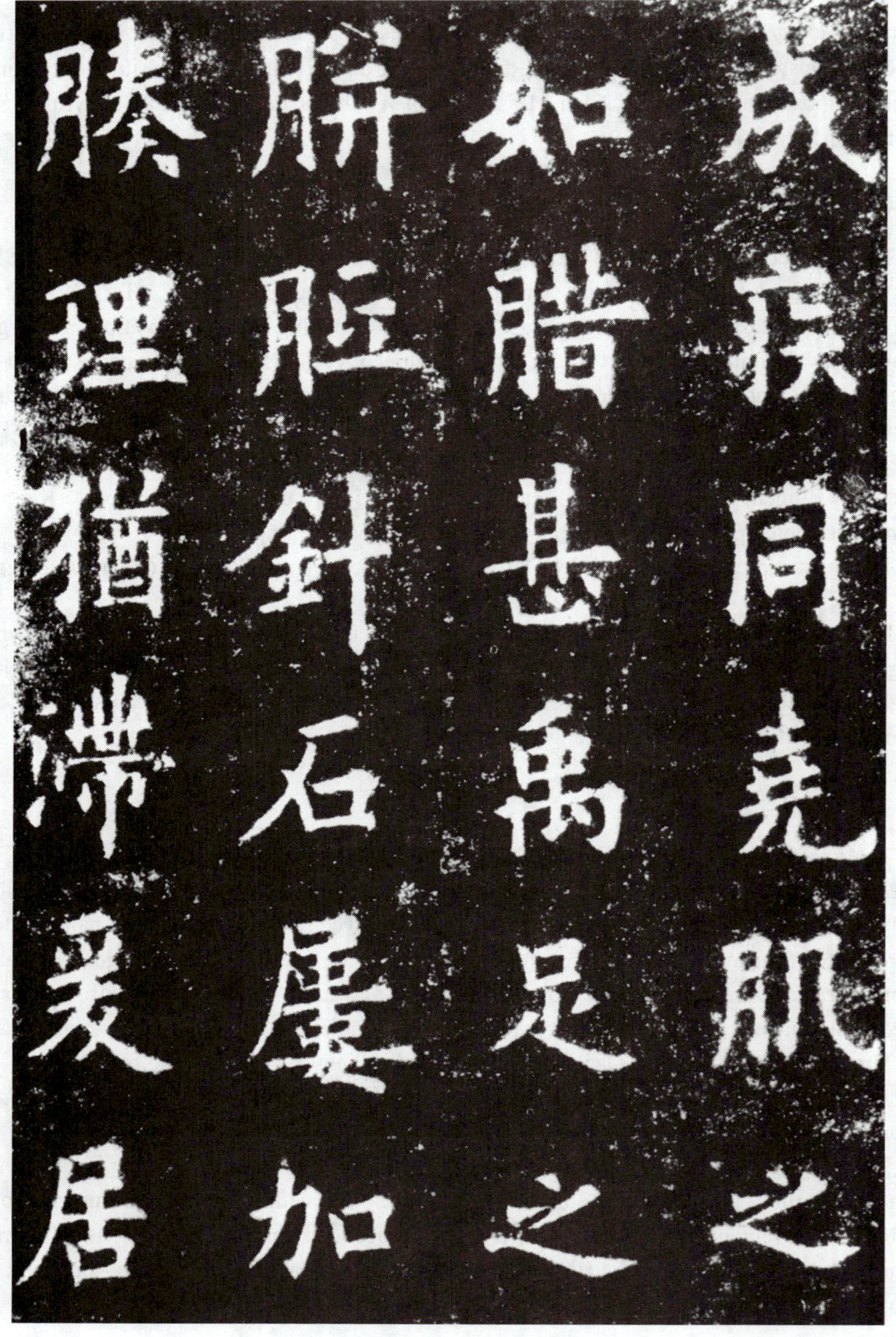

图 134　唐·欧阳询《九成宫醴泉铭》

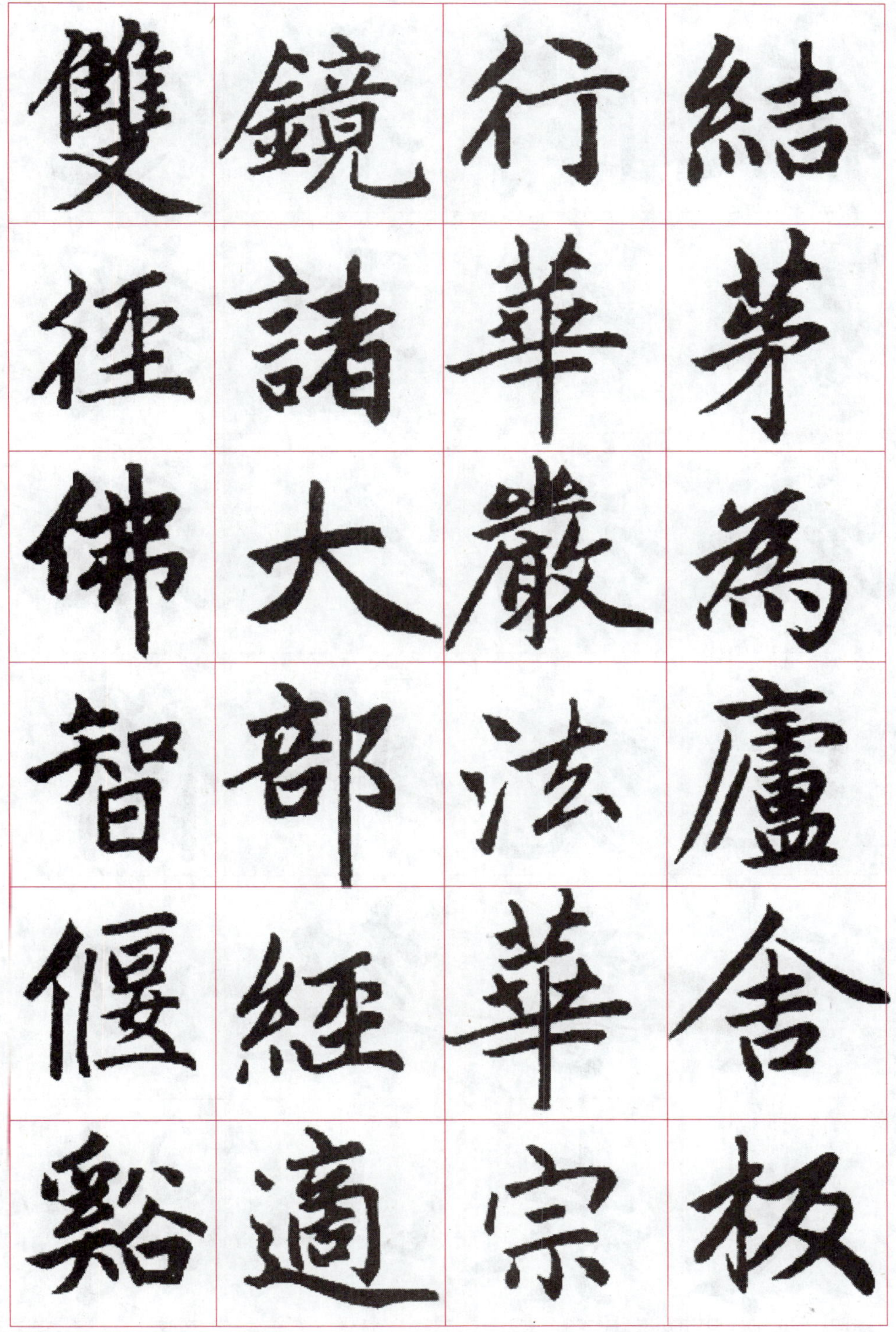

图 135　元·赵孟頫《妙严寺记》

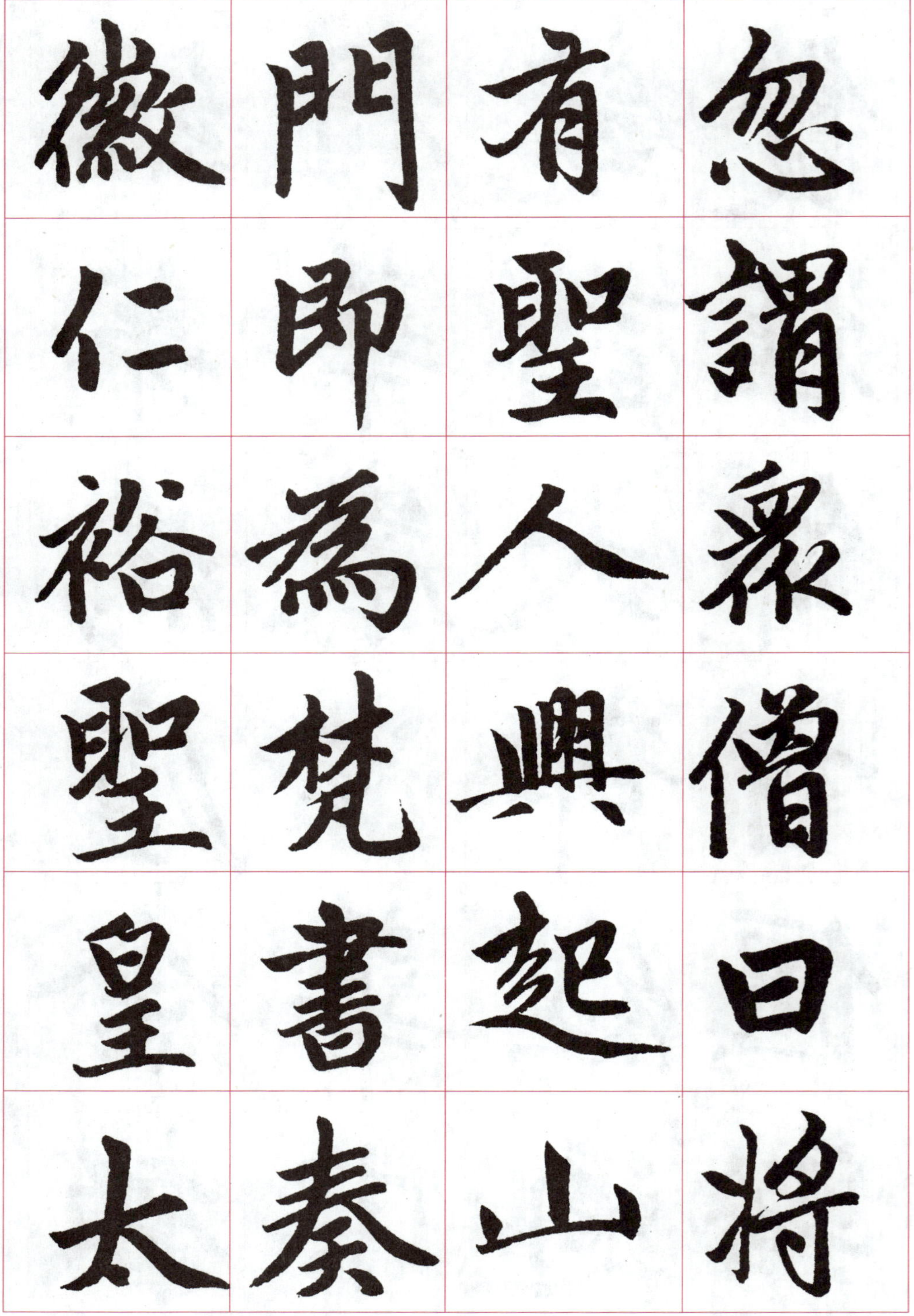

图136 元·赵孟頫《胆巴碑》

第 十 二 章

Chapter 12

练 习

Exercises

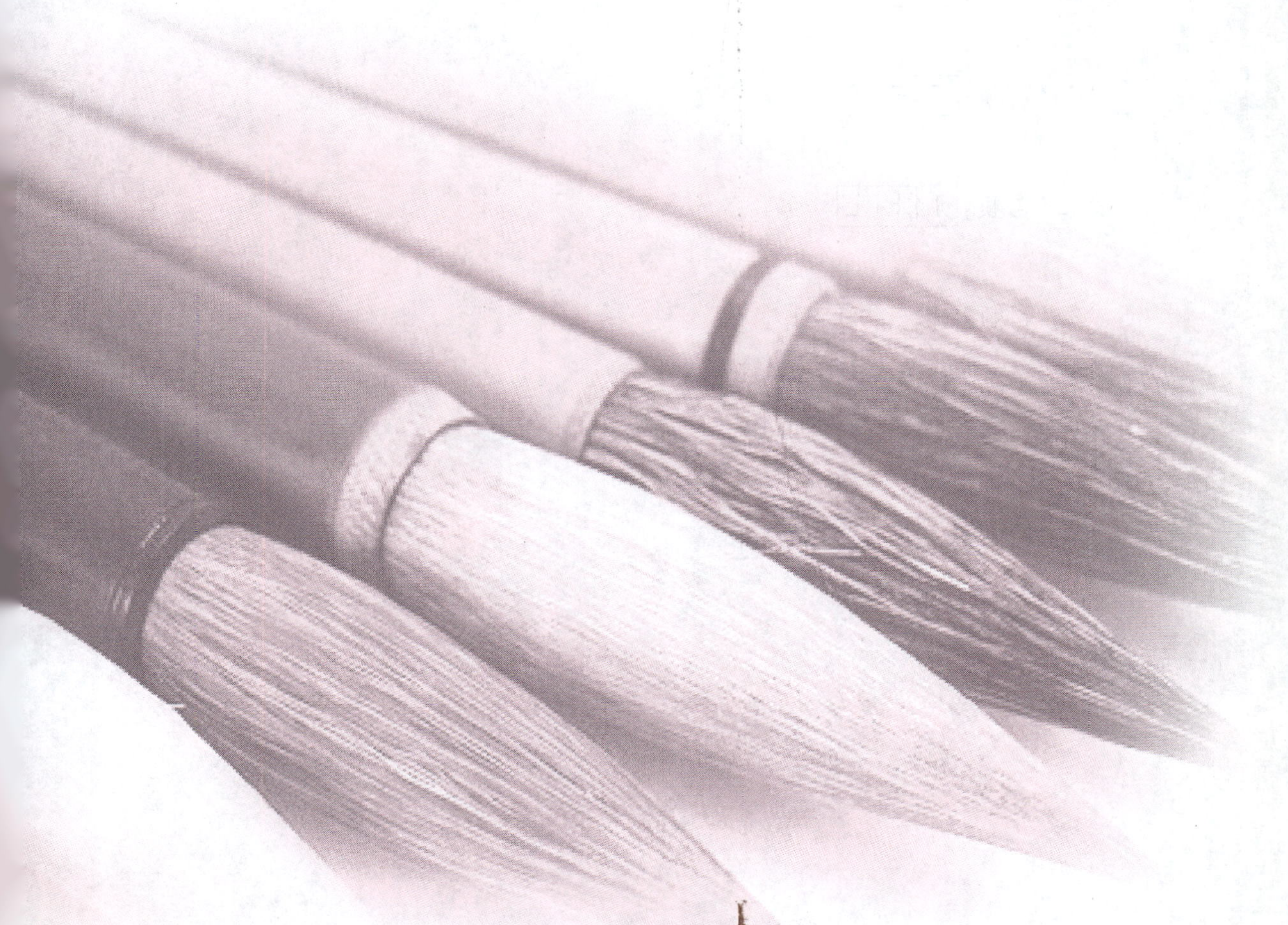

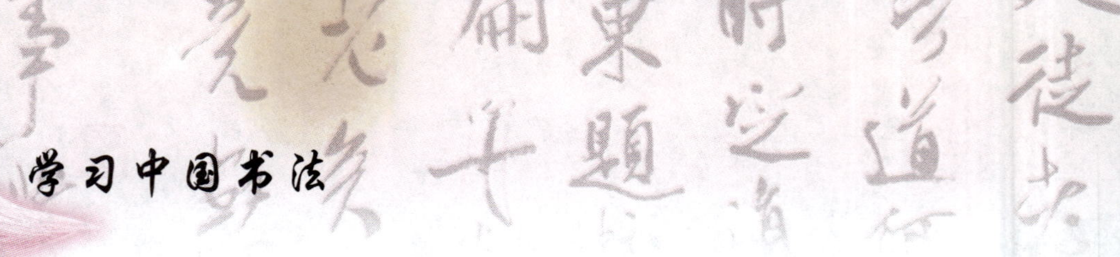

(1) 练习一：横画、竖画练习

练习长横、短横、垂露竖、悬针竖的写法。

"三"笔顺：一 二 三

"十"笔顺：一 十

"工"笔顺：一 丁 工

"土"笔顺：一 十 土

"士"笔顺：一 十 士

"干"笔顺：一 二 干

"上"笔顺：丨 卜 上

"王"笔顺：一 二 干 王

"正"笔顺：一 丁 下 正 正

"耳"笔顺：一 丅 下 下 正 耳

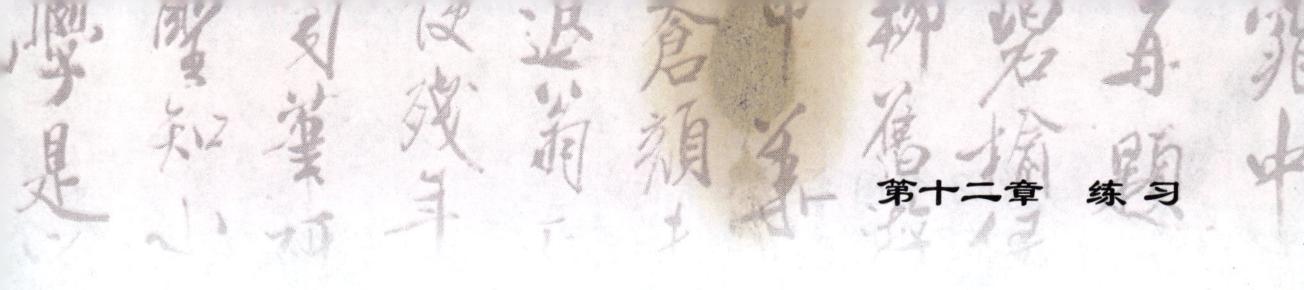

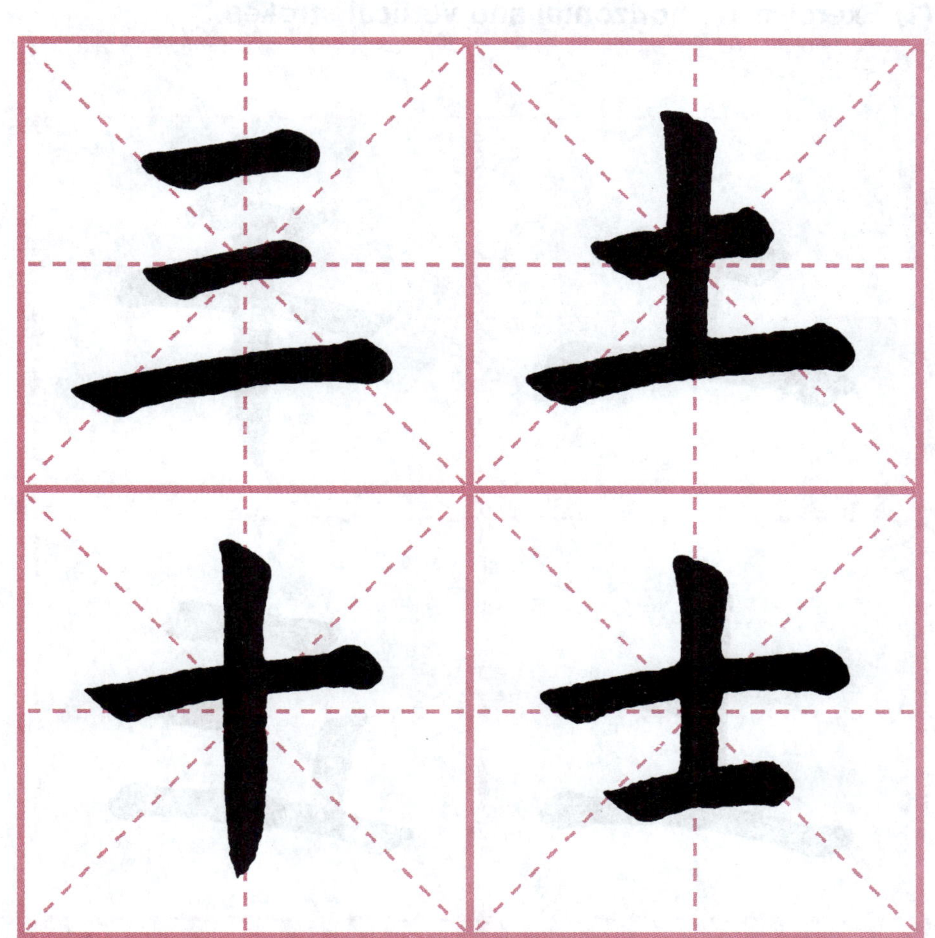

(1) Exercise 1   horizontal and vertical strokes

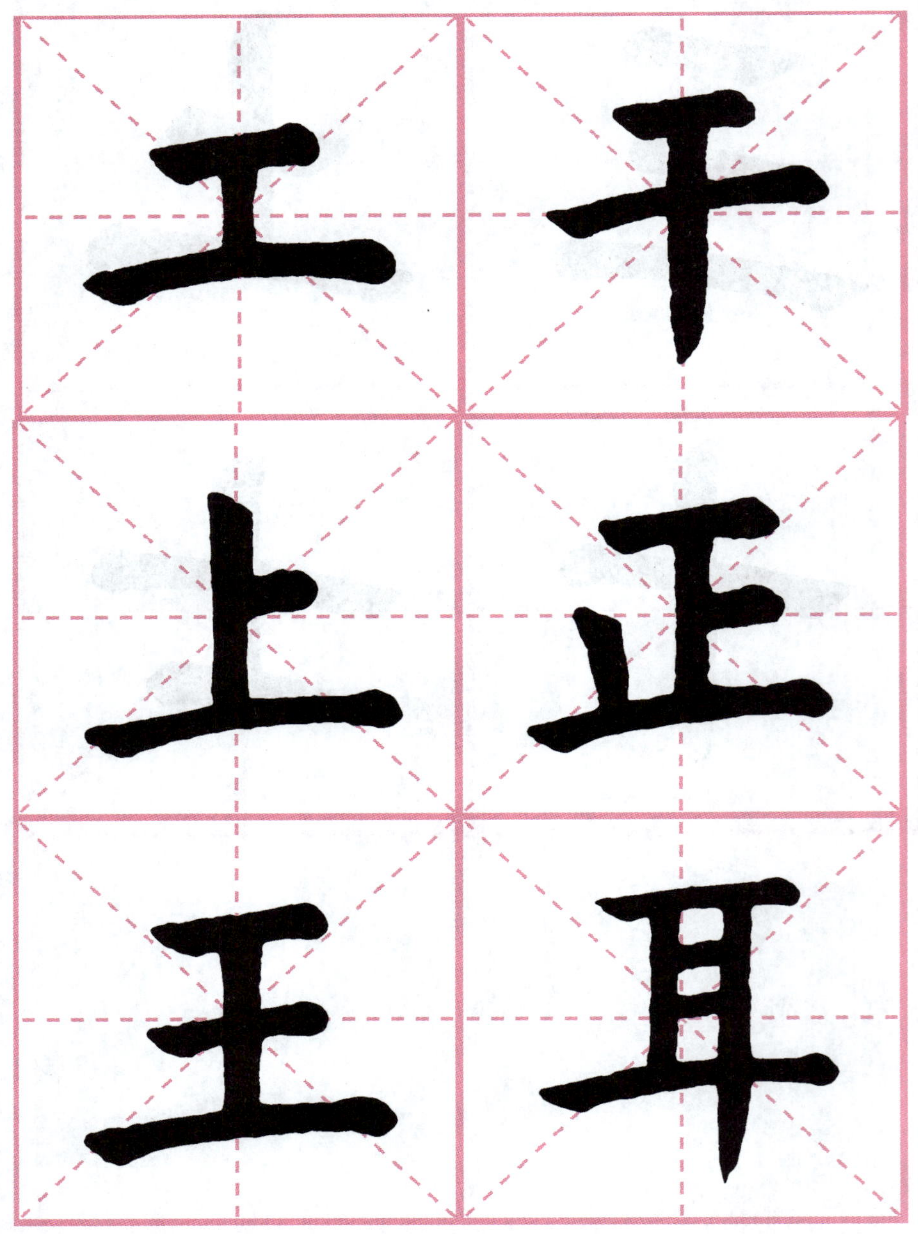

（2）练习二：点画练习

练习右侧点、左侧点、竖点、长点、出锋点、提点、撇点的写法。

"下"笔顺：一 丁 下

"卡"笔顺：丨 卜 上 卡 卡

"立"笔顺：丶 二 亠 立 立

"半"笔顺：丶 丷 丷 兰 半

"平"笔顺：一 丆 平 平 平

"六"笔顺：丶 亠 六 六

"羊"笔顺：丶 丷 兰 兰 兰 羊

"斗"笔顺：丶 丷 斗 斗

"江"笔顺：丶 冫 氵 汀 江 江

"其"笔顺：一 十 艹 艹 甘 其 其 其

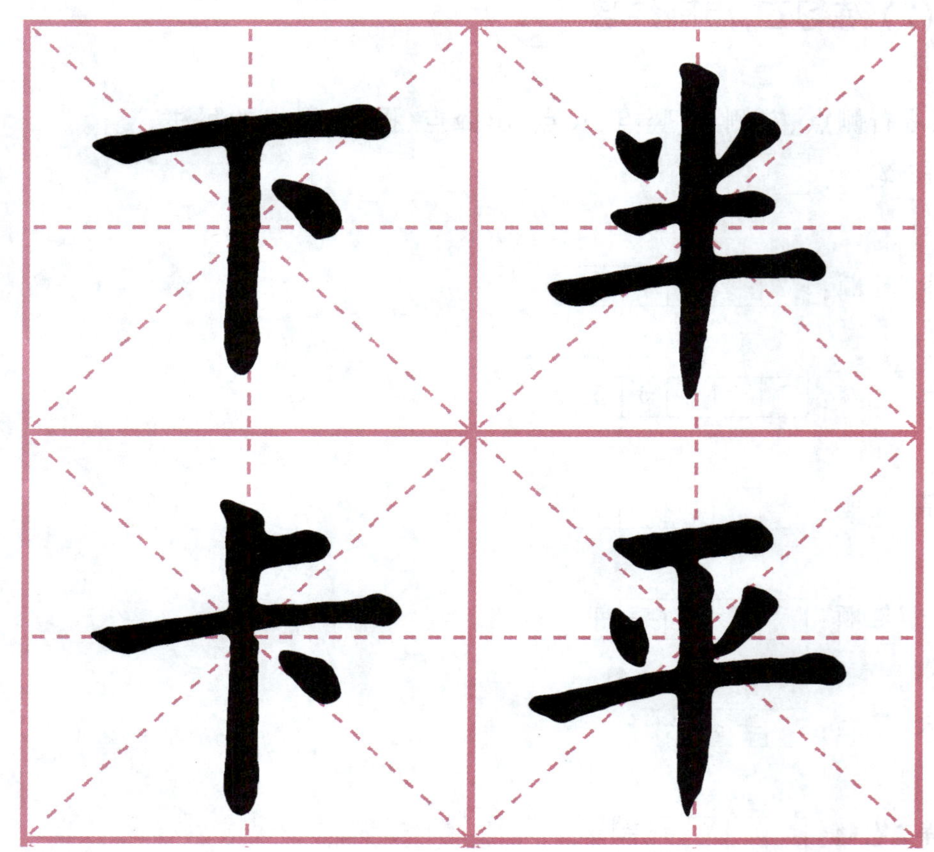

(2) Exercise 2　dot

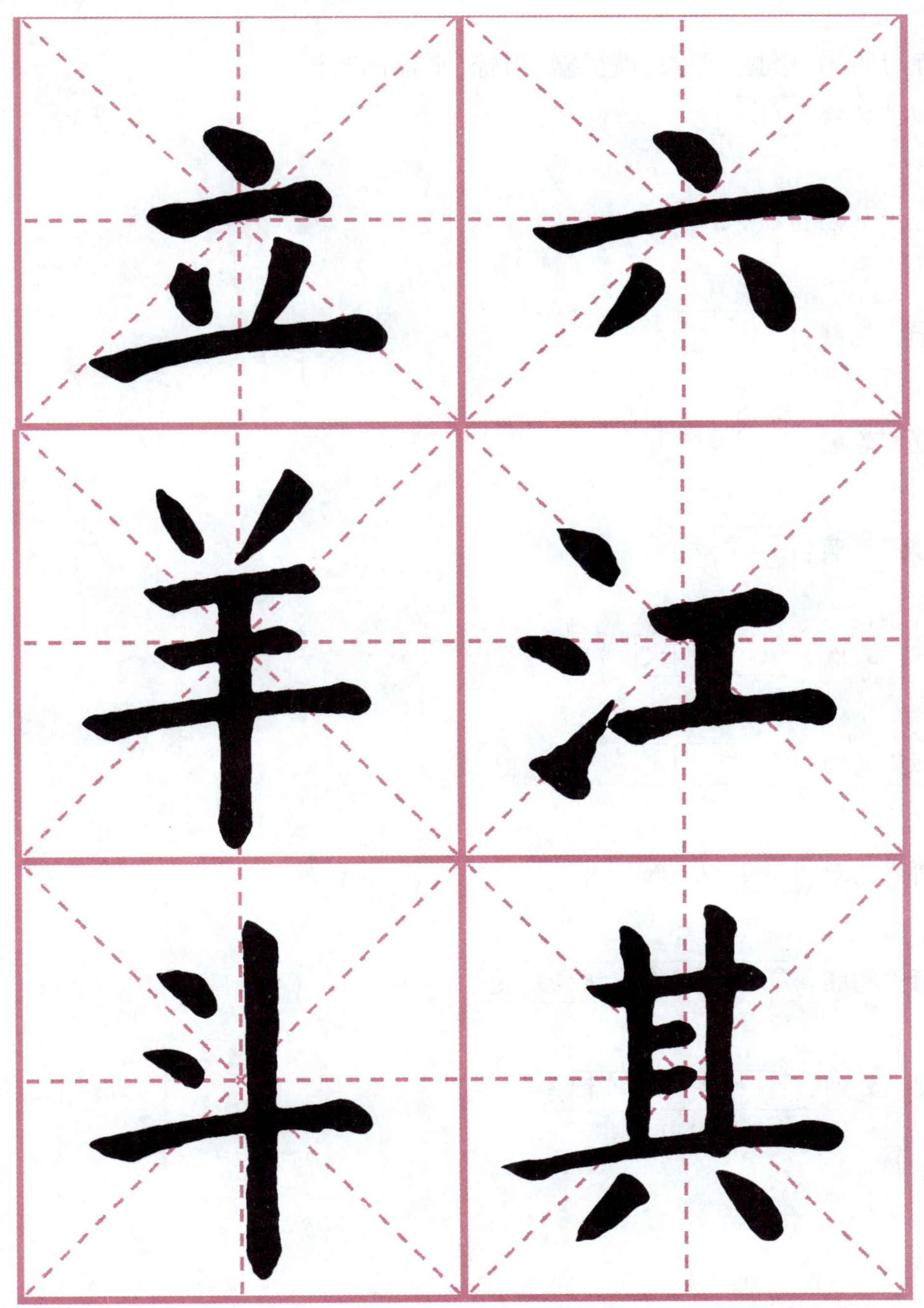

（3）练习三：撇画、捺画练习

练习斜撇、竖撇、平撇、横折撇、斜捺、平捺的写法。

"人"笔顺：丿 人

"八"笔顺：丿 八

"千"笔顺：丿 二 千

"斤"笔顺：丿 厂 斤 斤

"天"笔顺：一 二 于 天

"火"笔顺：丶 丷 少 火

"文"笔顺：丶 亠 ナ 文

"爪"笔顺：丿 厂 爪 爪

"受"笔顺：丿 爫 爫 爫 爫 受 受

"走"笔顺：一 十 土 キ キ 走 走

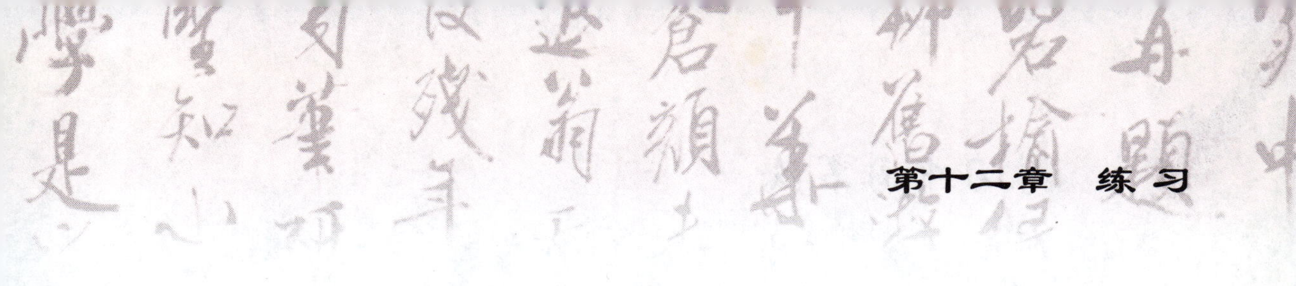

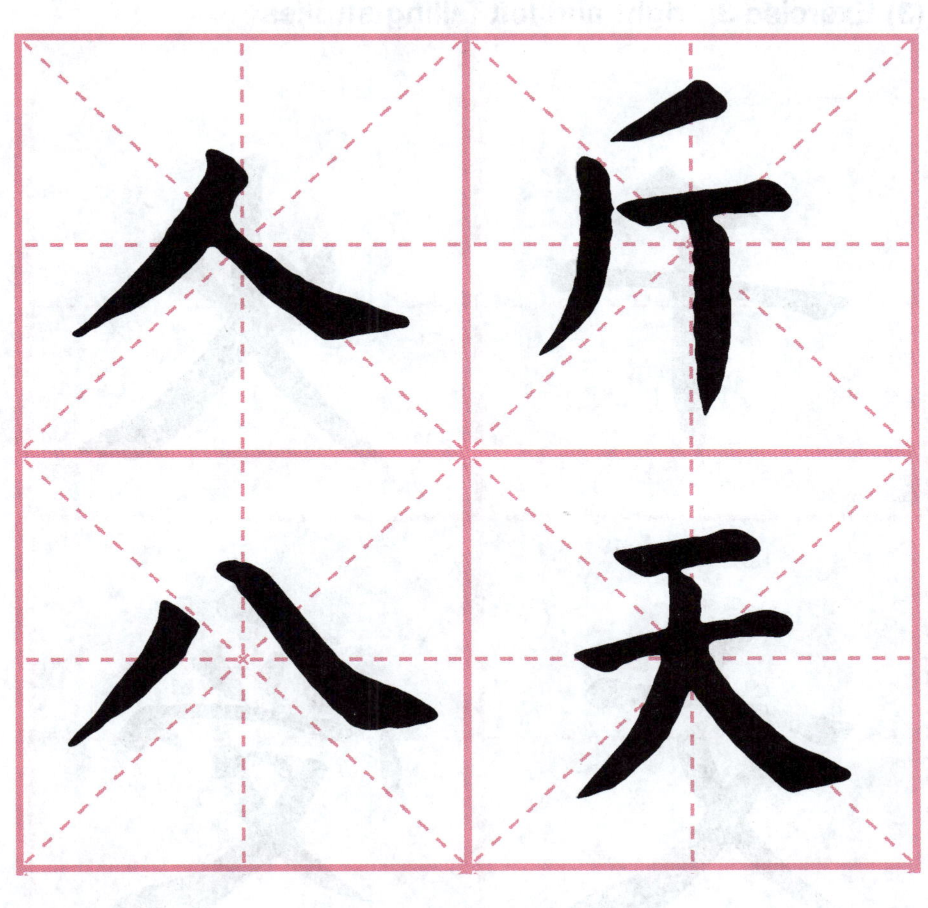

人
斤
八
天

(3) Exercise 3　right and left falling strokes

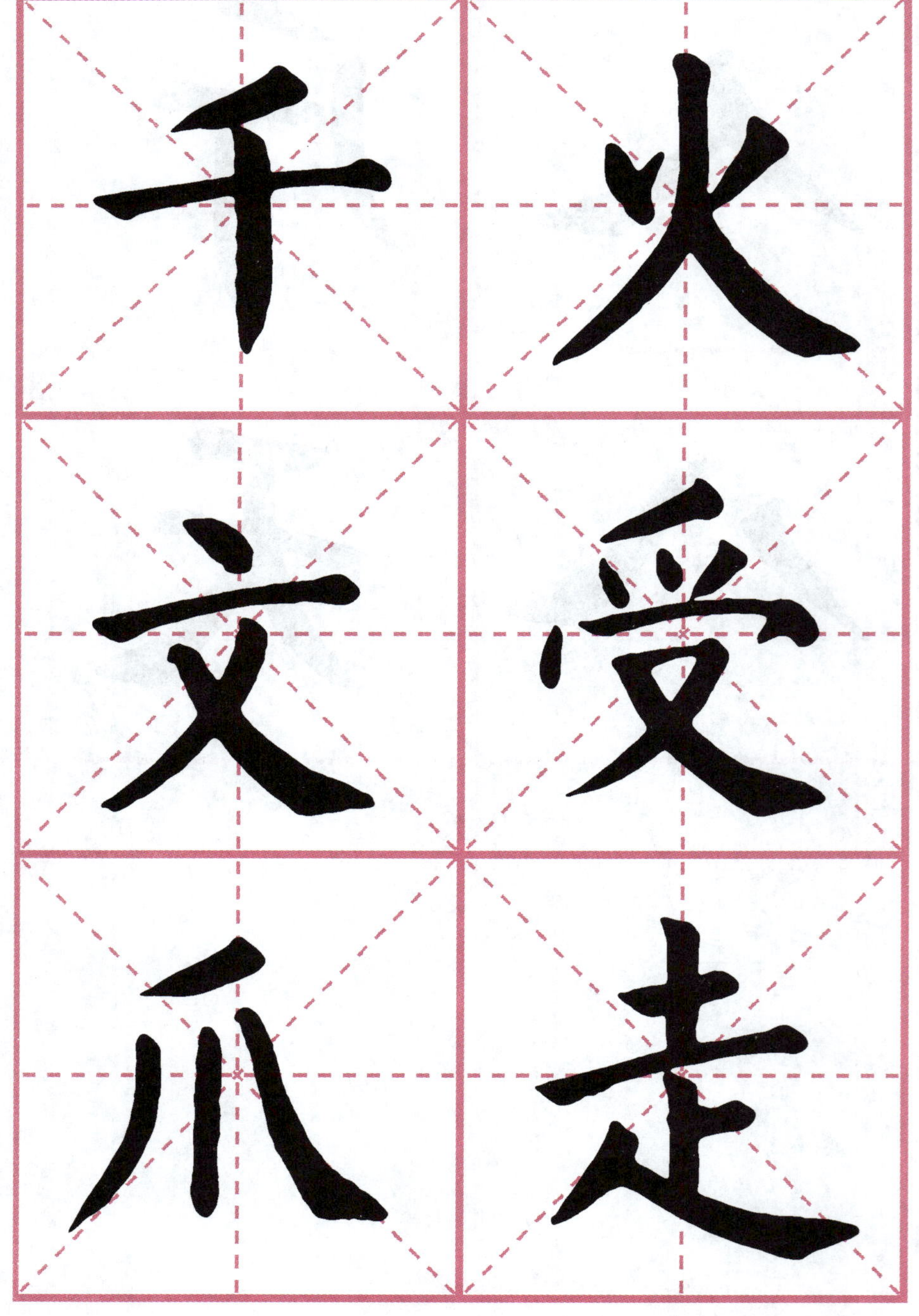

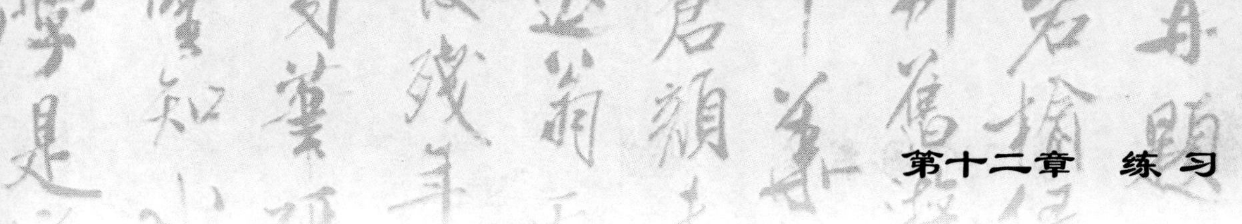

（4）练习四：钩画练习

练习竖钩、横钩、斜钩、反钩、竖弯钩、背抛钩、横折弯钩、横弯钩、耳钩的写法。

"木"笔顺：一 十 才 木

"乎"笔顺：一 丷 ⺍ 平 乎

"戈"笔顺：一 弋 戈 戈

"比"笔顺：一 比 比 比

"兆"笔顺：丿 丿 丬 北 兆 兆

"九"笔顺：丿 九

"凡"笔顺：丿 几 凡

"心"笔顺：丶 心 心 心

"毛"笔顺：丿 二 三 毛

"阮"笔顺：乛 阝 阝 阮 阮 阮

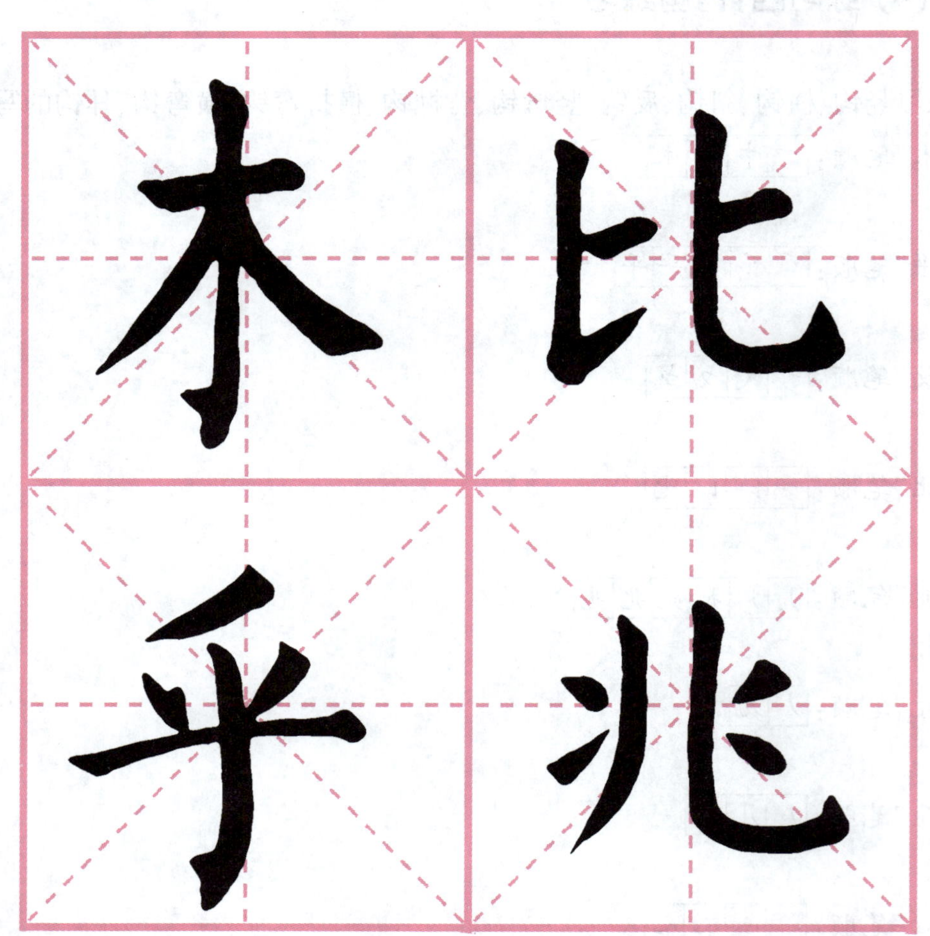

(4) Exercise 4　hook

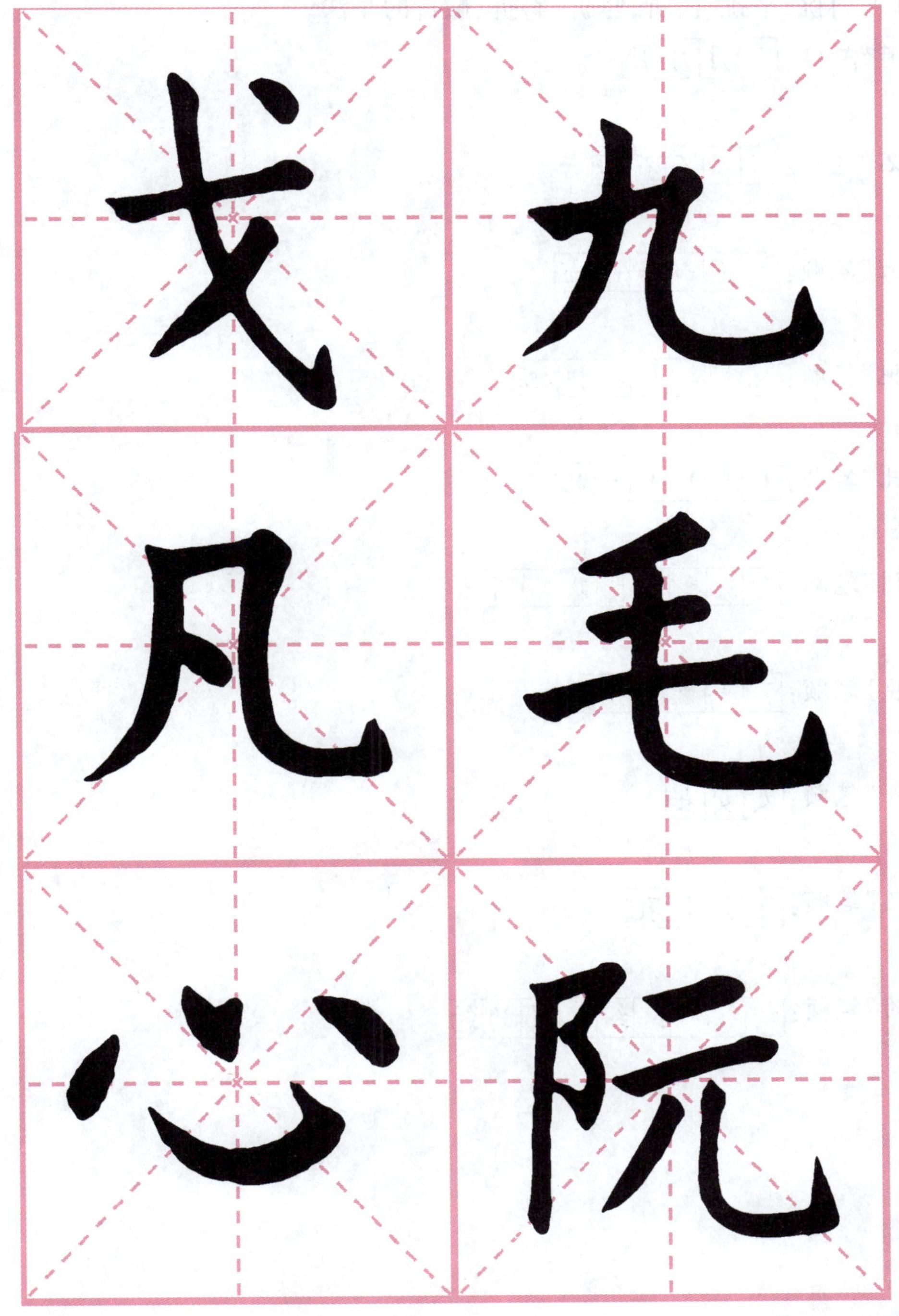

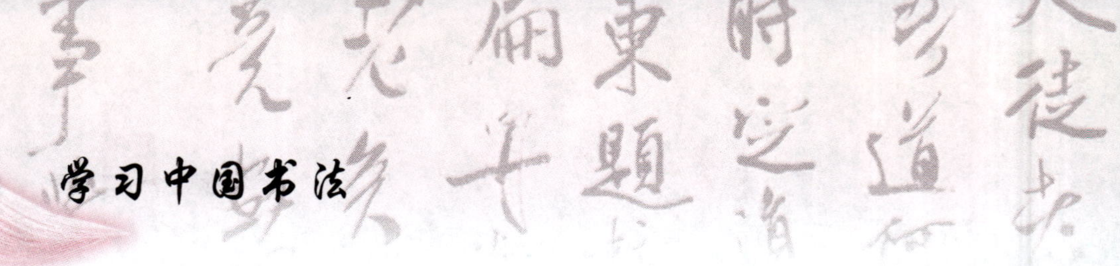

（5）练习五：挑画、折画练习

练习斜挑、平挑、横折、竖折、斜折、撇折的写法。

"月"笔顺：丿 几 月 月

"石"笔顺：一 ァ 不 石 石

"血"笔顺：丿 亻 白 血 血 血

"把"笔顺：一 十 扌 扫 扣 扣 把

"此"笔顺：丨 卜 此 止 此 此

"門"笔顺：丨 ㄱ ㅋ 月 門 門 門 門

"臣"笔顺：一 ㄷ 三 臣 臣 臣

"女"笔顺：乙 女 女

"孔"笔顺：乛 了 子 孔

"約"笔顺：乙 幺 幺 幺 糸 糸 糸 約 約

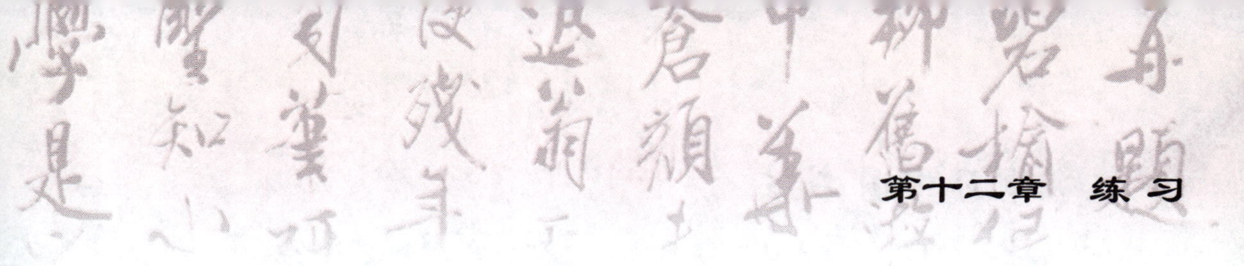

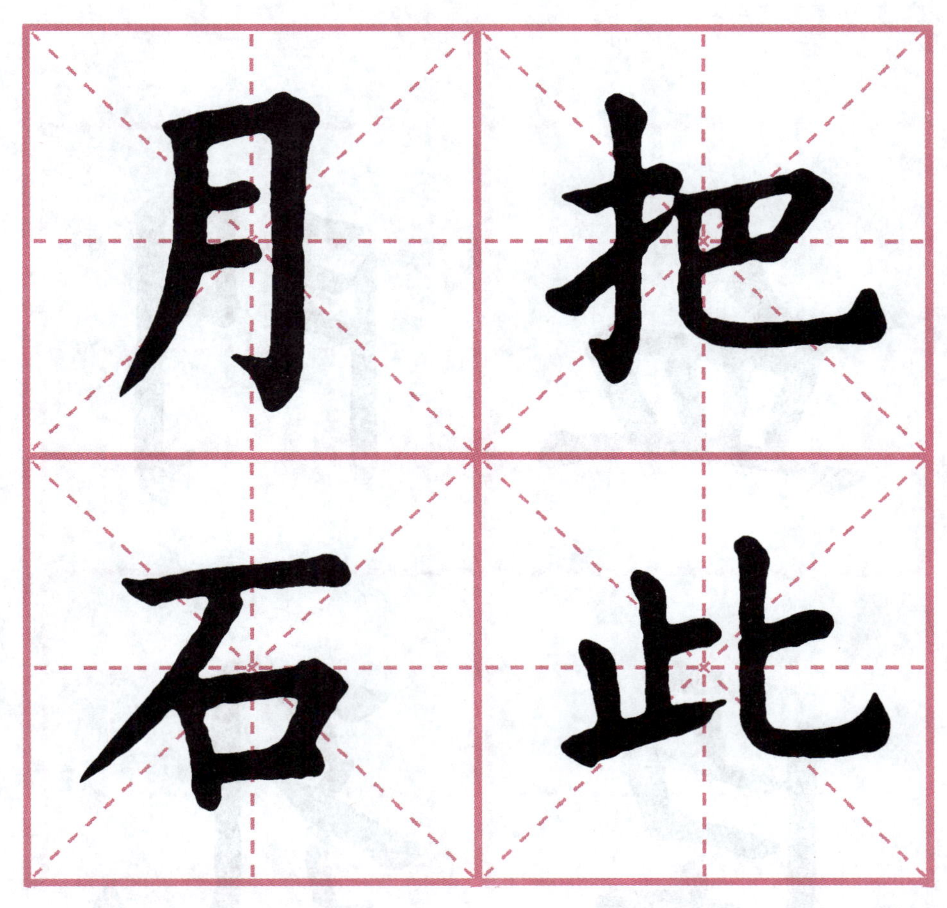

月 把
石 此

(5) Exercise 5　right rising strokes and turning strokes

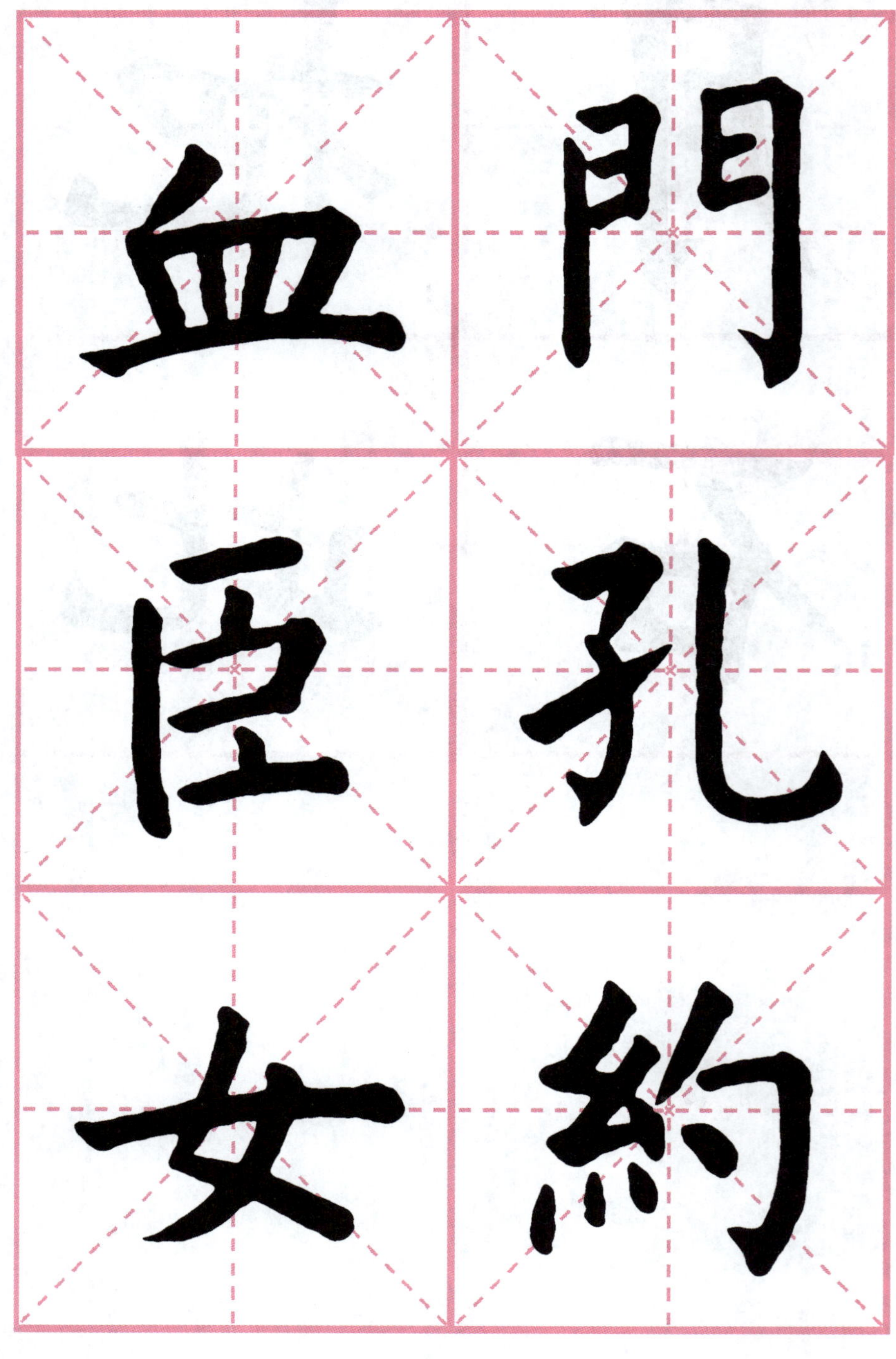

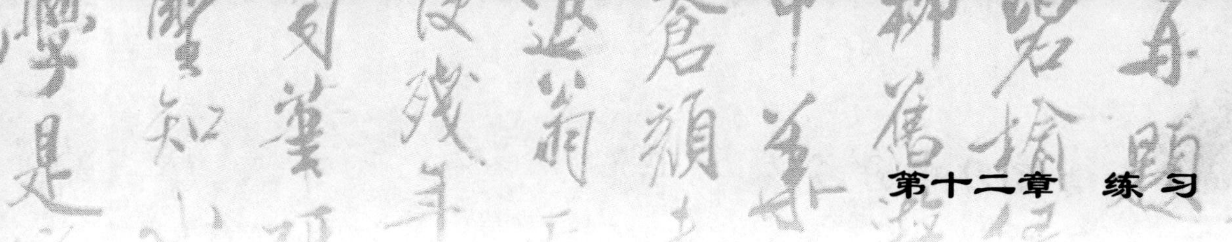

(6) 练习六：八种笔画综合练习

"句"笔顺：丿　勹　勹　句　句

"充"笔顺：丶　亠　云　云　产　充

"成"笔顺：一　厂　厂　成　成　成

"思"笔顺：丨　冂　囗　田　田　田　思　思　思

"以"笔顺：丨　乚　以　以　以

"好"笔顺：乚　夊　女　女　好　好

"母"笔顺：乚　母　母　母　母

"無"笔顺：丿　七　仁　仁　仨　無　無　無　無　無　無

"雲"笔顺：一　厂　冖　干　干　雨　雩　雩　雲　雲　雲

"風"笔顺：丿　几　凡　凡　凨　凨　風　風　風

"底"笔顺：丶　亠　广　户　庐　庐　底　底

"都"笔顺：一　十　土　尹　耂　者　者　都　都

句 思 充

以 成 好

(6) Exercise 6　combination of different strokes

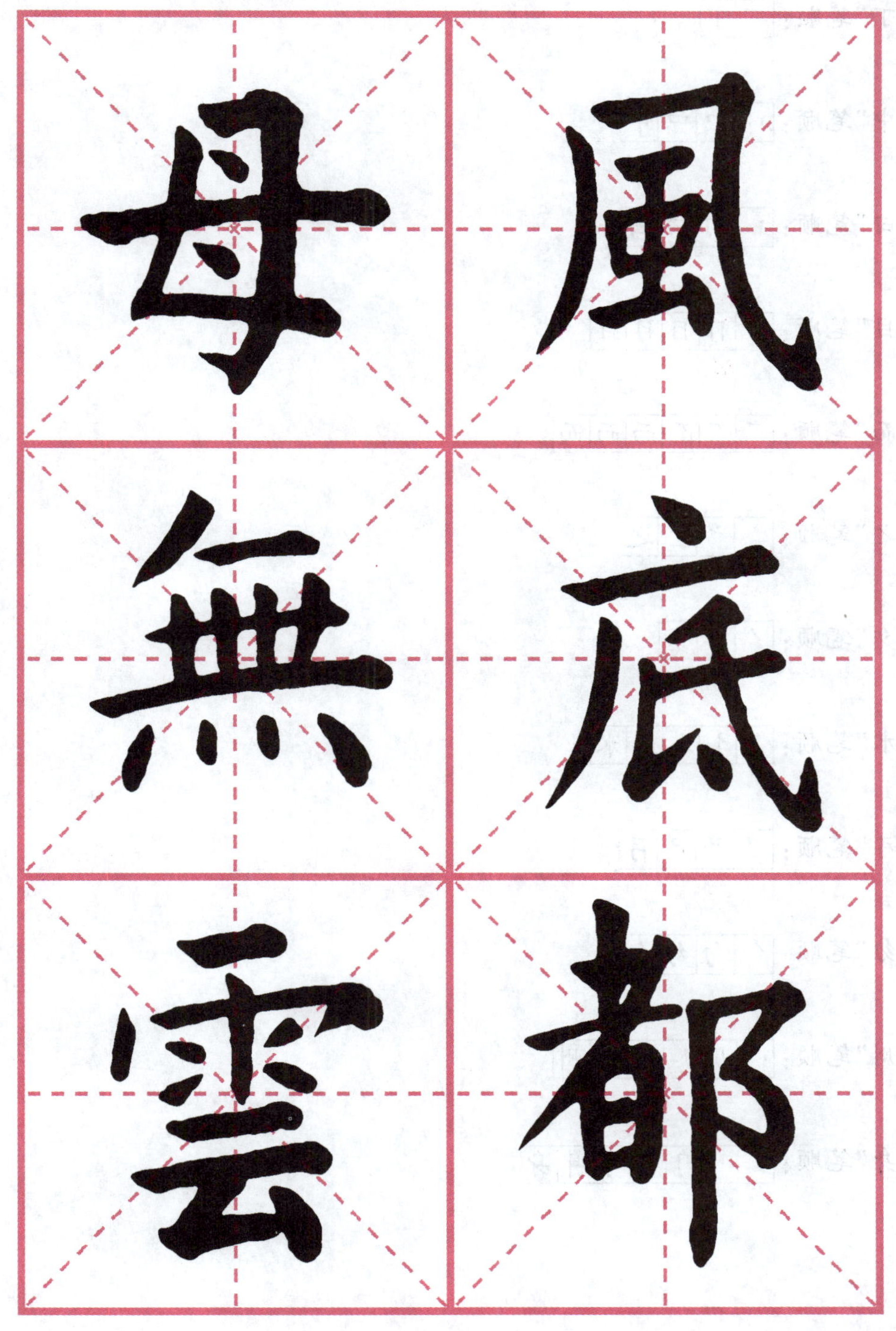

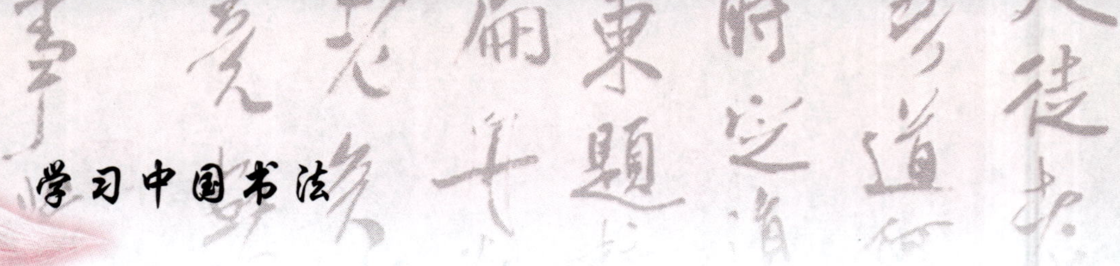

（7）练习七：笔画与独体字结构练习

"丁"笔顺：一 丁

"中"笔顺：丨 冂 口 中

"日"笔顺：丨 冂 日 日

"目"笔顺：丨 冂 月 月 目

"而"笔顺：一 丆 厂 丙 而 而

"之"笔顺：丶 冫 ㇇ 之

"夕"笔顺：丿 夂 夕

"水"笔顺：丨 ㇀ 水 水 水

"弓"笔顺：一 ㄱ 弓 弓

"勿"笔顺：丿 勹 勹 勿

"州"笔顺：丶 丬 少 州 州 州

"身"笔顺：丿 ㇀ 勹 自 自 身 身

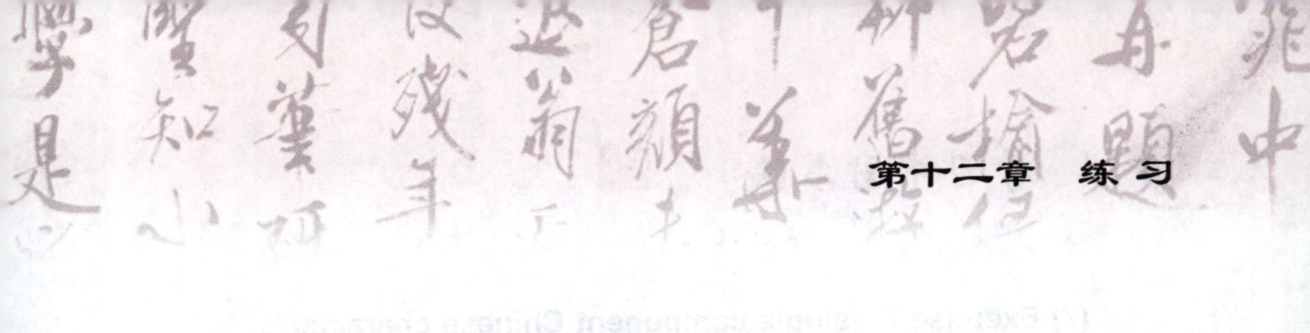

丁　目　中

而　曰　之

(7) Exercise 7　single component Chinese character

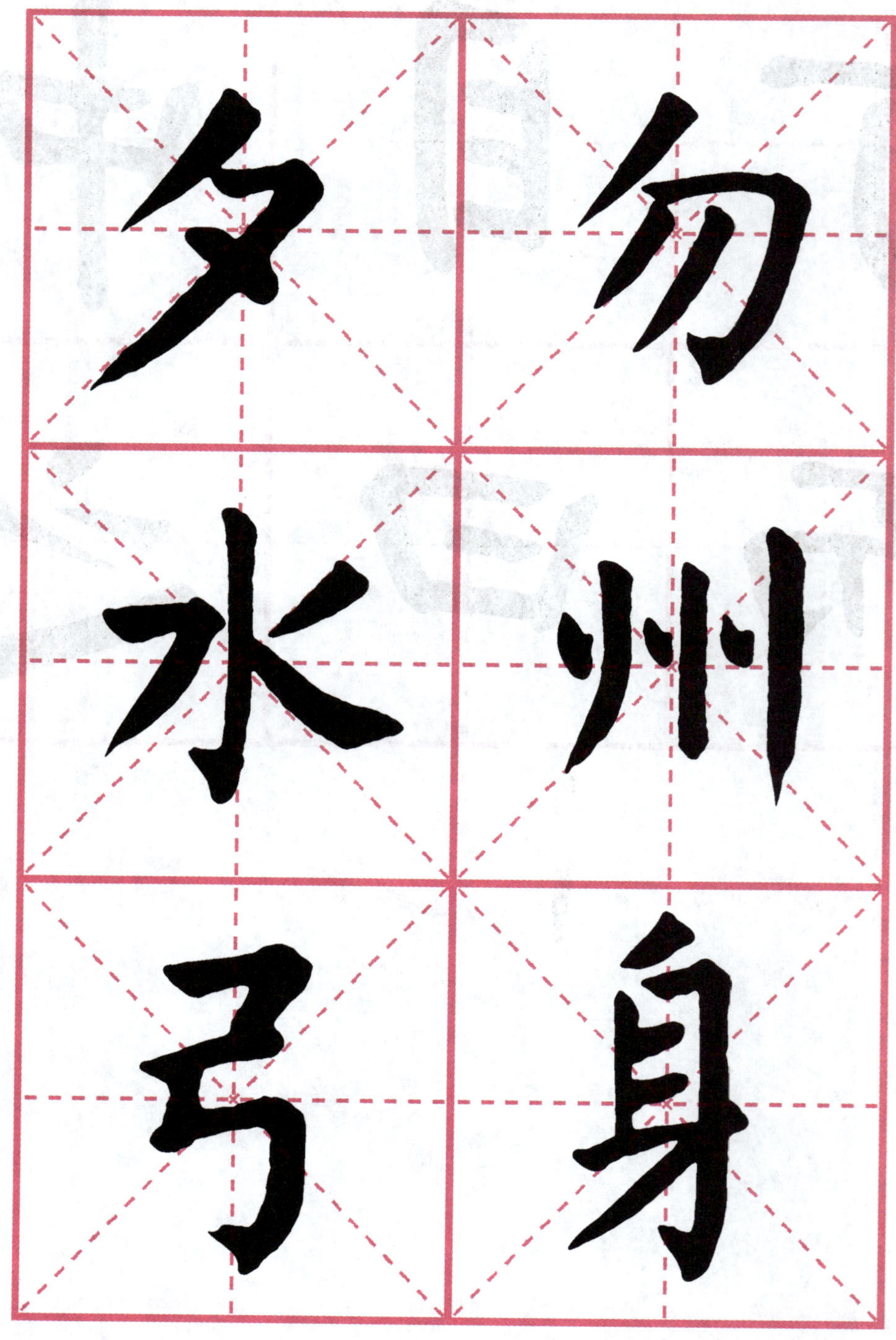

(8) 练习八：笔画与左右结构字形练习

“信”笔顺：

丿	亻	亻丶	亻亠	亻亠	亻言	亻言	信	信

“浪”笔顺：

丶	冫	氵	氵丶	氵丶	氵良	氵良	浪	浪	浪

“塘”笔顺：

一	十	土	土丶	土亠	圹	圹	塘	塘	塘	塘	塘	塘

“刻”笔顺：

丶	亠	亠	亥	亥	亥	亥	刻

“林”笔顺：

一	十	才	木	木一	村	材	林

“锡”笔顺：

丿	𠂉	𠂉	乍	乍	钅	钅	钅	钅	钅	钅	钅	钅	锡	锡	锡

“印”笔顺：

丿	𠂆	𠂉	印	印

“部”笔顺：

丶	亠	亠	立	立	立	咅	咅	部	部

“初”笔顺：

丶	㇇	礻	衤	衤	初	初

“叔”笔顺：

丨	卜	上	未	未	未	叔	叔

“如”笔顺：

𡿨	女	女	如	如	如

“和”笔顺：

丿	二	千	千	禾	禾	和	和

信 刻 浪
林 塘 錫

(8) Exercise 8　Chinese character with right and left components

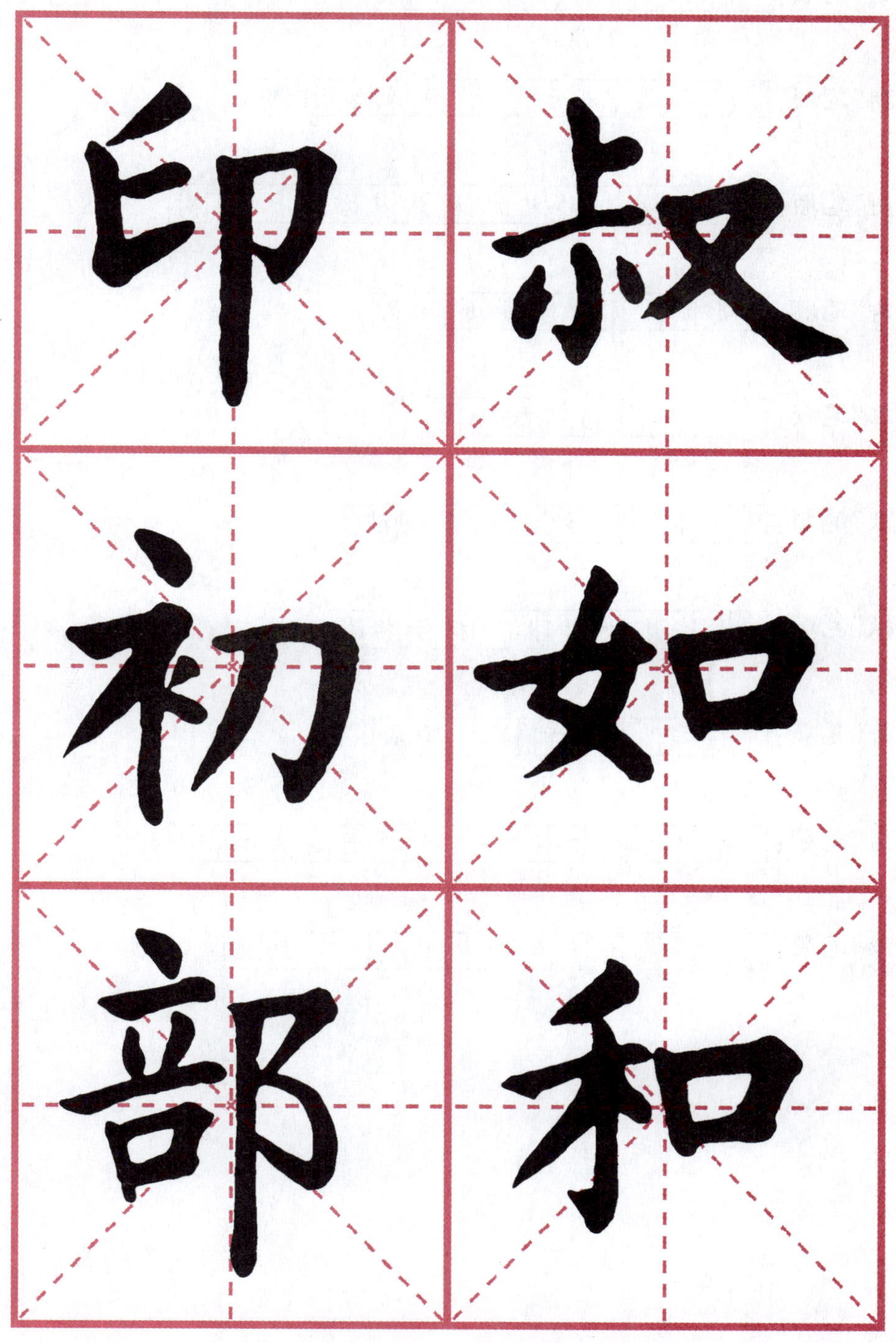

（9）练习九：笔画与左中右结构字形练习

"做"笔顺：丿 亻 仁 什 什 估 估 做 做 做 做

"潮"笔顺：丶 氵 氵 浐 浐 浐 泸 泸 洎 渔 漳 潮 潮 潮

"树"笔顺：一 十 オ 木 オ 村 杧 材 桔 桔 桔 桔 椲 椲 樹 樹

"脚"笔顺：丿 几 月 月 肝 肝 肚 胠 胠 脚 脚

"班"笔顺：一 二 干 王 王 班 玪 玪 班 班

"袱"笔顺：丶 ラ オ 衤 衤 衤 衻 衻 袱 袱

"揪"笔顺：一 十 扌 扌 扩 扩 抃 抃 抪 揪 揪

"聊"笔顺：一 丁 F F E 耳 耴 耴 聊 聊

"谢"笔顺：丶 丷 亠 三 言 言 訂 訂 訒 訮 謝 謝 謝 謝

"锄"笔顺：丿 八 乞 乍 乍 全 全 金 鈤 鉬 鉬 鉬 鋤 鋤

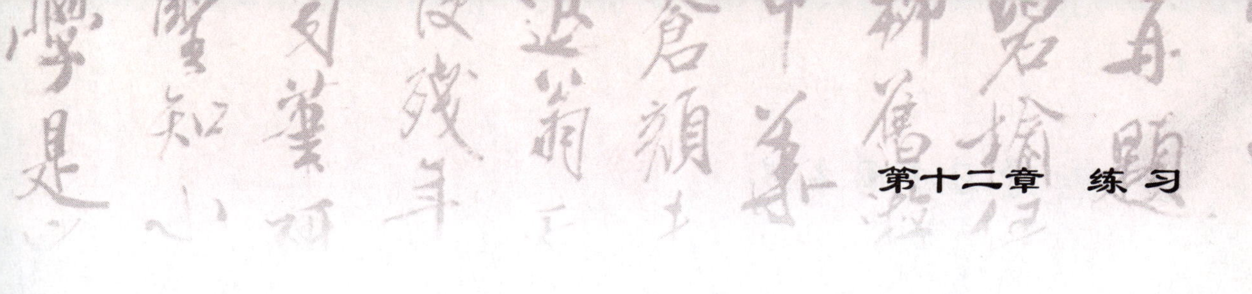

做　脚

潮　班

**(9) Exercise 9   Chinese character with three components:
left, middle and right**

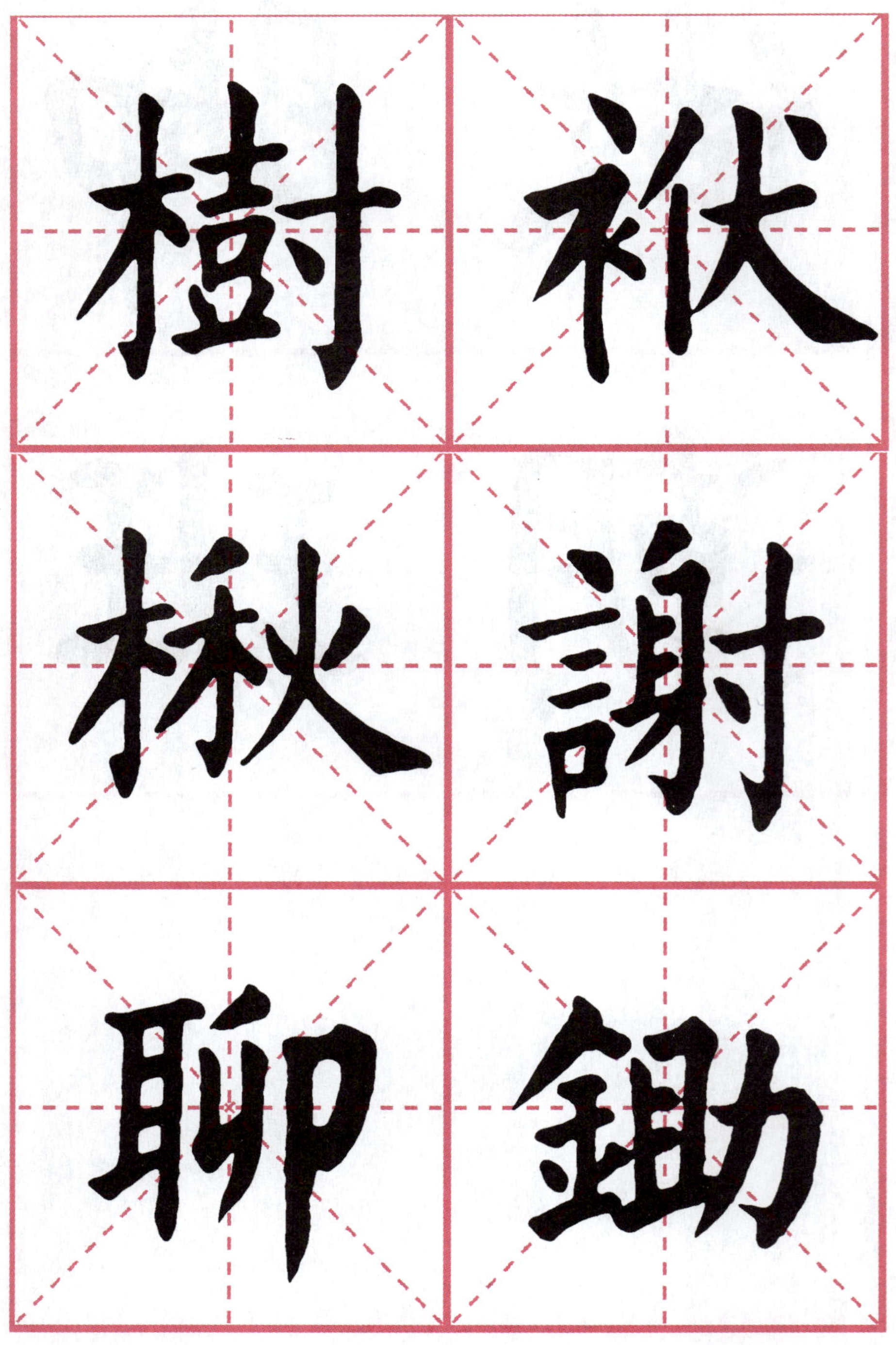

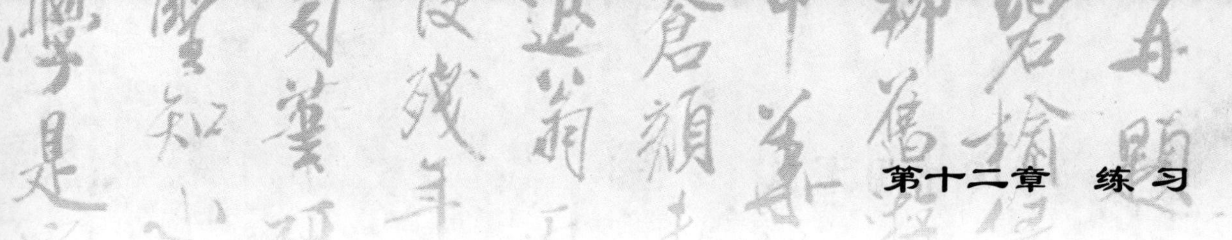

(10) 练习十：笔画与上下结构、上中下结构字形练习

"昌"笔顺：丶冂冂日旦昌昌昌

"多"笔顺：丿夕夕多多

"普"笔顺：丶丷丷广并并並並普普普

"奇"笔顺：一大大大奇奇奇

"奥"笔顺：丿冂冂冂冂向向向奥奥奥

"家"笔顺：丶丶宀宀宀宁宏家家

"需"笔顺：一一二千千雨雨雷雷需需需需

"賣"笔顺：一十士吉吉吉吉吉青青膏膏賣賣

"曼"笔顺：丶冂曰日旦昌昌昌昙曼

"墨"笔顺：丶冂冂冂四四里里里里黑黑黑墨墨

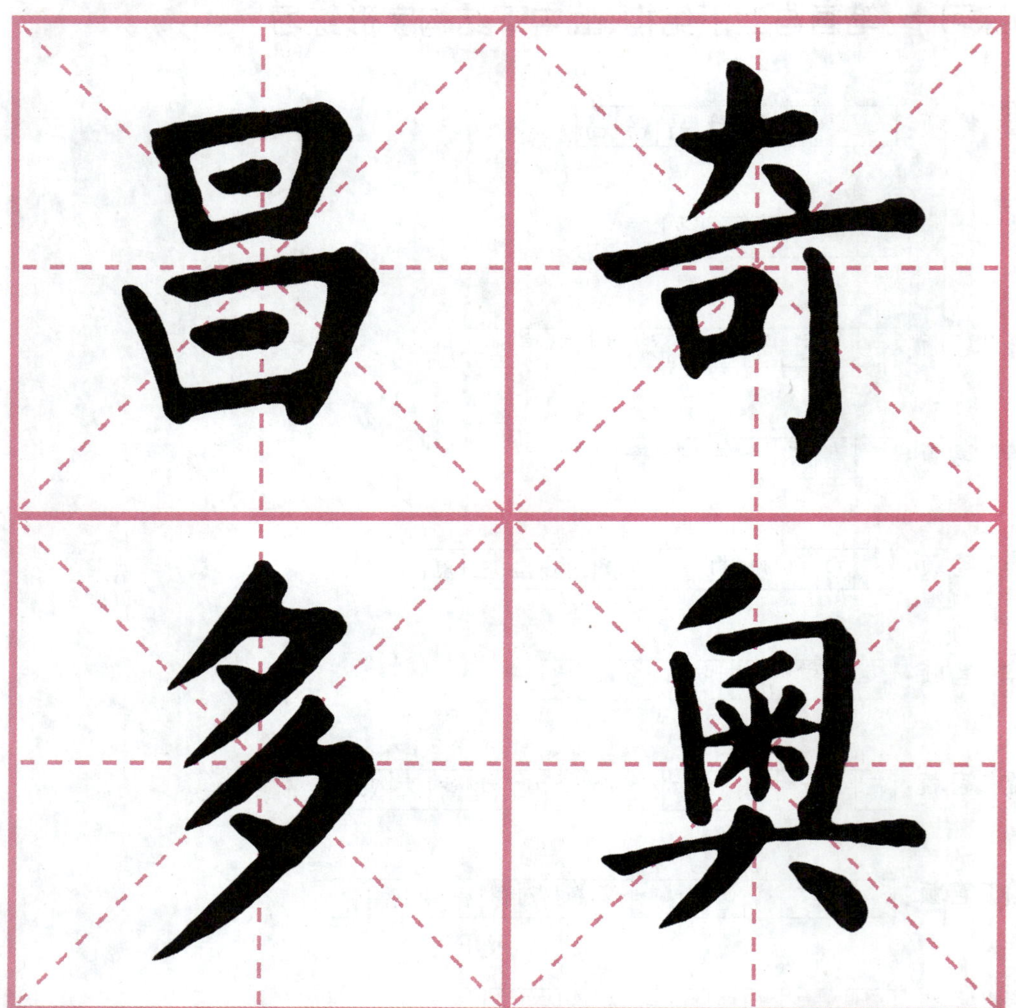

昌
奇
多
奥

(10) Exercise 10　Chinese characters with upper and lower component, upper middle and lower components

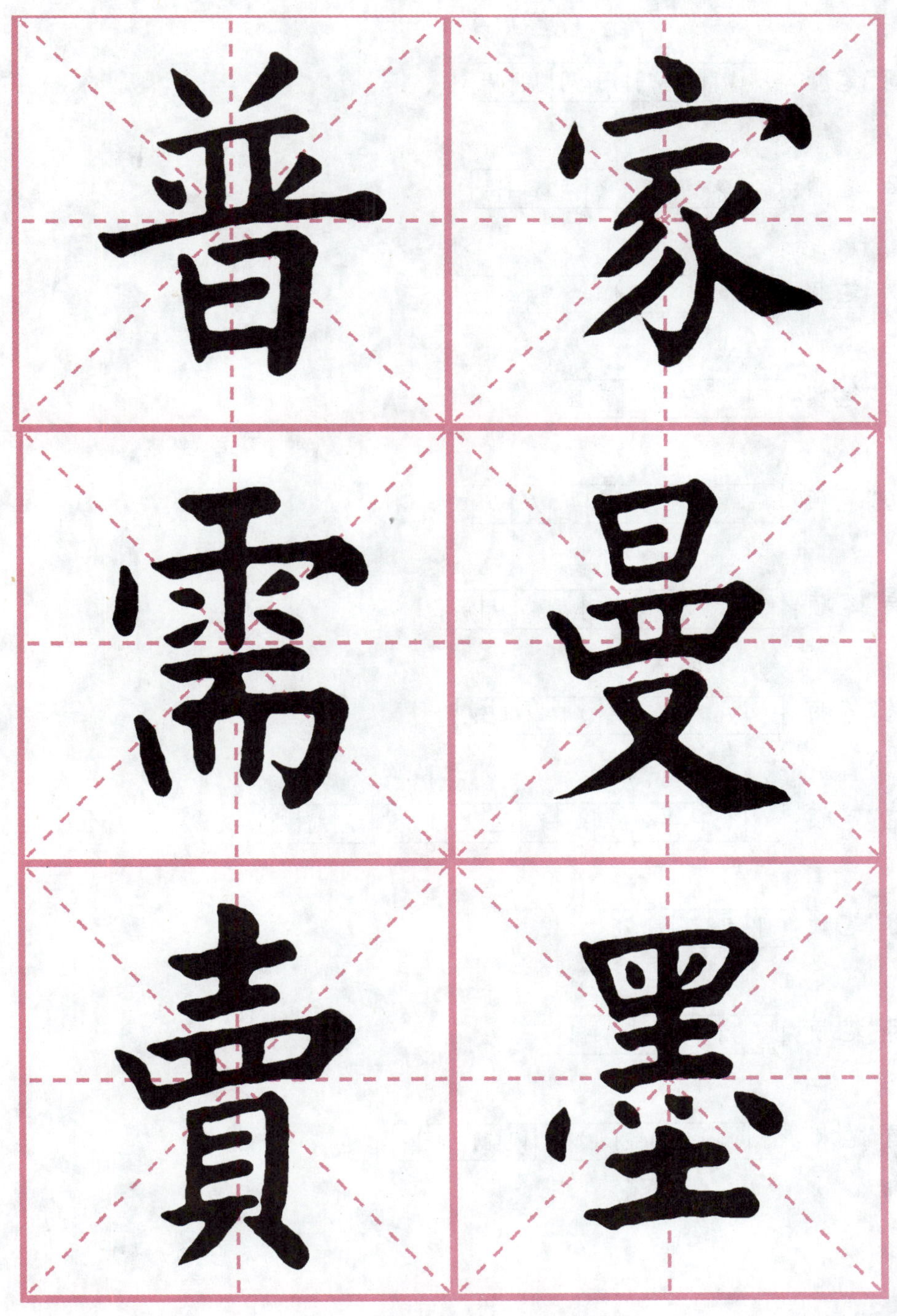

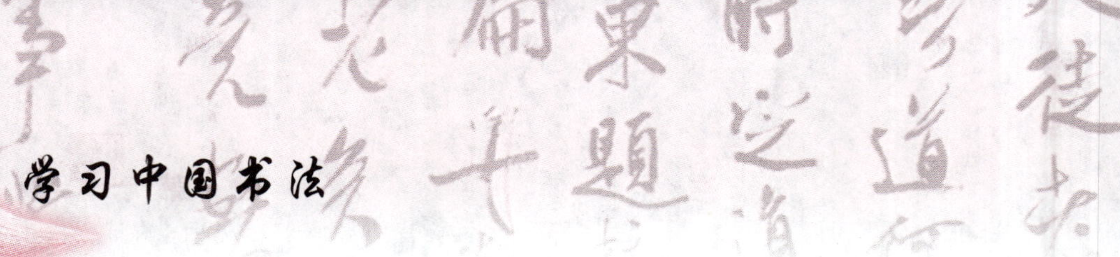

(11) 练习十一：笔画与半包围结构、全包围结构字形练习

"同"笔顺：丨 冂 冂 冋 同 同

"周"笔顺：丿 冂 月 冃 冄 用 周 周

"函"笔顺：乛 了 了 丐 丞 录 函 函

"幽"笔顺：丨 屮 纵 丝 丝 丝 丝 幽

"匠"笔顺：一 丆 厂 斤 斤 斤 匠

"居"笔顺：乛 コ 尸 尸 尻 居 居

"病"笔顺：丶 冫 广 广 疒 疒 疒 病 病 病

"送"笔顺：丶 丷 兰 兰 关 关 关 诶 送

"赵"笔顺：一 十 土 丰 丰 走 走 赵 赵 赵 赵 赵 赵

"司"笔顺：丁 刁 司 司 司

"因"笔顺：丨 冂 冂 円 因 因

"國"笔顺：丨 冂 冂 冋 囯 囯 囶 國 國 國 國

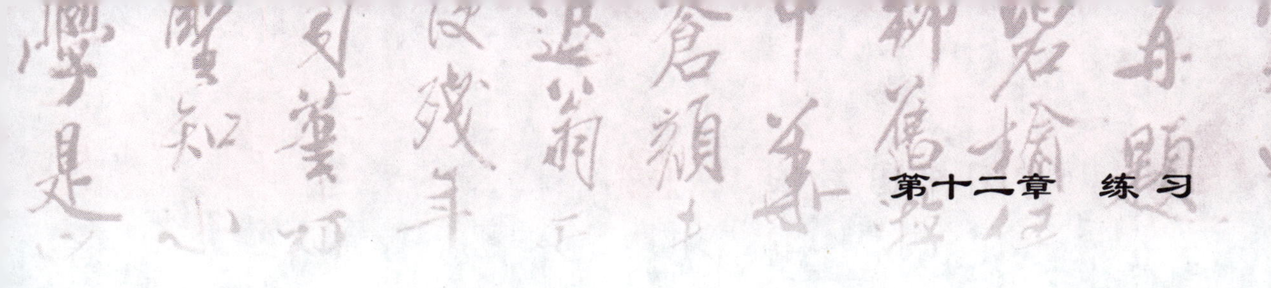

同　幽　周

匠　函　居

(11) Exercise 11　Chinese characters with partially enclosed and completely enclosed structure

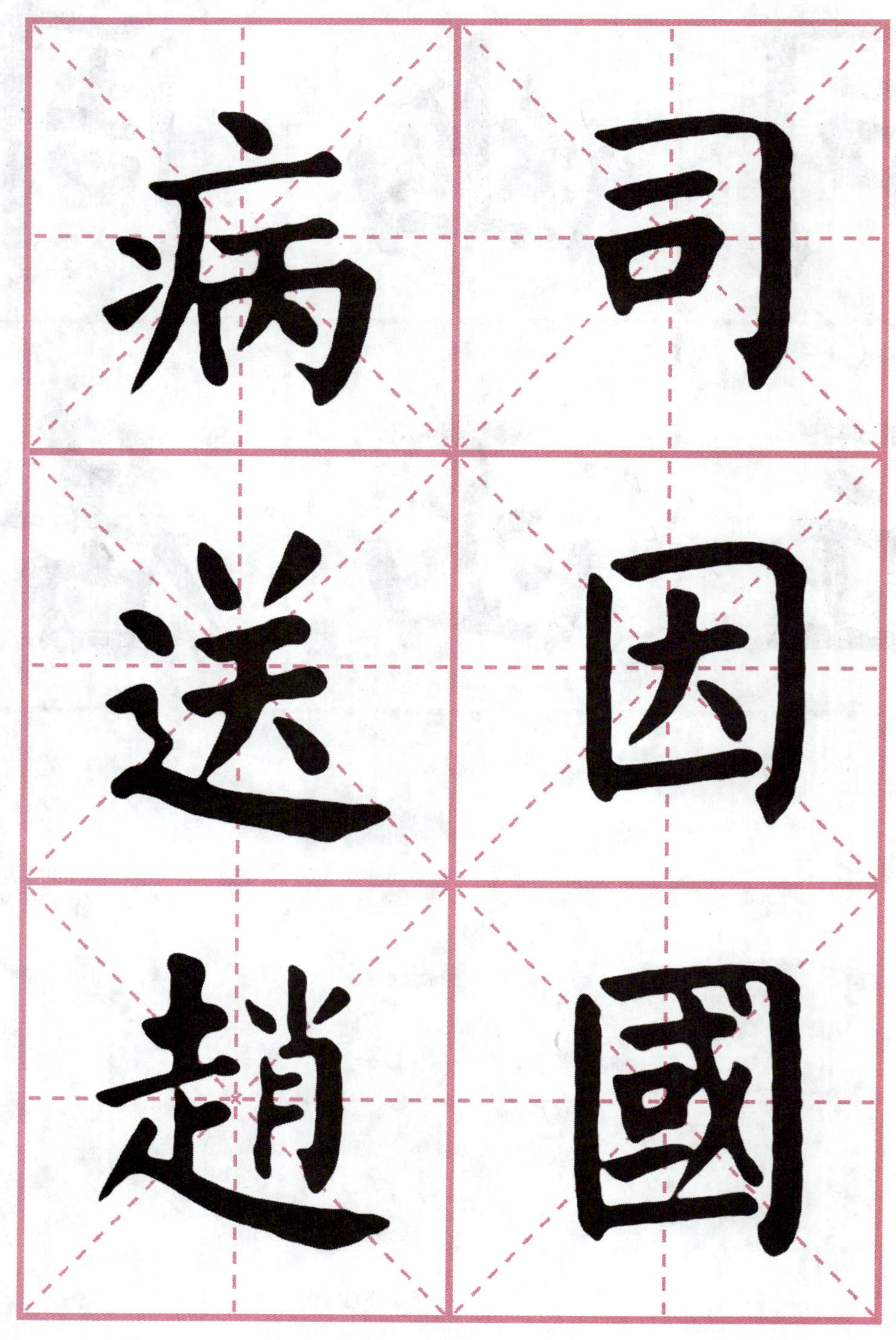

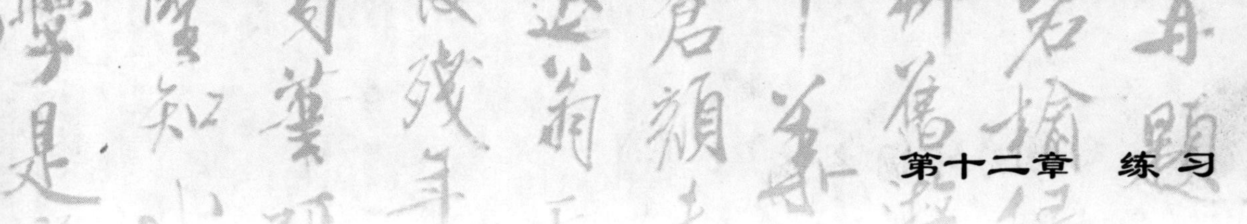

(12) 练习十二：笔画与复杂结构字形练习

"品"笔顺：丶 丨 口 口 吊 品 品 品 品

"處"笔顺：丶 卜 上 广 户 卢 虍 虍 虎 處 處

"婚"笔顺：乚 夊 女 妁 妒 妌 娇 娇 婚 婚

"婆"笔顺：丶 冫 氵 汀 汻 波 波 波 婆 婆

"案"笔顺：丶 丷 宀 宀 安 安 安 窀 案 案

"摩"笔顺：丶 二 广 广 庁 庁 庁 庁 府 麻 麻 摩 摩 摩

"嘉"笔顺：一 十 土 吉 吉 吉 壴 壴 壴 亭 嘉 嘉 嘉 嘉

"墜"笔顺：阝 阝 阝 阝 队 阵 陔 陔 隊 隊 墜 墜 墜

"盤"笔顺：丿 冂 刀 月 月 舟 舟 舟 般 般 般 般 盤 盤

"靠"笔顺：丿 广 牛 牛 牛 告 告 告 靠 靠 靠 靠 靠

"器"笔顺：丶 口 吅 吅 吅 吅 罒 咢 哭 哭 器 器 器 器

"腾"笔顺：丿 刀 月 月 月 胩 胩 胖 胖 朕 腾 腾 腾 腾 腾 腾 腾 腾

品　婆　處

察　婚　摩

(12) Exercise 12　complicated Chinese characters

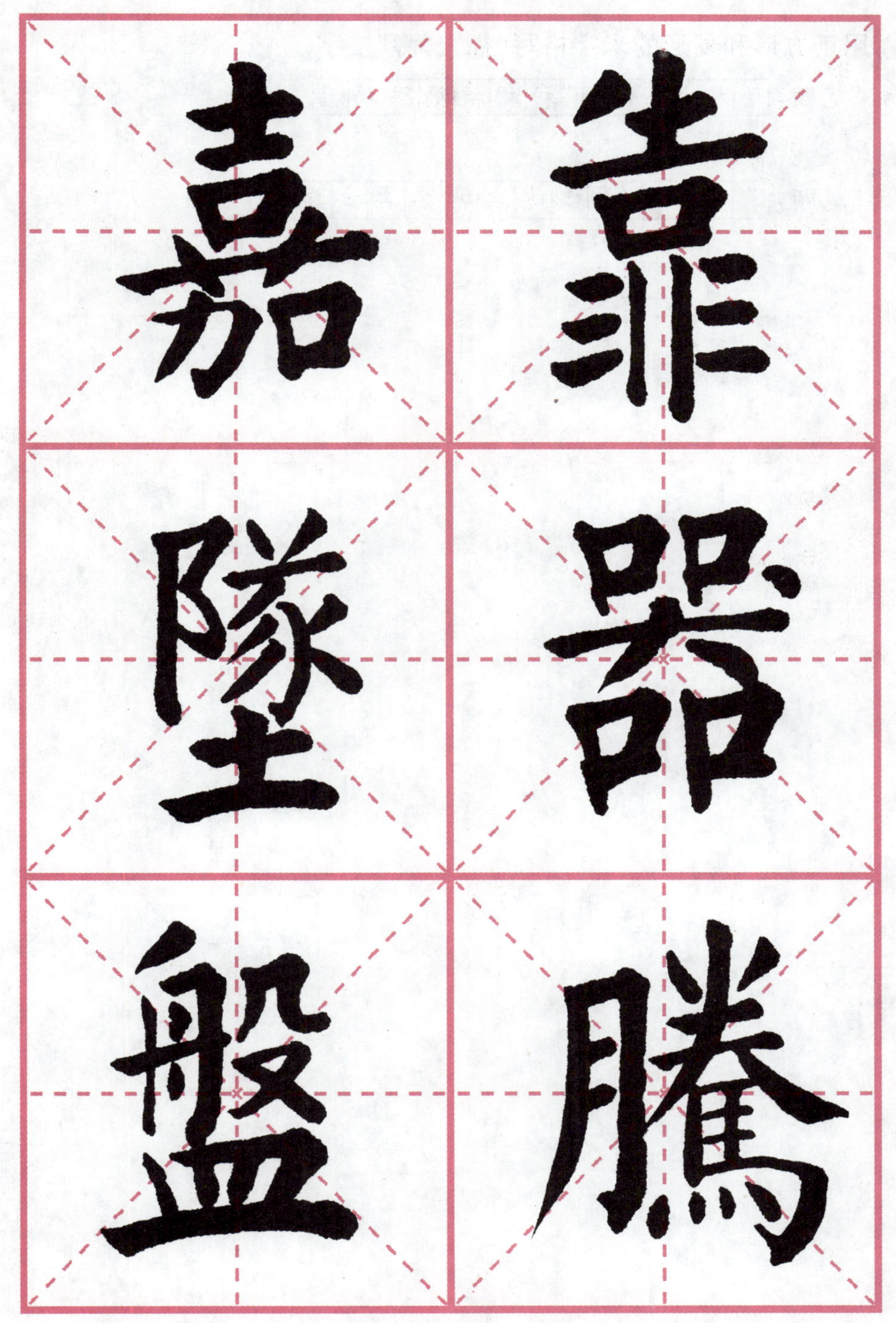

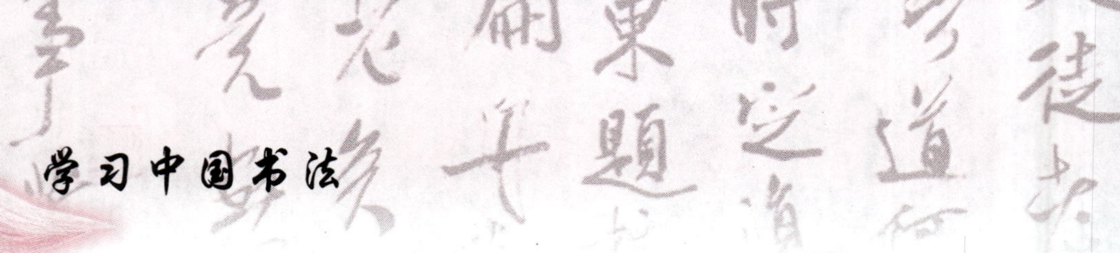

(13) 练习十三：综合练习（一）

1) 用正方形和菱形的米字格写"福"、"寿"二字。

"福"笔顺： ` ラ オ ネ 衤 祀 祀 祀 祀 禍 禃 福 福

"寿"笔顺： 一 十 圡 圭 丰 寺 寺 寿 寿 寿 寿 寿 寿

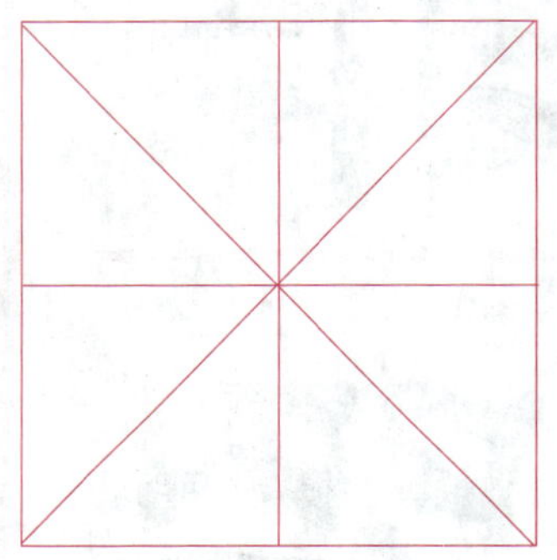

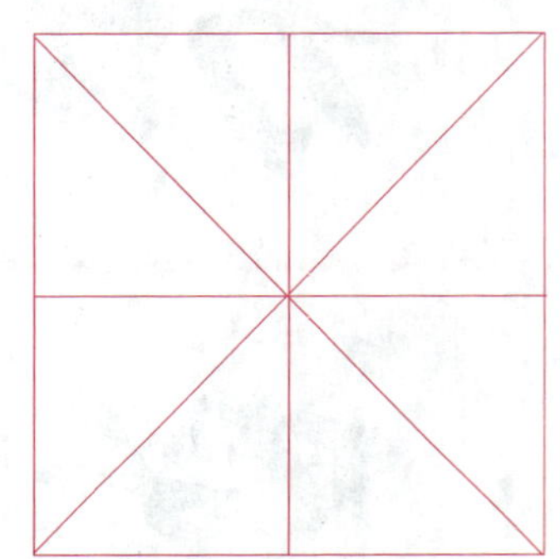

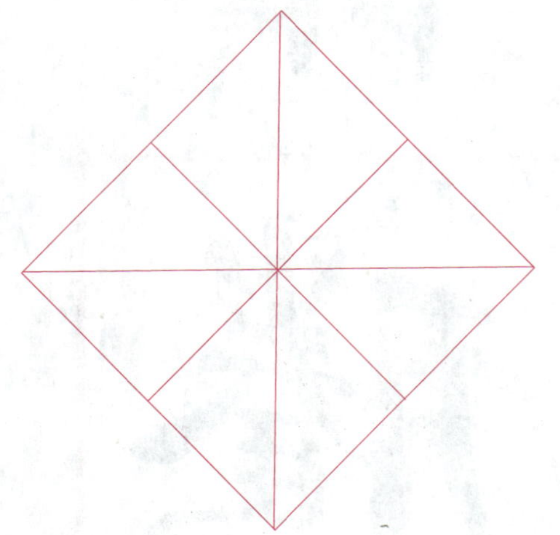

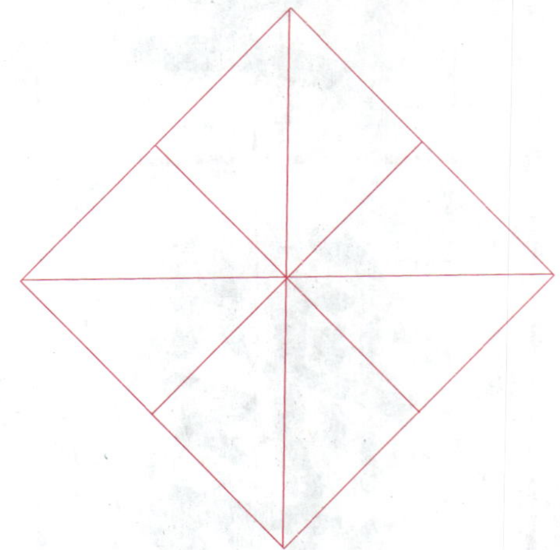

(13) Exercise 13　comprehensive exercise I

1) To practice the Character "福" and "壽" on pracrice sheets ("Mi Zi" and "Jiu Gong Ge").

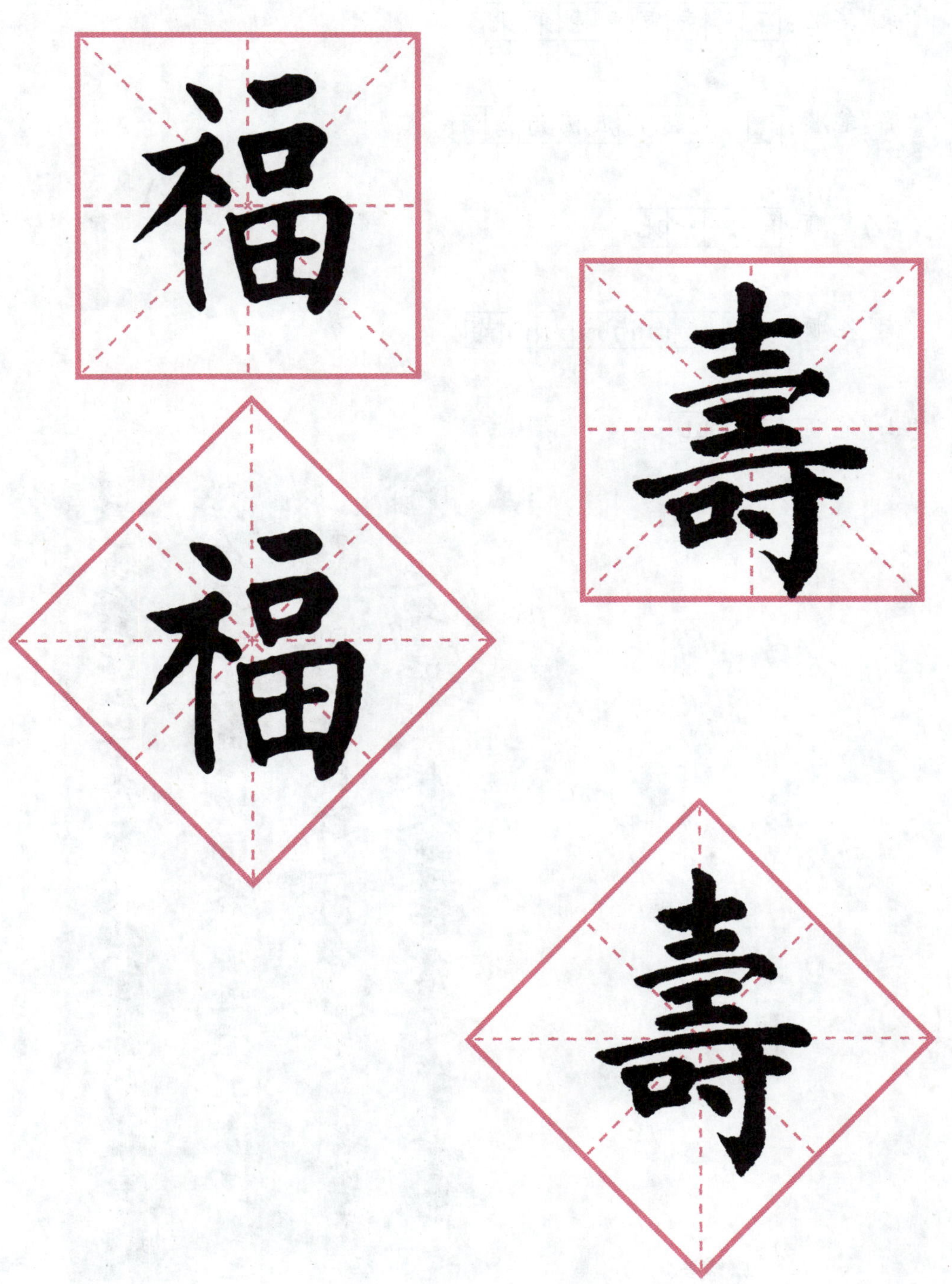

2) 用较大尺寸的宣纸写"福如東海，壽比南山"。

"如"笔顺：し 夕 女 如 如 如

"東"笔顺：一 厂 闩 甫 甫 東 東

"海"笔顺：、 冫 氵 沪 汇 海 海 海 海

"比"笔顺：一 上 比 比

"南"笔顺：一 十 十 内 内 内 南 南 南

"山"笔顺：｜ 凵 山

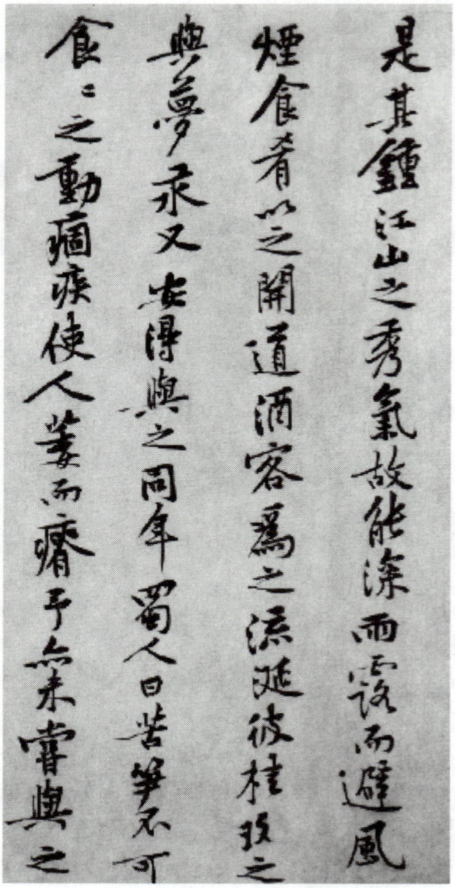

*《苦笋赋》

2) Use 2 feet or 3 feet "Xuan paper" to write the following couplet.

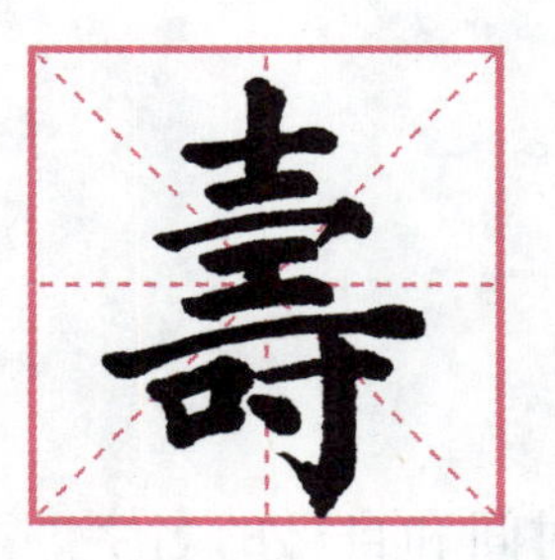 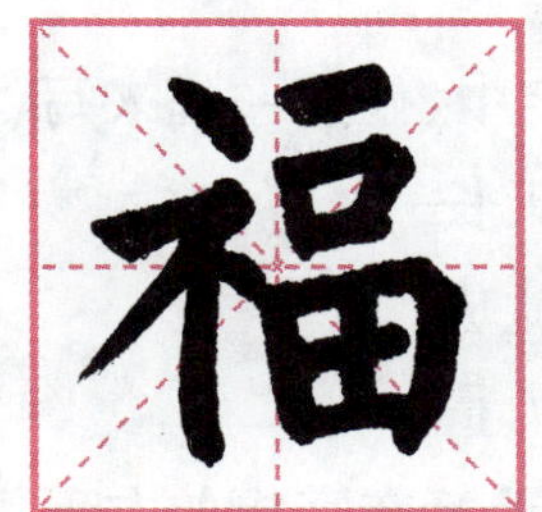

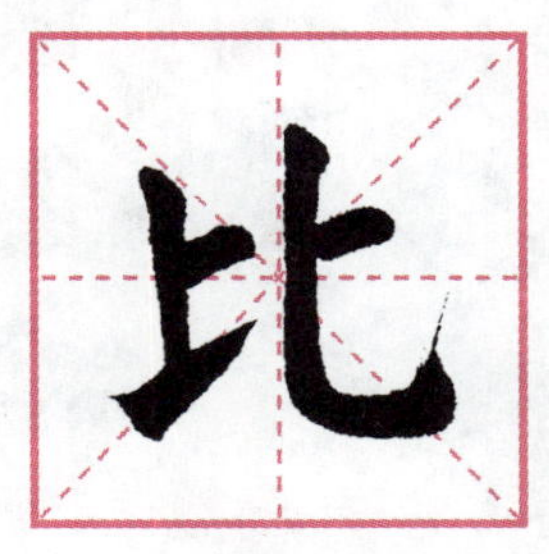 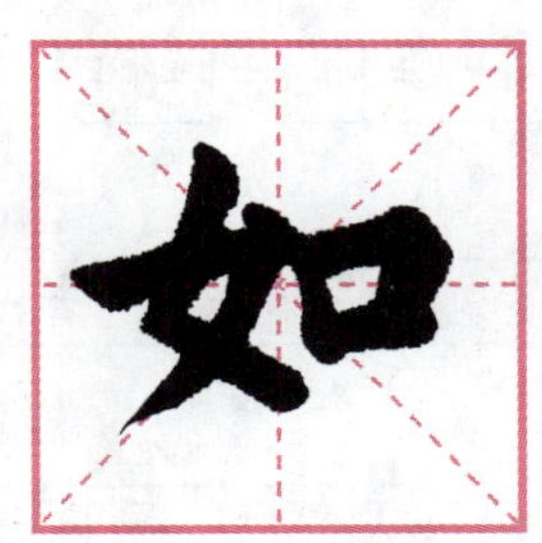

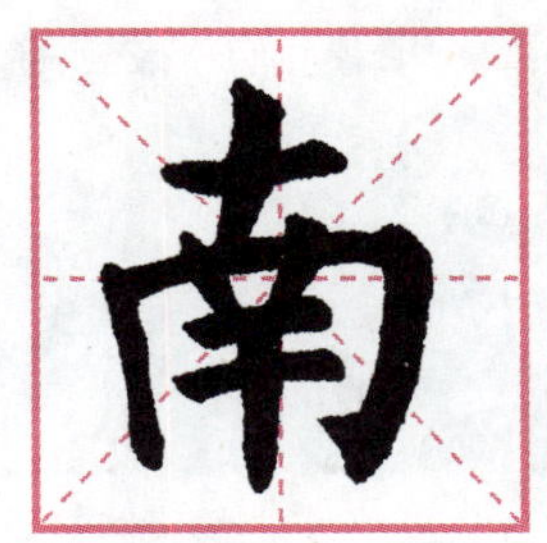 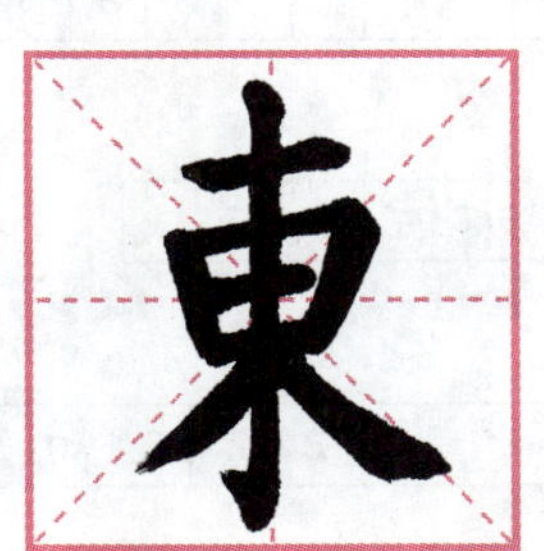

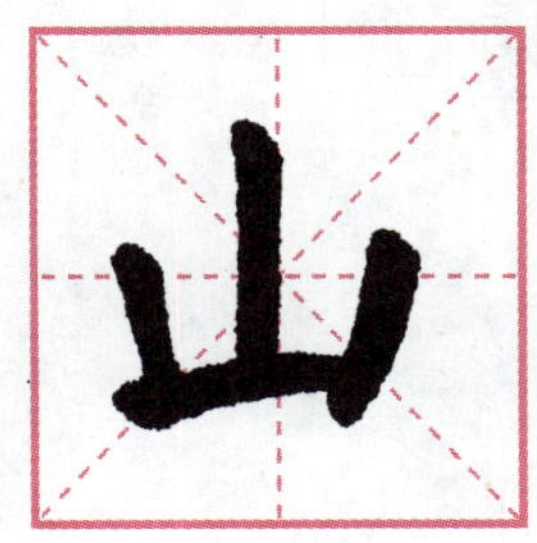 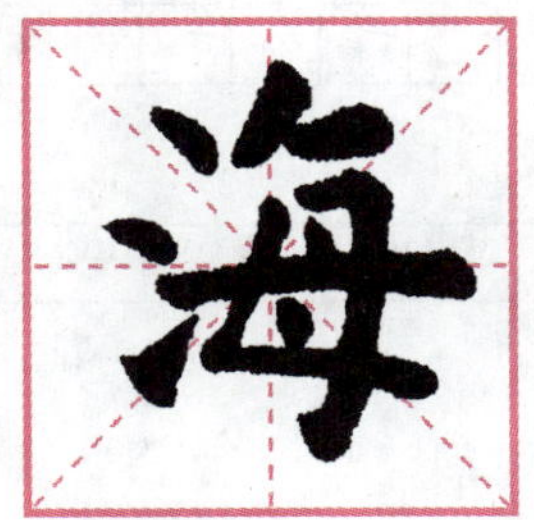

(14) 练习十四：综合练习(二)

在下面三幅字中,任选一幅来写,宣纸大小不限。

1) 友谊地久天长

2) 有志者事竟成

3) 知識就是力量

写完之后,用毛笔在字幅的左下侧写上书写的时间和自己的名字。

"有"笔顺： | 一 | ナ | ナ | 有 | 有 | 有 |

"志"笔顺： | 一 | 十 | 土 | 志 | 志 | 志 |

"者"笔顺： | 一 | 十 | 土 | 耂 | 耂 | 者 | 者 | 者 |

"事"笔顺： | 一 | 一 | 一 | 曰 | 写 | 写 | 事 |

"竟"笔顺： | 丶 | 二 | 十 | 立 | 立 | 音 | 音 | 音 | 竟 | 竟 |

"成"笔顺： | 一 | 厂 | 万 | 成 | 成 | 成 |

"知"笔顺： | 丿 | 仁 | 仁 | 矢 | 矢 | 知 | 知 | 知 |

"識"笔顺： | 丶 | 二 | 二 | 三 | 言 | 言 | 言 | 言 | 訂 | 訶 | 諮 | 講 | 諳 | 諳 | 識 | 識 | 識 |

"就"笔顺： | 丶 | 二 | 二 | 六 | 古 | 亨 | 京 | 就 | 就 | 就 | 就 |

"是"笔顺： | 丶 | 口 | 曰 | 日 | 旦 | 旱 | 旱 | 是 | 是 |

"力"笔顺： | 刁 | 力 |

(14) Exercise 14　comprehensive exercise II

Choose one of the following three sayings,　and write its Chinese translation on Xuan paper, (use any size of paper of your choice).

1) Friendship is forever.

2) Have will will succeed.

3) Knowledge is power.

"量"笔顺：丶 冂 冂 日 旦 咢 昌 昌 昌 量 量 量

"友"笔顺：一 ナ 方 友

"谊"笔顺：丶 讠 讠 讠 讠 言 言 言 讠 诌 诌 诣 谊

"地"笔顺：一 十 土 扌 坤 地

"久"笔顺：丿 夕 久

"天"笔顺：一 二 于 天

"长"笔顺：一 二 三 长 长 长 长 长

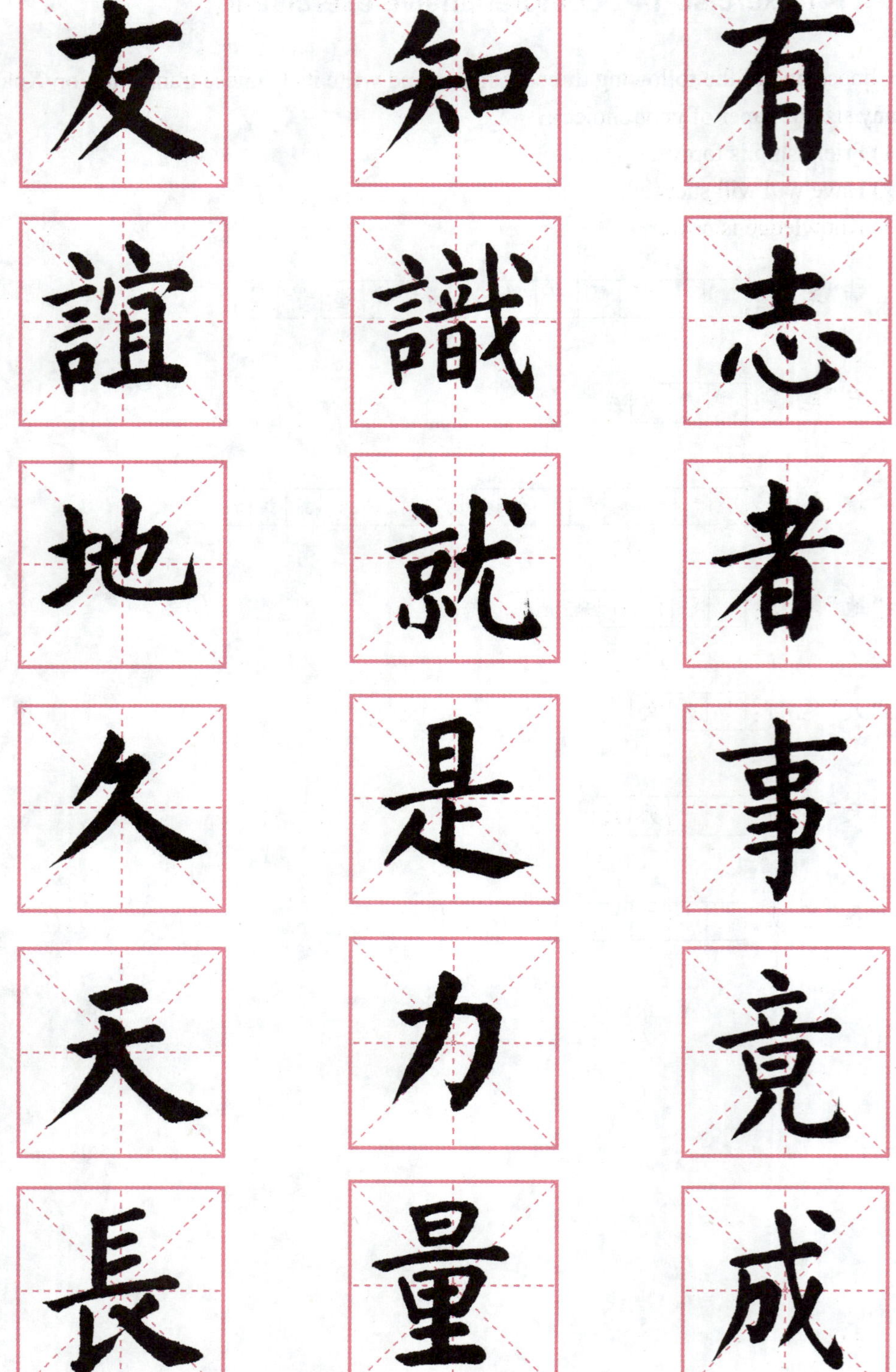

有志者事竟成
知識就是力量
友誼地久天長